GET CLOSE

GET CLOSE

Lean Team Documentary Filmmaking

Rustin Thompson

OXFORD
UNIVERSITY PRESS

OXFORD
UNIVERSITY PRESS

Oxford University Press is a department of the University of Oxford. It furthers
the University's objective of excellence in research, scholarship, and education
by publishing worldwide. Oxford is a registered trade mark of Oxford University
Press in the UK and certain other countries.

Published in the United States of America by Oxford University Press
198 Madison Avenue, New York, NY 10016, United States of America.

Library of Congress Cataloging-in-Publication Data
Names: Thompson, Rustin, author.
Title: Get close : lean team documentary filmmaking / Rustin Thompson.
Description: New York : Oxford University Press, [2019] |
Includes bibliographical references and index.
Identifiers: LCCN 2018020400 | ISBN 9780190909895 (cloth) | ISBN 9780190909901 (pbk.)
Subjects: LCSH: Documentary films—Production and direction.
Classification: LCC PN1995.9.D6 T46 2019 | DDC 070.1/8—dc23
LC record available at https://lccn.loc.gov/2018020400

9 8 7 6 5 4 3 2 1

Paperback printed by WebCom, Inc., Canada
Hardback printed by Bridgeport National Bindery, Inc., United States of America

CONTENTS

ACKNOWLEDGMENTS

I am greatly indebted to my editor, Norman Hirschy, for his insight, encouragement, and patience in seeing this book through from first proposal to publication. I also need to thank the anonymous peer reviewers whose critical feedback pushed me to continually revise and rework the manuscript. Most important, I want to thank my family. My daughter, Claire, for her copyediting skills, my son, Nick, for his close reading of content, and my wife, Ann, for making sure I was saying what I meant to say. The book would not have been written without their confidence, inspiration, and love.

INTRODUCTION

Lean Team Filmmaking Will Liberate You

In the 1980s, working as a broadcast cameraman, editor, and producer, I made documentaries for the local TV news. One of these was called *The Money Maze,* which concerned the thrilling topic of, wait for it . . . financial planning! To spice things up, I asked the TV station's design department to construct a cardboard maze and place it on a tabletop. I bought a four-inch-tall, windup penguin and set it loose in the maze. The sight and sound of that 99-cent toy waddling around in search of sound financial advice was perhaps the only memorable thing about the doc, but I sure had fun pulling off the gag. The station was a great playground for trying stuff out, learning on the job, and getting actual airtime, all while bringing home a steady paycheck. Every chance I got I tried to take advantage of my access to the station's equipment and talent by injecting imaginative visuals into the pieces I worked on. In reality, though, I was just biding my time. I'd always planned on an eventual career as a director of Hollywood features.

Then I saw Errol Morris's *The Thin Blue Line* in 1988. The film, deeply cinematic and narratively rich, opened my eyes to new possibilities within the documentary form. There was no droning voice-of-God narration or eat-your-vegetables educational component or do-gooder sermonizing. It was a crime thriller about a man wrongly convicted of murder told in the tenor of a pulpy film noir. The subject matter served the film's visionary style, composed of straight-to-camera interviews that looked like police blotter interrogations, expressionist crime scene reenactments using (gasp) actors, and repeated close-ups that took on the iconic weight of incriminating evidence. *The Thin Blue Line* was a startling revelation that changed the way many people thought about documentary filmmaking. But it also provoked a backlash against the movie's rule-breaking narrative strategies, which continue to be discussed, vilified, copied, and admired.

The Thin Blue Line's mischievous visual sense stayed with me. More than a decade later, it inspired me to finally make my first independent documentary, *30 Frames a Second: The WTO in Seattle*. The movie was a one-man-band, first-person account of my transformation, during the five days of the 1999 World Trade Organization (WTO) demonstrations in Seattle, from an objective photojournalist to a subjective witness of my own consciousness-raising. I was thrilled that I was able to shoot, write, and edit a compelling feature-length documentary film all by myself, with total creative license to insert playful visual and sound motifs. I made the film with very little money and even less regard for how it would be received. I simply shot it, cut it, and sent it out to a handful of film festivals (see Figure I.1).

30 Frames went on to screen at more than fifteen festivals, winning the Grand Jury Prize for Best Documentary at the Chicago Underground Film Festival and other best-of-festival awards in Seattle, Columbus, Ohio, Vancouver, BC, and Portland, Maine. The American Library Association even named it one of the top ten videos of 2001 (don't smirk; a lot of people watch movies from their local libraries). The film cost me about twenty-five hundred bucks to make. Now, nearly two decades later, I continue to license footage from the film to other documentaries and it's available on multiple streaming platforms.

I'll write more in Chapter 1 about how *30 Frames a Second* came about, but in the years since, working often with my wife, writer and producer Ann Hedreen, I have made

FIGURE I.1 A scene from *30 Frames a Second: The WTO in Seattle* (2000), written, directed, shot, and edited by Rustin Thompson. (Screen capture from digital file.)

five more feature-length nonfiction films: *Quick Brown Fox: An Alzheimer's Story*, *The Church on Dauphine Street* (a post–Hurricane Katrina film), *False Promises* (about Native American fishing rights), *Zona Intangible* (set in a human settlement outside of Lima, Peru), and *My Mother Was Here* (a first-person account of my mom's last two years of life). We've also made more than 150 short, doc-style films for organizations such as the International Rescue Committee, Ocean Conservancy, the Sierra Club, and many other nonprofits based in our home city of Seattle. These films are the main source of our income.

All of our independent documentaries have been distributed in educational markets (we work with the long-established companies Bullfrog Films, Women Make Movies, and Alexander Street Press) and are streaming on portals such as iTunes, Amazon, Google, and Hulu. All have shown on PBS stations and public TV networks in other countries, and we continue to get requests to screen them. They are also available on Vimeo on Demand as pay-per-view titles. Our films have made money, although never enough for us to live on.

We've produced our work while sticking to the same principles: We keep our budgets small, our subject matter engaging, our equipment simple. We like to have fun and we like to be efficient. We never let projects, large or small, drag on for too long. And, most important, we keep our team *lean*. For nearly all of our films, our production crew has consisted of just the two of us or only me, wearing all the hats of producer, director, writer, cinematographer, soundperson, and editor.

It's a way of working that has allowed us to make many films in the past twenty years, to travel to fascinating places, to meet and talk to regular people, to hear their stories, and to indulge our creative urges. We have no complaints.

But in order to maintain our independence, we've had to continually readjust our expectations to meet the challenging new trends within the documentary film industry, an industry crowded with filmmakers who have embraced the easy access to low-cost cameras and editing software. They want to tell stories and illuminate issues they are passionate about, and some of them are also lured by the glamor that accompanies a successful film festival run or theatrical debut.

Because of this flood of films, trying to get your own film accepted, noticed, or respected by the industry has gradually morphed into a stressful, competitive, time-consuming, and expensive proposition. There is simply not enough funding, nor are there enough sales agents or top-tier film festivals or distributors, to go around. Filmmakers can feel like they're running a gauntlet of grant applications, pitch sessions, workshops, and festivals, all monitored by a maze of decision-makers who may welcome your film but are more likely to ignore it. Feedback is rare, and rejection is plentiful.

These challenges can often feel defeating and frustrating to filmmakers faced with negotiating a steeplechase of approbation in the documentary industry.

For starters, filmmakers may have to amass a personal war chest of cash in order to succeed with insiders. A 2017 article in *Cultural Weekly* estimated the average budget for documentaries screening at the Sundance Film Festival that year to be around $400,000.[1] In 2013, the executive producer of PBS's *POV* figured a budget average for docs of $1 million on the highest end and $200,000 on the lowest.[2] That's a lot of money at either end of the spectrum. A lot of responsibility in managing that money. And a lot of time spent looking for it.

Directors may also need to laboriously tinker with their project to satisfy investors and executive producers. Their films often need to reflect social issues and current events to be considered a good bet for these stakeholders. An article in the *New York Times* by John Anderson, with the headline "Documentary Filmmakers Find That an Agenda Helps with Financing," reported that much of the money available to current documentaries is "coming from institutions that place considerable importance on a film's cause and its outreach plan (the organizational networking necessary to reach the audience sympathetic to that cause)."[3]

These kinds of restrictions can inhibit cinematic risk-taking with the documentary form, forcing docs to follow unwritten rules of structure and convention and to be freighted with noble intentions in order to be taken seriously by the industry. These industry expectations also create a feeding frenzy around the networking events, pitch sessions, and production labs that annually announce open calls for submissions from filmmakers.

One such event is called Independent Film Week, held each September in New York and organized by the Independent Filmmaker Project (IFP), which offers programs that "help filmmakers navigate the industry, develop new audiences, and encourage close interaction between all participants."[4] In the early 2000s, the organizers of this event accepted nearly every film or rough cut submitted (as long as it was professionally produced), and you received a screening in an actual theater and a chance to meet with industry pros. This offered completely unknown, unfunded filmmakers a way to get their work in front of people who could help them. Two of our documentaries found a home with distributors as a result of IFP connections, and two fictional-feature rough cuts I've made at least got a test run with audiences. But in the past decade, the IFP has capped the number of films it accepts and made the application process more selective and competitive. These restrictions are obviously a response to the staggering number of films being submitted, but they make it harder for all filmmakers to get a foot in the industry door.

Some filmmakers are responding to these barriers by opting for self-distribution, uploading their film to their own website or, after paying a fee, placing it on sites such as Vimeo on Demand or Tugg and keeping a majority of the profits. But this DIY distribution comes with a downside. You won't have the publicity or reach of a well-known worldwide distributor to increase the audience for your film, and you'll have to do the majority of the legwork to get your film in front of viewers.

Despite these challenges, more and more would-be documentary filmmakers continue to plunge into this world every year. They buy extremely affordable, high-quality cameras, sign up for online courses, attend weekend workshops, and embark on projects that, sometimes, they'll spend years working on. A stark example of this oversaturation could be seen during the 2016 Standing Rock protests against the Dakota Access Pipeline in North Dakota. "Dozens of documentarians have descended on the Sioux reservation— 34 teams, according to the tribal database," wrote Anderson in the *New York Times*[5] (see Figure I.2).

Thirty-four teams! Many of these filmmakers, to their credit, may finish their films and then send them off to compete in festivals—festivals that are routinely inundated with record numbers of submissions from filmmakers around the globe. Even small regional festivals are overwhelmed by the sheer number of films competing for a chance to be accepted. This deluge, unfortunately, also means a record number of rejections.

The current path for far too many filmmakers means working on one film for five, seven, even ten or more years, negotiating all the built-in hurdles of grant writing and funding cycles, crewing and staffing their project from preproduction to postproduction,

FIGURE I.2 A scene from *Beyond Standing Rock* (Brian Malone, 2017), one of thirty-four films in production during the 2016 confrontation. (Screen capture from digital file.)

shooting and editing their film in fits and starts, finishing it years after they shot their first frame, waiting months to hear back from film festivals, and endlessly researching potential distributors. When the marathon is over, these filmmakers may be so exhausted they may never want to make another movie, and in some cases, their films will already feel dated. Other would-be filmmakers are so overwhelmed they never even get started. And others are stuck in limbo somewhere along the way, out of money or out of gas, their project withering on the vine.

I write about all of these trends in more depth throughout this book, including a section that maps the formidable trek through the jungle of film festivals. My purpose is not to discourage you from making docs, but to *encourage* you to make them in a way that will be both financially viable and artistically rewarding. You can do this by keeping your team lean, your expectations realistic, and your eyes wide open.

It's true that more and more filmmakers are already working as one- or two-person teams, at least when they begin a new film. Some of these lone wolves are inexperienced and would like to hand over the reins of shooting so they can concentrate on directing or producing; others are comfortable running sound but not the camera; others feel they can tackle all the production team roles but are unsure how much to film, whom to film, when to stop, or what they're going to do when it comes time to edit. All too often their lean films start putting on weight as the process grows more complex, as they stare at their towers of hard drives containing the footage they shot and begin to plead for help. They add assistants, executive producers, editors, more assistants—all of which extends the time and especially the costs of their movie from conception to completion to festivals to distribution. Meanwhile, their original artistic vision has begun to fade.

It doesn't have to be this way.

The dream of making a documentary film remains a palpable one. Every time I feel stymied by gatekeepers, my disappointment disappears as soon as I'm sparked by a new idea for a film I want to make or I see a movie that surprises me with an inventive point of view or a bold stylistic approach. Although *The Thin Blue Line* remains a landmark in documentaries, recent films such as *Pina, Manakamana, Homo Sapiens, Manufactured Landscapes, The Joy of Life, Untitled,* and *Sacro GRA* are just as inspiring. They represent fresh takes on the documentary form that keep me dreaming about the movies I want to make. The fact that you're reading this book means that dream is alive for you, too.

It's easy to see why.

The field of documentary filmmaking continues to present fascinating ways of telling a story or bringing characters to life. It engages vivid aesthetic possibilities that can be realized with a few simple and accessible tools and techniques. It offers a realm of creative opportunities and a deeply satisfying sense of giving back to the world. The pursuit of this art need not be a bank-breaking, hair-pulling, inexorable exercise in frustration. It should and can be a medium for self-expression, for revelation and illumination, for intimate, personal storytelling.

The goal of this book is to map an invigorating new path to realizing the dream of becoming the author of your own film. It's called lean team documentary filmmaking, a term I will sometimes refer to in the book by its acronym, LTDF.

Get Close: Lean Team Documentary Filmmaking strips away the barriers to this authorship. It demystifies and declutters the way docs are produced today, removing the need for bloated crews, flocks of assistants, and executive overseers. I hope to entice you with the hands-on rewards of engaging with and perhaps even mastering the skills involved in nearly *all* the steps of the filmmaking process. I'll show you how you can plan, produce, fund, shoot, write, edit, and distribute a feature-length documentary at a tiny fraction of the runaway costs typical of documentaries today, with a lean team of one or at most two people.

In Chapter 1, I'll start by telling the story of how I pivoted from a career as a TV news cameraman to one as a filmmaker. It was during my time as a freelancer that I first learned that *getting close* to the subject matter was the key to working fast and efficiently. I used that experience to make my first lean team documentary in 1999, at the same time that affordable digital cameras and revolutionary nonlinear editing tools such as Final Cut Pro came on the market.

In Chapter 2, I'll show you how to embark on your potential project using the *get close, LTDF strategy* as a guide. You'll get a sense of how to develop your visual thinking skills, how to evaluate the potential of your story and define your characters, how to assess B-roll possibilities, locations, and the logistics of equipment, and how to consider all of this in service of eliminating or reducing the barriers between you and your subject. You'll also see how you should begin to think about funding, audience, and distribution in terms of what's realistically possible with a lean budget and a lean crew.

In Chapter 3, I'll lay out the list of essential gear you'll need as a lean team filmmaker, starting with seven basic tools that anyone can use to shoot an entire film. I'll then add to those basics more gear that can enhance your production values but is still easy for you to use as a standalone filmmaker. This chapter is not written for gearheads. It contains understandable descriptions of cameras and accessories and how to use them.

In Chapter 4, I'll describe how to work in the field as a one- or two-person team: how to practice a type of arm's-length cinematography that allows you to get close and stay close to your characters or subject matter; how to move the camera while covering the geography of a scene, from shooting the basics to experimenting with new angles and points of view; and how to think about editing with every shot or scene or sequence. I'll talk about recording sound with your essential audio gear and about lighting with your minimal lean team lighting package. I'll include a section on interviewing and I'll help you to continue to find or adapt your story while in the process of shooting (see Figure I.3).

In Chapter 5, I'll cover techniques for organizing the editing process, with a few simple strategies to get you started structuring a film. Then I'll discuss working with a timeline, interviews, B-roll, sound, music, on-screen text, and narration. The key to sticking with your lean team principles in editing is knowing your footage and knowing your story, a process made easier because you were already thinking about editing while you were shooting in the field.

In Chapter 6, I'll survey the current state of film festivals and distribution. I won't pull any punches in this chapter. Except for a few name-brand directors, getting a doc into festivals can be a frustrating experience, and it has dispirited many a filmmaker. But I will offer helpful advice on how to traverse this daunting landscape, or how to avoid it altogether, while exploring the many accessible avenues for getting your film distributed or broadcast.

Throughout, I'll use examples from my own work to highlight the successful strategies I've used—and the dumb mistakes I've made—as well as examples from dozens of other movies. I'll offer appraisals and critiques of films that are all easily found via streaming websites, DVDs, or your local library. Many of these movies are nurtured and distributed by the documentary industry; others are unconventional gems found outside the mainstream.

FIGURE I.3 The author filming within arm's reach of his mother in *My Mother Was Here* (in production, 2018). (Still capture from digital file.)

I'll draw on material from a few of the books that have come before this one, including Barry Hampe's *Making Documentary Films and Videos*, Sheila Curran Bernard's *Documentary Storytelling: Creative Nonfiction on Screen*, Alan Rosenthal and John Corner's *New Challenges for Documentary*, Scott MacDonald's *Avant-Doc*, Liz Stubbs's *Documentary Filmmakers Speak*, and Bill Nichols's *Introduction to Documentary*. These books do an excellent job of covering topics such as film history, theory, ethics, and various documentary modes or styles, while also examining the genre as an honorable way of illuminating the world. Some of these books break down the process of filmmaking; others conduct interviews with key directors.

What *Get Close: Lean Team Documentary Filmmaking* does is to gauge the current demanding landscape of doc filmmaking—the ever-changing technical tools, the funding challenges, the exorbitant costs, the stress of networking, the time it takes to get from conception to distribution—and confront those realities with a much more positive, energizing reality: the power that documentaries have to engage your artistic senses. This book will encourage you and help you gain the confidence and skills to realize that artistic potential while you're working by yourself or with only one other person, to take creative risks, to find your authorial voice, to reduce costs, and to spend less time making each film so you can make more films. This book will embolden you to pursue documentary filmmaking for the joy of it.

Your own filmmaking adventure may very well conclude with a successful experience within the documentary industry. Documentaries that premiere at Sundance, SXSW, Tribeca, and other fests usually started their public journey with industry funders and mentors, and these are the films most viewers hear about, ones that illuminate hot-button issues or that profile celebrities and politicians. These films are to be respected. But they too often serve as the only examples for filmmakers who want to try their hand at doc filmmaking, and they set an impossibly high bar of achievement.

Many worthy documentaries are made every year that don't screen at most of the important fests but are made with just as much care and passion. I saw a strange documentary about water dowsers (people who search for groundwater with a bent stick) more than fifteen years ago that has stuck with me ever since, even though the title, and the movie, faded into oblivion. Another, called *Children of the Kalahari*, directed by Velina Ninkova, which I saw at the 2017 edition of the Paris Ethnografilm Festival, was made with special calm and patience. Though the scope of the film was limited, I was impressed by the filmmaker's comfort with her own modest ambitions.

A movie about a persecuted Iraqi immigrant called *Barzan*, made by Seattle colleagues Alex Stonehill and Bradley Hutchinson, which I programmed for a weekend series I curated a few years back, made a forceful impression on the small audience that attended the screening. The film was quiet, thoughtful, and well crafted, and even though it may not have been earth-shattering or widely seen, the filmmakers were proud of it. Like many of these types of films, it can now be viewed on popular media streaming sites such as iTunes and Amazon.

Our own films have had eccentric journeys; though they've started out tentatively, they've eventually ended up finding their footing. *Quick Brown Fox,* our feature-length film about my mother-in-law's Alzheimer's disease, was very close to being purchased by HBO in 2006, until they decided a short film they'd programmed a decade before, *Complaints of a Dutiful Daughter,* had covered the subject matter adequately enough. *Quick Brown Fox* went on to be acquired by the distributor Women Make Movies, to screen on national television in Israel and Finland, and to play regional PBS stations in the United States; it was purchased by libraries nationwide and then streamed on video-on-demand platforms. We now sell the film on Vimeo and, fifteen years later, still get requests to show it. Meanwhile, HBO went on to produce their own ambitious multipart series called *The Alzheimer's Project.*

The idiosyncratic success of our films has led me to embrace the philosophy that life is too short and there is too much else I want to do as a filmmaker besides jump through the innumerable hoops of fundraising and endorsement-seeking. This conviction has limited my success in the industry but liberated me to make films on my own terms and my own schedule. My hope is that by reading this book, you will be liberated as well.

/// 1 /// MY LEAN TEAM EPIPHANY

The Revolution *Was* Televised

The call came on a Sunday evening in late November.

"This is Jennifer, CBS News in Los Angeles. Can you work for us tomorrow? A WTO story?"

"I think so, yeah."

I'd been wondering if I'd get this assignment. I'd been freelancing as a cameraman for network television news for nearly ten years. The soundperson I worked with, Pat Craft, and I were based in Seattle, and CBS was one of our most reliable clients. With the WTO (World Trade Organization) meeting in our city in 1999 for its annual round of negotiations, I knew there would be work coming our way. But just in case CBS passed on the week's events—after all, it looked like they were going to consist of a lot of stuffy meetings and arcane trade talk—my wife, Ann, had arranged for the two of us to get press credentials. She was contracted to do media relations for environmental groups, and with her background as a TV news producer, we figured we might get some spur-of-the-moment work shooting interviews and B-roll for NGOs (nongovernment organizations).

The CBS job would probably turn into several days of work. At the going network rate of $1,500 a day for a two-person team, and more with overtime, it was a no-brainer to say yes to the assignment. Yet I hesitated.

What CBS didn't seem to realize was that the WTO conference in Seattle that year was showing signs of being anything but business as usual. It was going to be a showdown. On one side were the bureaucrats, trade wonks, lobbyists, and political schmoozers. On the other side were busloads of citizens—students, environmental activists, anarchists, union workers, mothers, grandmothers, and Quakers—all there to demonstrate against a myriad of issues: sweatshops, unrestricted free trade, genetically modified food, environmental destruction, corporate greed; the list went on. A lot of people had something to protest and they were all gathering in Seattle. Word on the street was that the demonstrations were going to be massive. Coordinated blockades. Multiple marches. Sit-ins. A storm of nonviolent but unrelenting civil disobedience.

The Canadian documentary filmmaker Mark Achbar (*The Corporation, Manufacturing Consent: Noam Chomsky and the Media*), who was staying in our spare bedroom, had attended a meeting of demonstration leaders, and he told us, with a get-ready-for-this urgency, "This thing is going to shut down the city." The police had some idea of what was coming, but there was a feeling among the underground organizers that the cops had seriously underestimated the size of the resistance.

As it turned out, CBS didn't have a clue either.

"We want to send you to Wenatchee [an agricultural town two hours east of Seattle] tomorrow to do a piece on the apple industry and how the trade negotiations will affect it," Jennifer said.

Wenatchee? Was she kidding?

"Uh, you do know there are going to be major demonstrations in Seattle?" I said. "Probably starting tomorrow. They're predicting confrontations between the police and protesters. You heard this, right?"

"We don't really care about a bunch of people in sea turtle costumes waving signs. It's not a story."

At that moment, I knew I had to make a choice. I wasn't the only cameraperson in Seattle. If I said no, CBS would book the next crew on its list, and that crew would almost certainly be called back from Wenatchee to work twelve- to sixteen-hour days for the next week on the streets of Seattle, and that same crew would move to the top of the list for future assignments. There was little loyalty in the freelance world.

I also knew that if I said no I was cutting Pat, who was a good friend, out of a soundperson's percentage of the fee as well. We were a team. Passing on this lucrative gig would annoy Pat, endanger my freelance career with CBS, and impoverish my family for the coming winter.

Why the hell was I hesitating?

Because there was something else going on with me at the time. It involved the question of how I wanted to continue to live my professional life, what I wanted to accomplish with the skills I had, what I wanted to say creatively with those skills.

It had never been my dream to be a freelance television news cameraman. I'd gone to the University of Washington in 1976 hoping to study film, to make movies, to become the next Martin Scorsese or Steven Spielberg. After I realized the UW didn't have much of a film program and I didn't have the money or the self-confidence to go to film school in

Los Angeles or New York, I drifted quite willingly into broadcast journalism. The school had a thriving curriculum in radio and TV. I became a DJ at the university station, KCMU (now KEXP, a respected national voice in independent music). I learned the broadcast basics of announcing, interviewing, writing, shooting, lighting, and editing.

Around this time, handheld video cameras were a relatively new and exciting technology. Yeah, they were clunky and ugly, and dialing-in a correct white balance was like tuning a spark plug, but I liked the idea that I could just check out one of these new toys from the university's broadcast department, shoot some images and record some sound, and then come back to the school's editing stations and make little three-minute movies. Within two months of graduating in 1981, I got my first professional job at KCRL, the ABC affiliate in Reno, Nevada. Every day I was reporting and writing stories about plane crashes and train derailments, rodeos and potato farmers, city council meetings and gambling commissions. I'd sometimes shoot my own stand-ups, then return to the station and edit my footage. Six months later I got hired at a station in Colorado Springs, and a year and a half after that I went to work at the CBS affiliate KIRO-TV in Seattle, only thirty-five miles north of my hometown of Puyallup. I worked there for four years (see Figure 1.1).

FIGURE 1.1 The author, in 1987, shooting in the Dominican Republic for Seattle's CBS news affiliate, KIRO-TV. (Photo by Ann Hedreen.)

During my entire time in local television news I shot, edited, recorded audio, wrote, produced, and reported on hundreds of stories, features, specials, and documentaries. It was a fantastic training ground.

At KIRO, I was no longer the one-man band I had been in Reno and Colorado Springs. I was working with talented reporters, producers, and writers (one of them was Ann, whom I married in 1987) and getting experience in every genre of TV news: features, sports, politics, breaking news, live shots. After a couple years of exclusively shooting, I began editing all my own footage, delighted by the freedom I had to craft stories from the top down, to even imprint these pieces with signature shots and techniques (such as a frequent use of foreground, which I learned from watching movies made by—you guessed it—Scorsese and Spielberg).

Ann and I left KIRO in 1987. We were itching to travel, so we pooled our savings and backpacked around the world. Ten months later we returned to Seattle cash-poor but culturally rich, looking to do something more challenging than returning to the grind of local TV news. Ann began working in public relations at the Seattle Art Museum, we had a daughter, and I bought a $30,000 video camera to freelance for anyone who would hire me.

The freelance lifestyle was exciting and lucrative. In addition to the $1,500 a day, we got time and a half for overtime, per diem for meals, and "golden overtime" for working through the night. It was laughably easy to make quick money.

But after a few years, the work grew repetitive and the constant travel became a drag. My marriage, my relationship with my kids (we now had a son), and whatever dreams I'd had of creative fulfillment were threatened by the handcuffs of a lucrative but increasingly dull job. I'd call Ann from my comfortable hotel room and she'd either be dealing with a child-rearing headache or recounting a memorable moment with our kids. I felt awful I was missing these milestones (the good and the bad) and guilty when I complained that the hotel where we were staying didn't have microbrews on tap. At the same time, the work itself had become dreary.

When I started shooting for CBS, it was for news magazine programs like *48 Hours, Street Stories,* and *Before Your Eyes*. I covered breaking stories such as the shooting spree at a high school outside Eugene, Oregon, and the Tonya Harding fiasco in Portland. But I wasn't editing anymore, and the few times I urged producers to edit sequences in a certain way, based on how I shot them, I was ignored. When I watched the stories weeks later on TV, I could barely recognize the footage I'd contributed.

It seemed like Pat and I spent most of our time now setting up two-camera shoots with questionable journalistic appeal in $200-a-night hotel rooms. This involved working with another camera crew, flown in from San Francisco or Denver, and spending two hours putting up eight or more lights for a two- or three-hour interview, during which time the crews engaged in a competition over who had the best, the newest, and the most expensive equipment. I began to question why it was important to interview the crazy father of an even crazier serial killer or to pry tears from a poor woman whose baby was decapitated by an exploding air bag (true stories, both). Pat and I bickered like an unhappily married couple, and we grew more and more bored and disgruntled with the work. I was watching my artistic ambitions curl up and die in the corner.

Luckily, around this same time—it was the late 1990s—camera and editing technology began to change dramatically.

I'd been shooting with a $40,000 digital Betacam, the Sony 400A, soon to be made obsolete by a new camera that would cost me $60,000. The videotapes were the size of a hardback book, and they had short run times of thirty minutes. Editing was still based on rigid, linear technology. But small, high-quality, inexpensive digital cameras were coming on the market. You could hold them in your hand and record onto MiniDV tapes the size of a matchbox, and the footage could be ingested directly from the camera into a computer, where it could be edited in nonlinear fashion on a new computer-based system called AVID. I bought one of these cameras in 1998, the Sony TR-V9, a step up from the consumer models and a little pricey at $1,000, but a thrill to play around with. I shot a short documentary for a homeless advocacy organization and edited it on AVID. I was itching to try it out in a real-world, news-style situation (see Figure 1.2).

The camera was sitting on my dining room table when Jennifer called me up the night before the WTO shit hit the fan.

"I'm going to pass," I said.

A short silence followed.

"You sure?"

"Yeah, I am," I said. "I've been thinking of doing my own thing this week. Go down on the streets, just start shooting. Things might get wild, and I want to be there."

I'm sure Jennifer was already fingering her Rolodex when she asked, "Okay, can we check in with you later this week if the need arises?" Part of me wanted to say, "No. Fuck it. You guys are dinosaurs. I'm tired of watching my creative juices pool on the floor while I'm shooting those two-camera interviews. I'm nothing more than an overpaid electronic stenographer." But I didn't say that. My wife had taught me that it was a lot easier to not burn bridges than to apologize for the ashes later.

"Sure," I said. "No problem." But as I hung up the phone I knew they wouldn't call, and I wouldn't answer if they did.

FIGURE 1.2 The Sony TR-V9, used by the author to make *30 Frames a Second* (2000). (Photo by Rustin Thompson.)

The next morning, I was on the streets. I had my Handycam and a waist belt stuffed with batteries, several tapes, a couple of granola bars, and a water bottle. I used nothing but the camera's built-in shotgun mic for sound.

The shooting I did that week in Seattle turned out to be among the most memorable and rewarding professional experiences of my life. I was in the thick of the action, stimulated by the passions of the protesters, invigorated by their commitment to fierce civil disobedience and with my own lukewarm political awareness suddenly turned up to boiling. I was also putting all of my professional skills to work in a dynamic cauldron of marches, speeches, confrontations, riots, and arrests. I was free to roam (or sprint) through the streets with a camera the size of a beer bottle in my hand, answering to no one but myself. Something was happening on every street corner, from the quirky (giant puppets) to the strategic (people blocking roads by sitting with their hands locked together inside PVC tubes); from the inspiring (marchers in, yes, sea turtle costumes, protesting polluted oceans) to the infuriating (cops randomly assaulting peaceful demonstrators with pepper spray); from the calm (Native American drumming) to the chaotic (a standoff between police armed with rubber bullets and tear gas, and protesters armed only with gas masks and bandanas).

On that first day of shooting, I would periodically rewind my footage in the camera and check to make sure I was getting usable stuff, thrilled that it looked and sounded so good. I watched the network camera crews position themselves on street corners (there were dozens of them by the second day, including several from CBS), shooting stand-ups, trying to keep up with the rapidly changing events, while I was dashing ahead of them from one flash point to the next.

The evening news reports were typically one-sided, insulting the peaceful demonstrators by lumping them together with a handful of black-hooded anarchists who broke several windows and provoked a few of the cops. Most of the trade issues were minimized or ignored. The images broadcast around the world were of riots and chaos, chants of "The whole world is watching" providing a soundtrack to the demeaning picture the mainstream press painted of the activists. But on the street, enveloped by the spirited energy of this movement to shut down the global trade organization, the story was different and much more stirring.

I'll have more to say in later chapters about the techniques of shooting and recording sound in that kind of atmosphere, but for now the important point is this: saying no to a major news network was a moment of reckoning. I was moving on from my life as a gun-for-hire shooter into something new and unknown. I was working completely alone, with bare-bones equipment, and capturing intense, dynamic pictures, guided by nothing more than my own filmmaking instincts, responding immediately and spontaneously to events as they unfolded. It was a pivotal moment, and I was ready to grab it (see Figure 1.3).

But then what?

I sat on the footage for a month after the WTO demonstrations ended. Yes, I'd shot a bunch of visually exciting material, but do I sell it to a news station? Give it away to guerrilla media outfits to bolster court cases against the cops? When I started shooting I wasn't really thinking of turning it into a documentary; I was just doing what I always did as a journalist: covering all the angles, interviewing people, trying to get both sides of the story. I booked editing space at a nonprofit media center in town and put together a short trailer for how a documentary might look. It was clumsy and impersonal and played too much like a standard news piece. Colleagues urged me to try again. I decided to rent an AVID edit system and install it in a spare room in our house (I could afford to rent it for only a week at a cost of $2,000). I transferred all my footage to Beta SP tape, recorded narration, and fed all the material into the AVID. At the end of my seven-day window, I had a finished film.

I called it *30 Frames a Second*, a riff on a line from the Jean-Luc Godard film *Le Petit Soldat* (1963), in which the main character, a photographer, refers to cinema as capturing truth "twenty-four times per second."[1] When I first tried putting the movie together,

FIGURE 1.3 The author filming close to the action in *30 Frames a Second* (2000). (Screen capture from digital file.)

I opted for a straightforward, third-person-narrator approach, much like a standard-issue documentary. But I quickly realized this would drain the film of a sense of urgency. I needed to bring the energy of the streets and the day-to-day chaos alive for the viewer. I also felt that my experience during that week—my political awakening, if you will—was something others could identify with.

I decided on an unwavering first-person point of view, a strategy that invited the viewer to live through the events with me. I tried to be true to my subjective experience, and I ended up including the process of actually making the film within the film. I shot myself at the editing table, scanning footage and rewinding scenes. I included extreme close-ups of the digital time code reader on the playback deck. I created a dronelike music track using a portable electric piano I had bought for my kids. I recorded the voice-over into the shotgun mic on my Betacam. I inserted clips from the Godard film, from John Ford's *Grapes of Wrath,* and from the brilliant Haskell Wexler movie *Medium Cool,* a dramatic hybrid feature he filmed during the 1968 Chicago Democratic Convention. I didn't pay for these excerpts, crossing my fingers that I could invoke the fair use laws to justify their inclusion (fair use rules have become more favorable to filmmakers in the past few years; learn more about them at the Center for Media and Social Impact and other websites).[2]

In other words, I used only the tools immediately and cheaply available to me and worked furiously to complete the editing in one week. There was no color correction and no postproduction sound mix. The film was rough, real, honest, and immediate. As I wrote in the introduction to this book, *30 Frames a Second* played in several film festivals and went on to have a long life in the educational distribution market, eventually ending up on Netflix for several years. I never did pay for those film rights.

Emboldened by the film's reception and excited by this digital turn of events in my career, I bought two products new to the burgeoning DIY video market: the first version of the nonlinear editing program Final Cut Pro and a sharp, beautifully designed camera, the Sony PD-150, with three chips of resolution and low-light capability so good it was as if I could see in the dark. David Lynch made an entire film, *Inland Empire,* with a European version of this camera. These revolutionary tools enabled me to make my final break from the stodgy world of network news and to embark on a path to the creative freedom of self-employment.

My work as a broadcast journalist provided a good foundation for this leap in a new direction. I'd worked in the field for almost twenty years. I'd earned several photojournalism awards, regional Emmys, and a national Emmy Award for my work on a series of stories about famine in North Korea. All the skills I have in filmmaking I owe to that on-the-job training.

Now I apply those skills to making documentaries and to our business producing documentary shorts for advocacy groups. Ann and I approach these films as storytellers, defining an organization's mission and the people they serve in cinematic, focused, emotionally driven three- to six-minute films.

Though the tools continue to change and the digital industry has exploded into a far-reaching, immensely profitable universe unto itself, I've never wavered from my conviction that working lean—efficiently and inexpensively—is the only way to retain our creative freedom and financial solvency. The Chinese documentary filmmaker Wu Wenguang (*Fuck Cinema,* 2004) also discovered the independence of digital video around the turn of the millennium, rejecting the sanctioned formats of traditional documentaries: "I am very happy not to have anything to do with the kind of post-production that goes on in editing rooms, and not to have a voice from behind me telling me to do this or not to do that." He says he moved away from more labor-intensive films to become "an individual with a DV camera, filming as I please . . . because this approach doesn't cost much money I don't really care if it turns a profit" (see Figure 1.4).[3]

During the Great Recession of 2008, many local production companies and gear rental facilities closed up shop. They had too much overhead and too many salaries to pay in an industry where the tools and ways of working were becoming cheaper and more democratic. Even the television networks began thinning their crews and cutting back on expensive gear.

FIGURE 1.4 With a handheld camera and shotgun microphone, Wu Wenguang follows several young people trying to break into the Chinese film industry, in *Fuck Cinema* (2004). (Screen capture from digital file.)

Ann and I kept our business afloat through the lean years—and proceeded with caution even after things started picking up again—by staying small and nimble. This is the philosophy that defines our business and also my way of working in the field. Every one of our films, long or short, is founded on a simple method that can make lean team documentary filmmaking a reality for everyone. I explain this method in the next chapter.

///2/// GET CLOSE

Eliminate Barriers and Plan Your Project

When I was shooting for the CBS news-magazine show *48 Hours,* we always left the tripod in the van. In fact, we were *ordered* to leave it in the van. The series began as a CBS news special report called *48 Hours on Crack Street,* which aired in September1986. The idea was to send out multiple crews to cover a single subject and to do all of the shooting and interviewing in one forty-eight-hour period. The creators of the program realized that the best way to accomplish this was to hire small, mobile crews that could move fast, work long hours, and respond to changing conditions immediately. Gear packages were streamlined down to a few essentials: handheld cameras, onboard battery-powered lights ("sunguns," as they were called then), wireless microphones (sometimes four were used at a time), as many videocassettes as you could carry, and, most important, a wide-angle lens or adaptor that allowed for both macro-close-ups and zoomed-in telephoto shots.

The wide-angle was the signature piece of the package. This piece of glass allowed you to focus on infinity and refocus on objects extremely close to the camera. It allowed you to move with your subjects, following them through hallways, up stairwells, down rocky paths, with minimal camera shake, and without losing focus. It made it possible to keep two or three people together in the frame at the same time. Interviews were all shot off the shoulder, some in midstride. If one of the show's hosts was assigned to your team, you included that host in the interviews, either in a two-shot or by panning back and forth from reporter to subject. The wide-angle lens was critical to the aesthetic design of the program. But it was truly effective only if you remained as close as possible to the action. And the only way to do that was to eliminate the barriers between you and what you were shooting. This was where I learned the most important lesson of my entire career as a documentary filmmaker: *get close*.

Later, when I'd moved on from network freelancing, began making independent documentaries, and started my own business producing doc-style short films for nonprofits, "get close" became my mantra.

This idea of getting close is not something I invented. Former UN ambassador Samantha Power, in her 2016 speech to Yale graduates, told students, "No matter what you choose to do with your life, if you truly want to live fully and leave the world a little better than you found it, you have to *get close*."[1] The pioneers of cinema verité documentary—D. A. Pennebaker, Albert and David Maysles, and Robert Drew—working with new, light-weight, sync-sound 16mm cameras, reveled in the freedom they now had to hover close to their subjects. And the legendary World War II photographer Robert Capa uttered the famous line, "If your photographs aren't good enough, you're not close enough."[2]

But let's go back even further than the 1940s.

The sixteenth-century Italian painter Caravaggio could arguably be considered the world's first cinematic documentarian. He popularized the use of live models, he was attuned to the quality and source of ambient or practical light, his paintings had a star-tling three-dimensional sense of depth, and, most important, he got close to his subjects. Two of his most celebrated works, *Supper at Emmaus* and *The Taking of Christ*, are tightly composed medium shots that place the viewer into the action. *The Taking of Christ* is a freeze-frame of a climactic moment. Judas has just kissed Christ, revealing his identity to the Roman soldiers who will soon take him away for judgment. The scene is lit both by off-screen moonlight and by a visible lantern, which is clutched by Caravaggio himself, who has inserted himself into the scene. This deliberate anachronism is both audacious and impish, an admission by the painter that he is presenting a truth as only he, the doc-umentarian, sees it (a beautiful color image of the painting can be seen on the National Gallery of Ireland's website).[3]

The power of the painting comes from getting close. This should be part of the philo-sophical and aesthetic approach of filmmakers as well.

There is a kind of meditative awareness that takes over when I'm shooting close to my subjects, much like that of skiers or climbers who focus only on the physical elements right in front of them. The subject or character guides my eye, and my eye communicates with my hands, which then manage the camera's iris, shutter speed, zoom, and audio level. I'm always dealing with matters of exposure and composition and focus, but also with how my subjects are responding to my presence. I'm deeply aware of them as human beings and truly grateful they've allowed me to be this close to them so I can bring their story to a viewer, to make a connection.

This is the juice of documentary filmmaking, this closeness to your fellow humans, which dissolves borders of class, race, and language, at least temporarily. I don't want to suggest that this breaking down of barriers is permanent. You probably won't become longtime friends with your subjects, nor will the divides of class and race magically melt away forever, but for the brief time of your shoot you will be communicating almost non-verbally. The experience can be profound. Getting close has become my way of looking at the world, my philosophy of visual thinking.

Before shooting my first independent documentary during the WTO protests, I was nonpolitical and disengaged from current events. I knew the basics of what was going on in the world, but I never went beyond the superficial, never investigated the nuances. But just one week in the streets, within a few feet of protesters and police, talking to them or capturing fly-on-the-wall sound and then studying the issues in the evening, trying to catch up with what so many of these idealistic demonstrators already knew, changed me forever. Getting close to their passion ignited my curiosity. It taught me a new way of engaging with the world. It made me want to make films, both feature-length documentaries and short films for nonprofits.

Making these films introduces us to people who often come from other countries and whose circumstances or lifestyles are different from ours. They may be struggling with poverty or homelessness; they may be survivors of violence or learning to adjust to a change in their health; they may be targets of discrimination or exploitation. Often, they are activists and humanitarians rebelling against the label of victim, in turn forcing us to reevaluate our own privileges. Even after twenty years of doing this work, I am thankful for and honored by the opportunity to get close to their lives, if just for an hour or two.

Students and friends have asked me many times which I enjoy most, shooting or editing. I always think the answer will be editing, because that is where you turn raw material into stories, where the real creative process begins. But I think the two processes are linked. I'm energized by the characters I meet while shooting, by the reciprocal nature of our brief intimacy, by realizing that even though this situation is not new for me, it is quite possibly very new for them. This knowledge impels me to be alert and conscientious. The visuals acquire an innate energy, a role in the sequences I will construct later in editing. In that way, shooting and editing for me are inseparable.

To get physically close, the first thing I do is get rid of obstacles. I ditch the lights, the light stands, the flags, the reflectors, the slate, the boom microphone, the additional viewing monitor, the extension cords, the soundperson, the director (you are the director!), the unpaid intern, and, if I truly don't need it, the tripod. I attach everything I need to the camera or carry extra gear in a waist belt or knapsack. This helps me to get intimate, dynamic footage and greatly reduces the expenses and logistical hassles other crews or video production studios often feel they need. I can work alone and still capture exciting images and high-quality sound. (I'll go into the details of gear and shooting in the field in Chapters 3 and 4.)

Director and cinematographer Joan Churchill (*My Dinner with Haskell, Aileen: Life and Death of a Serial Killer,* co-directed with Nick Broomfield) learned how to pack light long ago in her career of more than forty years. "I've got it down to a bum pack (as we called it in the UK, where I lived for 10 years), which I wear on my front," she says. "It's not exactly a fashion statement, but it has everything I need for the day and it serves as my tripod . . . So when I go out for the day on a shoot, I must have everything I might need on my person, and still be able to jump in and out of cars while shooting."

Churchill rests the camera on her small pack instead of holding it on her shoulder, following the action from waist-high level. "I tend to work very close to people. I like them to be able to see my face which is why I will never go back to the shoulder mounted cameras. It provides me with an opportunity to relate to people. They can see my reactions and know that the power I wield by pointing a camera at them is nonthreatening."[4]

I advocate owning your own camera rather than using one you rented or borrowed. You simply can't know the ins and outs of a camera until you've spent time with it in real-world situations. Treat it like a precious friend. Learn its tics and foibles, it's annoying limitations and irritating quirks, but also its loyalty and companionship, its responsiveness and abilities, its gifts to you. Mistreat it and it will turn on you. Take care of it and it will love you back. I know, this sounds a little new age-y, like your camera is a therapy pet or talking crystal, but I've always believed having your own camera is worth the investment, even if you have to upgrade it every three or four years. Once you become close friends with your camera, you can then eliminate the obstacles that attach to it like leeches. Unplug and unscrew everything on your camera that slows you down or gets in your way.

For example, the adaptor affixed to the top of your camera that allows you to attach that pricey, blimplike shotgun mic? The smaller, less obvious shotgun mic that comes with the camera will most often do the trick. What about the "dual grip video stabilization shoulder systems" and "professional grade stabilizing action grips"[5] that announce you're a *serious filmmaker*? Don't buy a camera that requires a rig like that just to get a stable handheld shot. That's like putting steel bars between you and your subject. And do you really need the external audio recorder requiring an assistant to hold and monitor it? Just record sound directly into your camera via the XLR inputs. In fact, don't even think of buying a camera that doesn't have XLR inputs in the first place.

Not only does eliminating barriers clear away the physical space between you and your subject, it also removes emotional space. When it's just you, your camera, and the person you're filming, your camera acts as an extension of your body. It is a way of seeing and relating to the world inside your frame.

I'm always impressed by how quickly those I'm filming seem to accept the transaction we've made: I observe, they go about their business. We've made a bargain in which they are willing to be documented if I respond to who they are and what they're doing without manipulation or intrusion. It's remarkable how close I can get—within inches of their face—and they respond as if I'm not there. I believe that this sort of acceptance of my presence, and a character's naturalism in front of the lens, are possible only because it is just the two of us in the room.

The masterful photographer Mary Ellen Mark believed in taking photographs almost immediately after meeting her subjects. According to her photo editor at *Fortune* magazine, Michelle McNally, Mark "could randomly approach people in the street and get them to cooperate with her, and then in minutes she'd be able to capture the essence of a person or a group of people in a very short period of time, so she never wore out her welcome."[6] She didn't keep her camera in its bag while she hung out for days or weeks getting to know people. Whether documenting street kids in Seattle or circus performers in India, she demonstrated her talent for intimate portraiture; her pictures shot on film sets or inside celebrities' homes captured movie stars in emotionally revealing poses. But she established right away the transactional nature of her relationship with her subjects. She was a professional there to do a job; she became friends or confidants with many of her subjects in the process of doing her work, not before.

"A person with a camera has an obvious job to do, which is to film," believes the Australian ethnographic filmmaker David MacDougall. "The subjects understand this and leave the filmmaker to it."[7] Nick Broomfield, the energetic director of *Biggie and Tupac* and *Kurt & Courtney*, finds "that you get much more offhand things from people . . . more revealing (footage) in the first five minutes than you do when they are all settled down."[8]

Many of the great lean team documentary filmmakers of the 1960s and '70s also worked like this. They arrived at a location and began shooting right away, feeling out their subjects as they went, getting closer and closer. In Albert and David Maysles's *Salesman*, from 1969, they began by focusing on an ensemble of four characters, with the central character gradually emerging from the footage as they were filming (see Figure 2.1). This is not to say that spending time getting to know your subjects *before* turning on the camera—gaining their trust, living with them, and becoming, in a sense, part of their lives—is not an acceptable and honorable method. It just isn't always feasible or affordable. This kind of approach requires a continuous funding stream and a luxury of time many filmmakers simply don't have.

FIGURE 2.1 Albert and David Maysles get close to their main character in *Salesman* (1969), one of the first lean team documentaries. (Still capture from DVD.)

The late Austrian filmmaker Michael Glawogger was able to take that kind of time. He built relationships with potential subjects months in advance, before he brought his cameraperson along. "When I come to a country I don't know," Glawogger said, "I think, 'Everything here is so interesting that I could film it'—but I stay in the country until the very moment when I think, 'Everything here is so boring; I should go home.' And *that's* the moment when I actually start filming, because when you feel that, then you can connect with the real lives of the people there."[9] Glawogger reported that he shot *Whores' Glory* in thirty days, though his research time was much longer.

There are other drawbacks to this approach. It requires an ability to not fret over missing many filmable moments. Your subjects could tire of you before it comes time to shoot, or the social or political reasons for making the doc in the first place could change and render your project moot. More important, the daily stress of making such a long-term film could drain your creative juices and put a strain on your family and relationships. A more viable approach is the swifter one: You are there to do a job; your subjects are allowing you to do it. They are participating willingly in the work you're doing. If your film takes place in a location or with people already familiar to you, then this research phase has probably been ongoing throughout your daily life. You don't need to spend weeks in advance getting to know your subject matter.

When I describe to students this idea of getting close, they nod as if to say, "Sure, of course. Get close. I get it." But then I demonstrate that getting close means getting *really physically* close, as in Leonard Retel Helmrich's *Shape of the Moon*. In this study of changes in the lifestyle of an Indonesian family, his camera keeps inching ever closer to the faces of his characters, and it penetrates the natural world in macro-close-ups. To practice this approach takes skill, sensitivity, awareness of your surroundings, and a willingness to push the boundaries of personal space (see Figure 2.2).

Before I embark on a new project, I always evaluate my idea in light of the lean team documentary filmmaking, or LTDF, model. The first question I ask is, "Can I get close to my characters or subject matter?" If the answer is no, then I don't make the film.

If the answer is yes, then the second question is, "What kind of film do I want to make?"

Is it a performance film (dance, theater, music)? This kind of film nearly always entails large crews and complicated logistics, which isn't a good fit for LTDF.

Is it an investigative doc? Will I be investigating a broad and multilayered topic or something more personal and accessible?

Is it a sports doc, an environmental doc, a celebrity doc? These genres can be made with a low-budget, lean team aesthetic, but they rarely are. Maybe it's an agenda-driven social justice film? This also seems to involve stakeholders and large budgets.

First-person films, character profiles, essays, activist and experimental works—these are all possible with a lean team, as are hybrid docs that walk a line between fiction and nonfiction. Ethnographic or observational films requiring immersion in a culture or place are sometimes best suited to working alone, but they can require infinite patience, time, and steady funding in order for the filmmaker to continue to live while waiting for the story to materialize.

In his book *Introduction to Documentary*, Bill Nichols describes various documentary styles as *modes*: poetic, expository, observational, participatory, reflexive, and

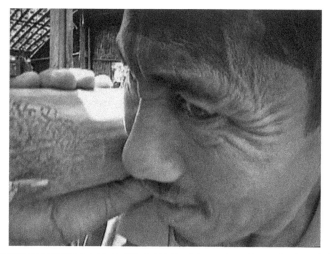

FIGURE 2.2 Director-cameraman Leonard Retel Helmrich works extremely close to his characters in *Shape of the Moon* (2004). (Still capture from DVD.)

performative. He acknowledges that documentary-makers are always trying to come up with new modes, or "different ways of representing the world."[10] This is especially true today, as filmmakers struggle to gain the attention of industry decision-makers in a crowded market. But Nichols cautions that "we do well to take with a grain of salt any claims that a new mode advances the art of cinema and captures aspects of the world never before possible . . . New modes signal less a better way to represent the historical world than a new way to organize a film."[11] The questions for you to ask are: Will the mode or style of my film be the best choice for structuring the story, will it be doable within my lean team limitations, and will it also yield artistically adventurous rewards?

In addition to modes, there are subgenres of the documentary style, seventeen of which are listed in a 2013 *New York* magazine article by David Edelstein, which trumpeted the sweeping digital changes within the industry.[12] Edelstein's list included verité films, personality profiles, investigative docs, diary or memoir movies, competition documentaries, nature films, and more. Some of his categories seemed invented for the purposes of his article—the "prank doc" is the niche for Banksy's *Exit Through the Gift Shop.* Today we can add virtual reality to the list. What is clear is that as more and more people make documentaries, the more blended and malleable the differing styles, subgenres, or modes become. The genres overlap. For example, Alison Klayman's *Ai WeiWei: Never Sorry* is certainly a portrait of a famous artist and celebrity, but it's also a film about political activism that *gets close* to its main character.

Edelstein's article includes a troubling observation, one worth remembering when you begin a film. He writes that "probably more people want to make docs than regularly go to see them in theaters." This is literally true, since very few documentaries actually receive a theatrical release these days. But it also applies to all of the docs that end up somewhere in cyberspace. How many people are actually watching them? You can take a wild guess based on user reviews from iTunes, Amazon, or Netflix, but these sites don't list total views. You can sometimes see viewing stats on Vimeo on Demand, but not for all films. Opacity seems to be the guiding philosophy for these online platforms, since true viewership numbers may be so low as to be discouraging.

That's why the payoff for all of your hard work, or at least the first reward in a potential string of rewards, must come from a personal sense of artistic satisfaction, a different set of expectations than fame or money. Yes, you are making your film for that splintered fragment of audience but also, perhaps most important, for yourself.

Be skeptical of making the claim that documentaries can "change the world." This is a noble idea, but it's an essentially meaningless phrase (as are its second cousins, "start a conversation" and "call to action"). Movies can illuminate or challenge the issues and causes they document. Movies can enhance or continue conversations already started. Movies can urge people to join an action already begun. But can they change the world?

Chris Boeckmann, a programmer for the True/False Film Festival, spent five years programming a monthly series of activist, issue-driven films before announcing, in an article entitled "Projecting Outside the Echo Chamber" for *Filmmaker* magazine, "After five years of earnest programming, I've come to the conclusion that I have wasted my time, and I suspect others' as well. Perhaps it generated some money or volunteer work for the partnering organizations . . . I'm certain it helped the filmmakers pay rent. But more than anything, it fed into the myth that this pervasive, pedantic sort of documentary can change the world . . . I've decided that I'm never touching another one again."[13] He goes on to confess that "nearly every one of these films has failed to leave an impression. They don't make me feel any more knowledgeable about the world, and they haven't inspired me to lift a finger."

A five-year diet of social agenda programming can turn almost anyone into a cynic, so I can see where Boeckmann is coming from. But then I encounter a film like Jennifer Brea's *Unrest,* which dramatically pulls the covers back on chronic fatigue syndrome, revealing millions of mostly young adult sufferers who spend their lives confined to bed. The movie may not move people to action, but it certainly exposes the misconceptions they may have about this devastating disease and may even make an impact on the search for a cure.

Impact. It's a word I'll come back to in a moment. But for now, let's talk about "access," the key component of every filmmaking seminar I attended in the late 2000s. Back then, your film had to stand out for its unique access to its subject matter. Nowadays, access doesn't seem quite as important as capturing the zeitgeist of current events. For example, as I write this paragraph in the summer of 2017, there are five fairly high-profile films available in theaters and online about the war in Syria: *Hell on Earth, Cries from Syria, City of Ghosts, Last Men in Aleppo,* and the Oscar-winning short *The White Helmets.* And then there are two more features and two more shorts airing at the same time on the PBS series *POV.*

Syria is a vast and complicated tragedy, but for my money, Sebastian Junger and Nick Quested's powerful and comprehensive *Hell on Earth: The Fall of Syria and the Rise of ISIS,* made for the National Geographic channel, tells the whole story. Do we need *nine films all at once* on the subject, especially since many of these films share the same approach and rely on graphic iPhone video shot by Syrians on the ground?

Times have changed since Ann and I made our post–Hurricane Katrina film, *The Church on Dauphine Street.* While we were shooting the movie, I tried to interest a New York distributor in the idea of our film but was quickly dismissed, told that "everyone is making a Katrina film." Yet only two films about the catastrophe, Spike Lee's epic *When the Levees Broke* and Tia Lessin and Carl Deal's *Trouble the Water,* broke through to the masses. We tried to make our film different by *not* including home-movie or news footage of the flooding, instead concentrating on the aftermath, but it made little difference. I sometimes wonder if Katrina happened today, we'd see a swell of shaky, iPhone-footage-based documentaries on the disaster.

If you spend a bit of time scrutinizing the current events issues making the rounds of funding organizations and festivals today—gender identity, political activism, refugees, minority oppression—it won't be hard to spot a new buzzword that has nudged "access" to a back seat. That word is, yes, *impact.*

The websites of several documentary-funding organizations prioritize impact, as in *social* impact, as a key component of your film's marketing strategy. The Jerome Foundation, the Fledgling Fund, the American Documentary Fund, the Miller/Packan Documentary Fund, Just Films, and many others state that the investors in their funds want to support films that make a positive impact on society. There is even an investment group called Impact Partners (one of the prime funders of *Unrest* and the 2018 Oscar winner for Best Documentary, *Icarus*), which represents a pool of around forty investors who select and steer a film toward a theatrical and multiplatform release, with the focus on earning a profit. Their goals include "raising awareness about critical issues facing our world today, reaching mass audiences on a global scale, and creating revenue for our films."[14]

"You need to have great characters," says Impact Partners' cofounder Dan Cogan. "You need to have drama, you need to have a three-act structure with a story that works just as well as a great feature film."[15]

Fine enough.

But as the critic Daniel Walber writes on the website Nonfics, there is "a sense that American documentary cinema remains firmly stuck in a rut of genre and form. The discourse lasts because of the continued proliferation of 'issue films,' calls to action that end with a website and an appeal for donations."[16] If your film does not strive for impact—if you don't have a Twitter hashtag in the final credits—then know you will have a much harder time finding money. If it does strive for impact, then know you will have a lot of competition.

This reality begs the question of how all the other types of films that aren't issue films will get made. These films, sometimes called "cinematic nonfiction," adopt more oblique approaches to subject matter and character. They are more concerned with impression and feeling, with immersion and ambiguity. They tell stories, but those stories might feel more like fables, and they may emerge organically from the images without explicit direction. These films are meant to engage, entertain, and even enlighten, but not always to educate. *Workingman's Death, Homo Sapiens, Approaching the Elephant, The Vanquishing of the Witch Baba Yaga, The Sea Stares at Us From Afar, Uncertain* and *Behemoth* are just a few of these types of documentaries.

These films and others that don't seem to push a particular agenda are often the ones that stay in your mind the longest and that can have a greater impact on your impression of a society, or even an agenda, than a film that preaches to the choir. Films that emphasize immersion and intimate character study, rather than talking-head experts and on-screen statistics, often do a better job of contributing to the understanding of a cause, or they entice a viewer into wanting to learn more. How do you explain your film's "impact strategy" to funders when it may be an unknowable quality, an element that becomes clear only once the film has been watched and reflected upon by individual viewers?

The British filmmaker Kim Longinotto says she tries "to make documentaries so they can give the audience the intimacy that only fiction tends to have. I don't want the viewers to feel separated from the film because they're given information and instruction." With tools such as Google and Wikipedia instantly available to all, Longinotto believes that "documentary filmmakers can cease to be the public service for answering basic questions. We can observe the world with finer precision, focusing on what's important to us, using the advantages of fiction storytelling."[17]

There are some funders who see the value in these kinds of movies. The Filmmaker Fund, Creative Capital, and the Sundance Documentary Fund are a few that don't always require a social impact plan as part of their application. I'll write more about funding later in this chapter, but realize that the cash for your more personal, experimental, observational, or non-social-impact movie will more likely come from crowdfunding sites or your own bank account.

The point here is to resist the temptation to assign your film a mission that is too lofty, too vast, too expensive, or just plain impossible to fulfill. If there is an issue or cause driving your film, fold it into the narrative through character development or a unique visual style. Avoid didacticism and lecturing. Try to look at your film through the lens of a lean team documentary filmmaker, adjust your expectations, and break down the elements of your project with these limitations in mind.

The rest of this chapter is a guide for doing just that: outlining your story and thinking about structure; identifying the visual material, the B-roll, of your film; determining the logistical challenges of locations and equipment; thinking about potential audiences and distribution avenues; and considering what funding sources, if any, may be available. In this first phase, you are mapping the *feasibility* of your film, from preproduction to distribution, within the LTDF model. While working through these steps, keep asking yourself, "How close can I get?"

STORY, STRUCTURE, AND CHARACTER

A good story is the spine of your film. Everything else—images, sound, interviews, music, text—forms the body of the film the spine supports. And a good story comes with strong characters. Sometimes the characters will be the spine, and the story they bring with them is the body. This is the premise of *The Fog of War* by Errol Morris, with its focus on Robert McNamara, secretary of defense during the Vietnam War; *Jim: The James Foley Story*, about the American journalist murdered by ISIS, made by his childhood friend, Brian Oakes; *Grey Gardens*, the classic portrait of the eccentric Beale sisters by Albert and David Maysles; and any number of celebrity or political profiles. But the majority of documentaries start with a story that *includes* strong characters.

In *Oil & Water*, by Laurel Spellman Smith and Francine Strickwerda, the spine of the film is a toxic oil disaster in the Ecuadorian Amazon, a potentially huge subject also covered in Joe Berlinger's *Crude*. To focus their approach, Spellman and Strickwerda concentrated on two young men passionately engaged in efforts to publicize the spill and cleanup the contaminated rainforest. The men were from different worlds and had met by chance years earlier, but in telling their stories and bringing them together, *Oil & Water* avoided polemics and ended up being an engaging movie about two individuals whose lives on our fragile planet mattered more than the cause that threatened to swamp them.

Characters are usually real, live people. But the main character of your film can also be a place (your hometown, a prison, the moon), a thing (an electric car, a lava lamp), an idea (time travel), or an animal (pick one). Much of Frederick Wiseman's oeuvre is concerned with the role institutions play in our lives, in films such as *Ex Libris* (the library), *National Gallery* (the art museum), and *At Berkeley* (the university). The institutions are his characters and the people are in supporting roles.

Sometimes powerful images alone are enough to form the basis of an entire film, as you can see in Nikolaus Geyrhalter's *Our Daily Bread*, about the mass production of society's food, and Glawogger's *Workingman's Death*, about the perpetually grueling nature of hard labor. Glawogger believed that "imagery is the essence of the art of cinema—and language, sound and story are the legs on which this painting-in-motion is standing."[18]

How do you know you have a story worth telling? Before you invest your time and energy, research a story's potential. In addition to finding the central characters, ask if the story has something valuable or important to say about the times we live in, even if it's a story about something that happened in the past. Will it offer twists and turns, surprises or intrigue? Is there enough potential material to make a feature film, or would a short film be better? Does the story have the properties of a setup, a conflict, and a resolution? Not that it needs to have these elements, but if it doesn't, what do you see as the propulsive energy, thread, or motivation within the story? What is the takeaway? What do you want people to feel? Has the story been told before? If so, is there anything left to say about it? Do you have special access to the story, its location, or its character that no one else has?

Sheila Curran Bernard covers all aspects of this craft in depth—from finding the story to exposition to structure to narration—in *Documentary Storytelling: Creative Nonfiction on Screen*. I'll touch on many of these elements throughout this book, as we explore the continual evolution of a story throughout the process of shooting and writing and editing.

When you're evaluating your project at this early stage, the most important thing for you to ask is, as Barry Hampe points out in *Making Documentary Films and Videos*, whether you're asking a question or making an assertion. "A question leads to a search for answers with the outcome not necessarily known," Hampe writes. "An assertion, on the other hand, starts from the conclusion and then piles up facts as proof."[19] A film that asks a question invests the viewer in the search for the answer. A film that makes an assertion is interested only in validating a point of view. The title of the 2006 documentary *Who Killed the Electric Car?* seems to imply that the film is asking a question, but what it really does is make assertions: that the car is dead, we know it's dead, we are mad about it, and we probably know who killed it (big oil, big car companies). The film spends ninety minutes making these assertions, all of which could have been perhaps more succinctly explained in a magazine article.

Films that make assertions add more noise to the echo chamber. Films that ask questions invite you to be surprised, or at least exposed to a place, a people, or an idea you may know little about. Which kind of film do you think is worth spending your valuable creative energy on?

Nina Davenport (*Hello Photo, Parallel Lines, Operation Filmmaker*) relies on a methodology that boils down to simply following her instincts. "I like filmmaking to be a process of discovery," she says, "to be able to start without anyone breathing down my neck, and to see where the process takes me."[20] This is one of the great advantages of documentary over fictional narrative: the promise of discovery. Keep this in mind when thinking about story. All you really need before you get started is a sense of the story and its potential elements and an educated guess about its trajectory and possible outcomes.

When we made our post-Katrina film, we knew that a team of volunteers was traveling from Seattle to New Orleans to help rebuild a church. We knew the church was the center of the deaf community, that the church was run mainly by two (hopefully charismatic) individuals, and that the volunteers would also include local union tradespersons, whose own homes were completely ruined by the hurricane. We had the elements of a tapestry.

Our job was to collect the various bits of material and start knitting. But we didn't know yet what it would look like when finished.

Since doc filmmaking is in a sense an expedition, you can consider yourself an explorer. Successful explorers are always well prepared, and preparing is what you're doing in this first stage: mapping out a route, identifying guideposts, considering who your companions (your characters) will be, and thinking about what you might collect along the way.

Start by making an outline to organize your thoughts. Nobody else needs to see this—it exists only to give you a visual idea of the potential worth of your film. Identify the big picture or theme (as mentioned earlier), make a potential shot list, jot down a few key plot points that may or may not occur, name a few characters (or a wish list of characters you hope to meet while making the film), and sketch out a possible trajectory or timeline of how you will organize your approach as a lean team filmmaker.

Move on to a general idea of the visual material the project presents. For our Katrina film, an initial shot list consisted mostly of wide-angle ideas: neighborhood, church, work crews, city atmosphere. We made six trips in all to New Orleans, and with each return trip our shot list grew longer and more specific. But think of this first stage as a way to entice you further into your project. You are making a *movie*. If you have trouble imagining the concrete images that will tell your story, this is the time to consider whether another medium is a better choice.

Also try imagining how your story will play out. Identify the inherent momentum that you want to capture. Not every story has to build up to a dramatic event or resolve itself with a positive or tragic denouement, but a story should have some kind of movement to keep a viewer engaged. Map out the plot points, the places where your story might turn corners or introduce surprises or reveal more depth. Again, don't reject your film simply because it doesn't contain "big moments," but be cautious about taking on a film whose small moments don't add up to anything.

Once you've decided your story offers enough material to sustain a feature-length film, you can start figuring out who your main character or characters are. Keeping in mind your stripped-down, LTDF approach, ask how accessible these characters are, how reliable, how comfortable you will be filming them, and how comfortable they will be being filmed. Is it possible to get the footage you need to illustrate these characters' stories all by yourself (or with only one other person)? Will there be rules or restrictions on where you can go? Will you be shadowed by handlers or bodyguards or assistants? Will the spaces in which the characters move have room for you?

Finally, take a cold, hard look at the timeline of your film. What will the project ask of you in terms of time and money and energy? If you're making a film about your hometown, can you capture the people, the places, the rituals, the businesses, and the barbecues working as a one- or two-person team? Will you be able to spend weeks or months documenting the natural flow of everyday life, or would you rather hire several crews to blanket the town for a weekend? The two approaches will render different portraits. The blanket strategy will yield an embarrassment of possibly superficial riches, while working as a single lean team will yield riches with more depth and meaning.

In his one-man documentary *The Overnighters*, Jesse Moss traveled to Williston, North Dakota, because he was curious about the fracking boom going on there and its impact on the people and the fabric of the town. In an interview on PBS's *POV* program he said, "From this big story of the North Dakota oil boom in which there are an infinite number of small stories, I was looking for a way in. A way to tell this larger story but on intimate terms."[21] He read about a local pastor who helped house and feed the large number of transient workers passing in and out of town, and he documented the controversies this act of kindness created and the revelations that followed about the town, its people, and the pastor. This is where Moss focused his filmmaking. *The Overnighters* didn't barrage us with dramatic facts, figures, graphics, and on-screen text about the oil boom; it conveyed the tangible dramatics of real people struggling to deal with the fallout of that boom, and Moss was able to do it by working alone.

In the work my wife and I do—the "for-hire" work, making short films for nonprofits— we are often told by the people we film that they were nervous before we arrived, that they were expecting a much larger crew, with grips and assistants and lights and a dolly. Even though we are working for a client, and the client suggests to us what to film and when, we come across as two people with a minimum amount of equipment who are there to hear our characters' stories. The barriers begin to fall away immediately. This is easily the most important benefit of the lean team approach. You present yourself as simply another human being, one to one, carrying a small, unimposing camera.

The esteemed feature and documentary filmmaker Werner Herzog works this way. In his twenty-six-part filmmaking course available on the Masterclass website, he says, "Become self-reliant. Make a film with only one or two people."[22] The crew for *Encounters at the End of the World* included just Herzog and his cameraman, Peter Zeitlinger. They would show up at a location and start shooting right away. Herzog interviewed people he'd met only minutes before. He and Zeitlinger gained immediate access to more intimate stories and spaces because there were just the two of them. The characters they profiled came alive.

After you've written your initial story outline—this first crack at visualizing your project—take a moment to stand back and ask yourself the most important question: Will you be able to pull this off as a lean team filmmaker?

POTENTIAL B-ROLL

I would like to assume that all aspiring documentary filmmakers know what B-roll is. It's a term that has different, sometimes disparaging meanings. Barry Hampe writes that "all too often journalists shoot illustrative B-roll while a documentarian looks for visual evidence."[23] He believes B-roll is filler, merely repetitive or uninspiring footage, video wallpaper.

I like the term "visual evidence," and since I started out in the broadcast news business, B-roll for me always meant exactly that: visual evidence supporting what the interviews or reporters were telling us or showing what a character's world was like. We simply couldn't return from the field with footage that didn't help tell the story or else we'd be out of a job. So for the sake of simplification, B-roll in this book means the same thing as visual evidence.

I feel it's better to use the term as an honest and convenient way to explain to your subjects what you need to shoot in order to visualize their story. "Thank you so much for taking the time to talk to me," I'll tell them. "Now I'd like to get some B-roll of you doing what you talked about in the interview." In fact, many people have suggested B-roll possibilities to me before I ask: "I'm going to feed the chickens now. Might make some good B-roll."

B-roll is everything else you shoot besides talking-head interviews. It doesn't necessarily mean archival clips, home-movie film, YouTube excerpts, etc., but if that is all you have to work with, then those elements do become your B-roll. *Amy,* a portrait of the late singer Amy Winehouse by Asif Kapadia, was constructed entirely out of existing footage, an ingenious workaround to replace the lack of original footage.

When we interviewed a union worker in New Orleans, he described the flooded house and streets he had to flee in his neighborhood of St. Bernard Parish. The B-roll consisted not only of shots of these same streets, but also of him driving his truck through the neighborhood, talking to us from behind the wheel, walking us through his abandoned home, flipping through the water-logged pages of a photo album. This was B-roll, the visual evidence.

The question you will want to answer before you embark on a shoot is whether it's logistically possible to capture the B-roll operating as a one- or two-person crew. You'll need to evaluate the location, the weather, the available light, and the dynamic or static nature of the subject matter with this priority in mind. Will you be able to shoot technically usable footage, meaning footage that is in focus, properly exposed, properly color-balanced, and with a variety of angles? Will you be able to move, adapt, react, and—most important—record high-quality sound given the conditions you'll be working in?

Let's say that you'll be shooting all or part of your film in an outdoor setting prone to blustery winds, interviewing characters or capturing important sound. Should you consider expanding your lean team to include a soundperson with a larger, higher-quality, wind-protected microphone attached to a boom? How will this choice affect your budget and the comfort level of your subject? In some veteran two-person teams, one runs the camera and the other the sound, and one or the other is the main "author" of their film (Broomfield directs and runs sound, as does Wiseman, who also edits). But still, you have to consider the presence of the boom mic as a possible distraction, a barrier, to the naturalism of the scene you are trying to capture.

Evaluate the "action" of the film. Will your subject be on the move, mostly static, or both? When we were making our documentary *Zona Intangible*, set in a large human settlement outside Lima, Peru, I knew we'd be filming a doctor treating patients in a clinic in a bustling squatter community. I knew the clinic would be busy, the location dusty and gritty, and most of what I would film was going to happen in daylight. All I needed was my camera, a short on-board shotgun mic, a wireless system, a belt pack for extra batteries, and a sturdy pair of shoes. I was well prepared (mostly; I left behind a critical light) when the doctor and his head nurse, a tough, athletic nun in her sixties, decided to make a home visit to a shack up in the steep hills near the clinic (see Figure 2.3). But I was well prepared only because I'd asked myself these questions when I was packing for the trip to Peru: Will I have to travel quickly through several locations to keep up with the doctor?

FIGURE 2.3 Because the author's gear was minimal, he was able to follow a doctor and nurse on an impromptu house call in *Zona Intangible* (2017), by Ann Hedreen and Rustin Thompson. (Still capture from digital file.)

Will I move with him or watch from a distance? Will I be alone with the doctor and one patient at a time in an examination room?

Remember the Tonya Harding story I mentioned in Chapter 1? Harding was the Olympic figure skater the media branded as a white-trash wild girl, who in 1994 was accused of covering up her ex-husband's role in the kneecapping of her rival, Nancy Kerrigan, and then found herself embroiled in a month-long tabloid-TV fiasco (the feature film *I, Tonya*, does a pretty good job of depicting the characters and milieu of the events). Pat and I covered this story for CBS News for thirty-five days, often working in the thick of chaotic perp walks and spontaneous courthouse press conferences, many of which turned into full-on media clusterfucks. We often had to film characters while walking backward through teeming masses of other camera crews who were also trying to film the same subjects while walking backward through the same teeming masses (although these moments were intense, they were never as rabid or ugly as they're presented in movies). It would have been nearly impossible to shoot professional-quality video without Pat grabbing hold of the back of my belt and leading me through the crowd, calling out obstacles (trash cans, stairs, trampled competitors) as we tried to stay in front of the action, with Pat, at the same time, recording audio.

What if the film you are making requires you, as a lone cameraperson, to shoot in a similar situation? If you want to stay lean and inexpensive, you will forgo the extra crew members (the soundperson clearing a path, the reporter shouting questions) and accept the reality that you will miss key moments others may get. It makes sense to understand this before you embark on your lean team shoot. The choice to work with fewer tools and people means you will make some sacrifices, but you will also be able to shape your film and your approach to gathering the B-roll you need with this limitation already in mind.

You can get a clear sense of the impact of these limitations by comparing two extreme examples of the so-called music documentary. *Dont Look Back* (the apostrophe is missing in the film's original title), a 1967 film chronicling a three-week Bob Dylan tour in England, was directed by D. A Pennebaker, who was also the cinematographer and lead editor. He had help recording sound, and three other cameramen contributed footage, but the majority of the film was shot by Pennebaker himself, who hung out with Dylan, Joan Baez, their friends, reporters, and other musicians. The loose, naturalistic scenes shot in hotel rooms, taxis, studios, and performance halls contributed to a teasing and complex portrait of the artist on the cusp of worldwide fame and controversy (the folk singer was only months away from "going electric" at the Newport Folk Festival). Two producers are credited, one of them Dylan's manager, Albert Grossman, who also appears in the film.

In contrast, the 2013 Oscar-winning *20 Feet from Stardom,* which explored the tentative desire for fame experienced by a few key female vocalists who sang backup for superstars (the most well-known being Darlene Love, who labored for years in the shadow of the notorious producer Phil Specter), featured a lengthy crew list. In addition to director Morgan Neville (who did not shoot or edit or run sound), ten producers, two cinematographers, three editors, three makeup artists, more than a dozen sound recordists, and a battalion of grips and camera assistants worked on the film.

The two movies are entirely different in many respects, although they both attempt to convey the personalities of the artists. But where *Dont Look Back* is raw and vital, with revealing off-the-cuff comments by Dylan and Grossman, and concert footage shot in a scruffy, you-are-there style, *20 Feet from Stardom* is heavy with glamorous, studio-mounted interviews (hence the makeup artists), multicamera concert interludes, and a kind of smorgasbord approach to character development. If the director had focused exclusively on the central, emotionally powerful story of Love, rather than cluttering things up with side characters and glitzy celebrity interviews with Bruce Springsteen and Sting, he would have made a more compelling and *much cheaper* movie. *20 Feet from Stardom* is entertaining and highly professional, and the music soars, but for my money, *Dont Look Back* is the more memorable experience.

It's important to be intentional about the narrative thrust of your B-roll. Does the B-roll have a storytelling function; does it enhance or advance the story? Or is it mere filler between talking heads, the wallpaper Hampe describes? I tend to call this kind of B-roll "cover footage." I often faced this problem when shooting TV news. We'd be interviewing a character describing something for which there was no illustrative B-roll. I would get a few shots of the person sitting at a desk, working on a computer, and talking on the phone. Or I'd be forced to settle for the shot of that person walking along a sidewalk for no discernible reason (22 million viewers got to see this ridiculously overused trope during Anderson Cooper's *60 Minutes* interview with Stormy Daniels). One piece of cover video I grew to hate was what I called *salad video.* This is the footage of last resort: you've just interviewed a couple in their home, and the only available B-roll is of them making dinner, which always includes a tossed salad. Try to avoid this at all costs.

Recently I watched two short films about the criminally mismanaged contaminated-water crisis in Flint, Michigan. Both films covered similar ground, and both had potentially powerful characters to help tell their stories: parents who watched their children develop rashes, pregnant women whose unborn babies could have suffered lead poisoning, ACLU lawyers angrily confronting government officials. But the films made the mistake of substituting droning talking heads for any dynamic footage of these characters in action. The filmmakers weren't thinking visually. They ignored the medium in favor of the message.

Another recent film, *Promised Land,* set out to tell an important story about the Duwamish Indians of the Pacific Northwest and their efforts to seek sovereignty for their tribe. But the film was a hundred-minute slog through a patchwork of dozens of talking heads endlessly repeating the same points, with an occasional cutaway to a standard-issue shot of a river or a few folks rowing a canoe that bore no straightforward or even metaphorical connection to the words being spoken. The B-roll was used as filler, not as a tool to advance or enrich the story, which suffered in the presentation. *Promised Land* was an academic lecture, what Hampe would call a "talkumentary."

Ask vital questions about your B-roll *before* you get started. If there are no creative or remotely compelling ways to tell your story visually, why make a film about it?

LOGISTICS OF LOCATION

Dont Look Back and *20 Feet from Stardom* also illustrate the importance of logistics. Imagine if Pennebaker had dragged a large crew (more than seven) or even a midsize crew (three to seven) around England with him for three weeks. Imagine him asking the mercurial, impudent Dylan to wait an hour while they lit the hotel room or laid dolly tracks for his arrival backstage at one of his concerts. The production would have ended before it began (remember that Dylan, ever the cranky iconoclast, initially brushed off the Nobel Prize he won for literature in 2016). In *20 Feet,* the producers decided on high-key gloss rather than intimate grit, using stages or elaborately lit homes where the subjects came to them.

When evaluating whether or not you can shoot your film in the lean team style, remember that while characters and B-roll can often be unpredictable, location tends to be fixed. Research your location, especially if it is unfamiliar to you. In fact, you should research not just your location but the entire scope of your film by looking at maps, reading books and articles, watching films (fictional and documentary), listening to relevant music, and talking to people—anything that brings your subject matter into clearer focus, that gives you a sense or flavor of the environment you'll be entering.

For *Zona Intangible,* we watched a fictional film that was shot in the very same human settlement as ours, a young city called Manchay, and we saw that it was built on a sprawling, dusty hillside, the houses connected by staircases, the neighborhoods by snaking gravel roads. We learned Manchay was thirty kilometers from Lima. We knew we needed to hire a car and driver to get us there rather than drive ourselves (as in many major cities in developing countries, traffic laws in Lima are mere suggestions; the city has the highest rate of traffic deaths per vehicle in Latin America),[24] and we knew we needed a translator (our Spanish was not nearly good enough to conduct interviews). These necessities increased our lean team budget. But we also knew, from our preproduction research, that we didn't need to hire a handler to open doors, we didn't need extra permits or licenses or clearances to film, we'd be able to get close and on the ground in our location with relative ease, and we didn't need extra gear or assistants. Shooting a lean team film in this location was entirely doable.

Perhaps the most important question to ask about your locations is one that may not occur to you: *Do I want to go there?* There are all sorts of places you would probably never go unless someone paid you. I once spent ten days in a dinky smudge on the map in northern Montana, ostensibly filming white supremacists for CBS News's *48 Hours*. Mostly I sat in my crummy motel room, waiting for the weekly shipment of semifresh broccoli to arrive so I could eat at least one green vegetable. Would I ever go back there to make an independent documentary? Not on your life. But I would go to Peru, or Bolivia, or the wilderness of the North Cascades mountains. In other words, if you're going to spend a few years and a few thousand dollars (but no more than a *few*) making a film that nobody told you to make or is paying you to make, why not pick a story in a place you've always wanted to visit and can see yourself returning to again and again? That's how my wife and I felt shooting our post-Katrina film. Each time we touched down in New Orleans we considered ourselves so fortunate to be helping tell the story of the rebirth of one of the most culturally rich cities in America (see Figure 2.4).

If you're a lean team documentary filmmaker, free of the editorial demands of investors or high-profile producers, why not make your movie where you want to make it?

LOGISTICS OF EQUIPMENT

The essence of LTDF often comes down to the phrase "just you and a camera."

It was just Jesse Moss and a camera when he shot *The Overnighters*. It was just Aaron Shock and a camera when he made *Circo*, a lovely tale about an itinerant family circus in Mexico. It was just Mark Grieco and a camera when he made *Marmato*, set in a Colombian mining town. It was Amanda Wilder working alone with her fly-on-the-wall camera recording the free-form learning going on in *Approaching the Elephant*. And it was Nina Davenport shooting as a one-woman band while making *Hello Photo* in India and *Operation Filmmaker* in the Czech Republic and London. Of course, you will need a few more pieces of equipment, such as microphones and batteries, to make your film (I'll get into the nitty-gritty of essential gear in Chapter 3). But you'll want to travel as light as possible, even if you're just going across town.

FIGURE 2.4 The author discovered many iconic images in post–Hurricane Katrina New Orleans while making *The Church on Dauphine Street* (2008) with Ann Hedreen. (Still capture from digital file.)

When thinking about the logistics of equipment, think small. Too much gear is intimidating. Too much gear creates a barrier to getting close. Too much gear slows you down. Too much gear is expensive.

Remember that when you're assessing the viability of shooting your documentary in the lean team model, the overriding question is: How can you shape the vision of the film you want to make within the limitations of the lean team strategy? If the logistics of your shoot blow past the limitations you've created, then maybe the film isn't the right one to tackle. Know what you're getting into long before you ever turn on your camera. Otherwise, just you and the camera could turn into you, the camera, the soundperson, the producer, the field monitor, the grip, the jib, the drone, the rental van, the financial overseer, and the exploding budget.

AUDIENCE AND DISTRIBUTION

The sheer bliss of creating art for the sake of it is sometimes the only motivation you need to go ahead and do it. But nearly all artists also desire some recognition for their work. Part of that desire comes from ego, part comes from an altruistic need to share the story they're telling, and part comes from a pragmatic reality: to signal to their funders or friends or family that what they're doing has a meaning that can best be validated if viewers see it and engage with it.

For these reasons, it pays to think about the future life of your film before you start and to recognize how the small-footprint approach you're about to take, or the *extremely personal* small-footprint approach, may limit your movie's exposure after completion.

As I stated in the introduction to this book, I'm puzzled by the bloated budgets of most mid- to high-profile documentaries, especially in a medium where the tools of creation are so cheap and accessible. Are large budgets meant primarily as a signal of a film's "importance"? It seems like there is a top 1 percent of filmmakers who get all the funding and festival exposure, backed by the marketing glitz of a handful of documentary production studios. "More than any other time in my 30-year career as a filmmaker," writes Renee Tajima-Peña, "the documentary world has become intensely stratified. There is a top tier, dominated by wealthy media companies, individuals and foundations, major film festivals and elite film schools."[25]

The films in this tier receiving theatrical exposure or exclusive deals with Netflix and Amazon Studios are packaged and promoted with the same splashy polish as high-profile fictional films. They have a long list of executive and associate producer credits, orchestra-rich music scores, and structures that echo three-act narratives. Some of the 2018 Oscar shortlist contenders, *City of Ghosts, An Inconvenient Sequel: Truth to Power, Icarus,* and *Jane,* exemplify a type of documentary that can be intimidating to lean team filmmakers.

For example, 2017's *Casting JonBenet,* in which the director, Kitty Green, auditions actors for a fictional film about the real-life death of the child beauty pageant contestant JonBenét Ramsey (a twenty-year-old tabloid story) and then turns those auditions into the subject matter of the documentary, is lavishly staged, lighted, and crewed. The documentary raises questions about motivation, not that of the six-year-old's murderer, but rather the director's reasons for making the doc in the first place. Is *Casting JonBenet* a layered meta-commentary on gossip and playacting, or is it a highly aestheticized stunt, a kind of challenge to other filmmakers to see how far they can twist the design and meaning of documentary? The movie boasts several funders (Sundance, Cinereach, Rooftop Films), two known documentary producers (James Schamus, Scott Macaulay), and a deal with Netflix, creating a formidably high standard that could convince the industry to close its doors even tighter to less connected, underfunded directors.

Lean teamers are already grappling with increasing demands to reshape their visions to fit the mold of funding organizations and investors. In "Documentary Filmmakers Find That an Agenda Helps with Financing," Debra Zimmerman, the executive director of the specialty distributor Women Make Movies, states that this situation is the "coalescence of a number of different trends, none of which has been really good for filmmakers who aren't interested in making social-issue docs." Commenting on the loss of regional grants from the National Endowment for the Arts (NEA) and decisions by both the Rockefeller Foundation and the MacArthur Foundation to stop financing films directly, Zimmerman added, "Unfortunately . . . we don't have any real national support for film as an art form."[26]

The Rockefeller and MacArthur Foundation grants have been rolled into other funds, such as the Sundance Documentary Fund, further narrowing the selection process. While these and the NEA grants claim to be directed more toward films with artistic merit than to those with a focus on advocacy issues, they are usually not awarded to filmmakers pursuing a mostly personal artistic agenda.

In addition, film festivals are falling into a pattern of accepting films that have been anointed by social issue or impact investors or those with deep-pocketed studios behind them. HBO, PBS, and Disney-owned A&E Indie Films had a startling total of twelve docs at the 2016 Sundance Film Festival. As Anthony Kaufman put it, writing for the online magazine *IndieWire*, "Old guard broadcasters were everywhere."

"Shouldn't Sundance," added Kaufman, "which values independence and has gone to great lengths in recent years to scale-back crass commercialism in its dramatic selections, apply this same intense regard for indie-ness to its U.S. documentary programming? If HBO had seven films at Sundance, that's seven documentary slots that could have gone to films not funded by Time Warner."[27] These high-profile "gets" bring in sponsors and audiences and reduce the desire of film festivals to take risks on blind-submission discoveries.

An industry programmer at Toronto's Hot Docs Film Festival told me that filmmakers' chances of getting a festival, distributor, or funder to pay attention to them are greatly enhanced if they have "a bankable Executive Producer or a known cinematographer" on their team. When I asked why—as in Why can't the quality of the film speak for itself?— she told me that it helps to have "reputable members of your team who have access to buyers and funders who know them and know their work . . . past achievements of the members of a creative team are a consideration."

By extension, then, these imprimaturs would seem to guarantee the quality of the funded film. So how does one explain a documentary as woefully insubstantial as Laura Dunn's *Look & See: A Portrait of Wendell Berry*, executive-produced by Terrence Malick and Robert Redford, shot by Lee Daniel (*Boyhood, Before Sunrise*), and partially funded by the Sundance Documentary Fund? *Look & See* "seems to have many objectives, yet accomplishes none of them satisfactorily," states a reviewer in the *Austin Chronicle*.[28] A movie that "encompasses two different films, and neither one of them . . . despite sincere intentions, is very good," writes a critic on RogerEbert.com.[29] Yet the picture's bankable producers and the known cinematographer helped attract funding, a film festival run, Netflix distribution, and a string of reviews, despite its questionable quality. The Sundance winner *Unrest* (a much better film than *Look & See*) lists thirty-four producers, co-producers, assistant and associate producers, executive producers, and co-executive producers in its extensive end credit roll. I present these criticisms to make the point that you, as a filmmaker, need to be aware of industry prerequisites that could pressure you into making creative or business decisions you don't necessarily want to make.

These pressures didn't used to exist in the documentary world. The one- and two-person teams behind Ross McElwee's *Sherman's March* and Albert and David Maysles's *Salesman* didn't have to consider the bankability of their films by attaching additional names to them. They simply produced stellar work. Robert Gardner went to India with nothing more than a film camera and a soundperson and made the seminal ethnographic essay film *Forest of Bliss*. The list of credits at the end of his movie is blissfully brief. Nina Davenport made her first feature, the sublime *Hello Photo*, completely alone. "Cinematography, sound & editing by Nina Davenport" reads her final credit (see Figure 2.5).

How would these films fare in today's marketplace? Would Gardner and Davenport have to rustle up a known executive producer—Errol Morris, Werner Herzog, Barbara Kopple, or Sheila Nevins (the powerful former president of HBO Documentary

FIGURE 2.5 Filmmaker Nina Davenport shooting on 16mm film and working alone in India for her directorial debut, *Hello Photo* (1995). (Screen capture from digital file.)

Films)—to legitimize their efforts? I don't mean to romanticize the past (well, maybe just a little), but if you are working mostly alone, with little funding, without executive producers or other connections to the industry, without the desire to submit to time-consuming and potentially disheartening rounds of pitch sessions, workshops, labs, etc., then you need to understand these new realities. It makes sense to adjust your expectations before you start.

At an Independent Filmmaker Project conference I attended called "Screen Forward," a panel of decision-makers (as they were described in the program) referred to a noticeable shift in the past five or ten years in how docs are judged and funded. They all agreed that your film must have incredible access, feature amazing characters, and be beautifully rendered in order to be seriously considered (and, as I said earlier, it must have a finger on the pulse of current events). The message to filmmakers seemed to be: don't even think about knocking on our company door unless your documentary is perfectly put together, passionate, impactful, and conforms to our idea of beauty. "So . . . ," I wrote in my notes, "making a successful documentary is like rushing a sorority."

Know that by opting for the lean team approach, you are opting for freedom, and that freedom may come at a price. Many of you won't know how your film will turn out until after you're finished. What started as a grand and important project may turn into a smaller, more personal achievement. What began as a small story you were making out of curiosity may take an unexpected, dramatic turn that propels your film to national awareness. Ask yourself what you will be satisfied with when your film is finished. Theatrical distribution? Broadcast on national or regional PBS stations? A run in major film festivals or a run in smaller regional fests? Maybe educational distribution? Or maybe streaming on your own website?

THINK ABOUT FUNDING

My response to funding has always been: just shoot it. Lean team doc filmmakers don't need collaboration, permission, approval, or even a whole lot of money to get started. Lean team doc filmmakers don't want to waste time filling out endless grant submission forms and then tapping their fingers for six months, waiting for an organization to get back to them, after which they will be either rejected or asked to progress to yet another round of evaluation. Lean team doc filmmakers will have a hard time getting money from the federal government.

Too many filmmakers begin a project by looking for the money first, which requires them to describe their film before they've even shot a frame of footage. This not only constricts filmmakers' sense of discovery but also forces them to make their vision conform to the desires of an unseen board of decision-makers, as described earlier.

In *Documentary Filmmaking: A Contemporary Field Guide,* by John Hewitt and Gustavo Vazquez, Sundance grant-winning producer Gary Weimberg describes fundraising as a "tough way to go. I found that if I put the same amount of effort into earning a living and donated that money to myself . . . in the end I was better off."[30]

If you do apply for funding, you'll have to come up with a budget, which Hewitt and Vazquez describe, accurately, as "a bit of a joke among producers—you don't have one budget, you have seven budgets,"[31] since often you have to adapt your budget to fit different-sized funding organizations. This time-sapping activity has little bearing on reality, but it's considered a must-do in laying out the vision for your film. My advice would be not to spend too much time on it, but at least give some thought to real numbers—most important, the cost of your *own* time and equipment, from preproduction to shooting to editing to postproduction.

The Sundance Documentary Fund and the International Documentary Association (IDA) have recognized the folly of asking filmmakers to tailor every funding application to each organization's demands. In response, they've created the Documentary Core Application Project, which brings together a number of funders to adopt a standardized set of proposal requirements. Right now, this still appears to be a work in progress. It's only a checklist, not an actual online form that can be saved and then submitted to participating grantees. This may mean spending a little less time on a process that can drain a filmmaker's creative energy, but it doesn't make it any easier to get your hands on that money.

One bright spot in the funding universe is that resources are slowly becoming more widely available, and more fairly allocated, for minority filmmakers. ARRAY, an organization founded by Ava Duvernay, the director of *13th,* is looking to help women and filmmakers of color. The NAMIC (National Association for Multi-Ethnicity in Communications) states they're on a "mission to educate, advocate and empower for multi-ethnic diversity in the communications industry." Firelight Media and the ITVS Diversity Fund strive to provide more distribution and funding opportunities for underrepresented racial and ethnic groups. A list of other organizations dedicated to cultural diversity in media can be found at the website Edit Media, which stands for Equity, Diversity, and Inclusion in Teaching Media.[32]

There is also a crowdfunding site dedicated solely to women entrepreneurs, called Women You Should Fund. With a model similar to Kickstarter, the six-year old platform was successfully used by filmmakers Jo Ardinger and Rosalie Miller to fund postproduction on their reproductive rights documentary, *Personhood.* Debra Zimmerman's Women

Make Movies has been distributing films directed or codirected by women since 1972, a vital outlet for stories that would otherwise go unnoticed by the greater documentary industry.

Unfortunately, this industry deems getting funding from approved sources (instead of, say, your rich college friend) a badge of prestige that filmmakers must display if they want to be considered legitimate or acceptable. At the highly competitive Hot Docs Forum, filmmakers are selected to pitch their project to distributors, broadcasters, and funders only if it has a *trigger financier* attached. This trigger financier—a term apparently invented by the documentary-funding bureaucracy—is a respected funding source that has already given you money. In other words, you must have money before you'll get any *more* money.

David Wilson, cofounder of the True/False Film Festival, told me his festival starts tracking films by keeping tabs on those that major donors are funding long before the films are ever completed. According to the No Film School website, "9 out of 16 of the documentaries in the 2014 U.S. Competition at Sundance were backed by well-known funding agencies" such as the MacArthur Foundation, Chicken & Egg Pictures, Cinereach, and the Fledgling Fund.[33] Filmmakers who apply for funding from these sources must be prepared to deal with possible rejection by the documentary industry before they've even turned on their cameras.

Take a glance at the most recent list of those who have received grants from the Sundance Documentary Fund, the gold standard of funding support in the doc world. Many, if not all, of the filmmakers receiving funds have track records of successful films, impressive pedigrees, and even previous funding from the same organizations. This is certainly understandable. It would be difficult for filmmakers to sustain a career without continued support from these sources. But it's hard for those on the outside looking in not to perceive bias in the process of deciding who gets picked.

One director in particular was celebrated as a MacArthur Genius Fellow, which comes with a mouth-watering $625,000 award spread out over five years. The director spent several years shooting a feature documentary and then received another $100,000 grant from the MacArthur Foundation (one of ten selected out of 540 submissions, a 1.8 percent acceptance rate) and another award for operational support. You would expect that, just maybe, the filmmaker had by now maxed out the limited largess funding orgs can afford. Nope. Those grants were followed by yet *another* generous grant from Sundance.

When one filmmaker receives close to a million dollars for a single film, a film still in production after twelve years, the phrase "share the wealth" may come to mind. I don't mean to suggest the director should share the money or refuse the grants; the problem here is with the granting organizations, not the artist.

To their credit, many funding organizations are aware of this inequality, and they make efforts to include a few first-time filmmakers in their granting cycles. It's vital to filmmakers that these foundations, as well as countless state, county, and city foundations, exist to help artists realize their creative dreams. But the odds are long. The Sundance website states, "We review up to 2000 proposals annually, but will generally fund no more than 60. We fund between 3-4% of submissions."[34]

The chances of getting funded are especially miniscule if you are an unknown film-maker. Liz McIntyre, CEO and festival director of the 2016 Sheffield Doc/Fest, said on the UK-based funding website Whicker's World Foundation, "It is clear that for the documentary art form to have a sustainable and brilliant future, the industry as a whole needs to consider how new and emerging talent is supported and enabled."[35] In a 2016 survey conducted by the foundation, many filmmakers agreed they could make an entire documentary for around $100,000, but it would probably be "a verité, observational doc with no archival material and limited music, where the filmmaker does all the editing and shooting herself." A budget the industry views as paltry, $100,000, is more than enough for a resourceful director to make a full-length feature doc. In other words, a lean team film!

The 2016 study concluded that "in a climate where funding for documentaries is often scarce and in decline, these findings provide insight into the financial challenges faced by documentary filmmakers." Jane Ray, the foundation's artistic director, admitted she was "shocked to realize that so many [filmmakers], 9 out of 10, are either chronically underpaid or apparently in a position to make documentaries without needing to pull a wage. Neither scenario strikes me as healthy for the future of documentary."[36]

I'm not sure what's more surprising about that statement—that most filmmakers are poor, that some are rich enough to treat doc-making as a hobby, or that Ray herself is "shocked" by all of this. Funders need to understand that even a sum of $50,000 granted to as many filmmakers as possible could help level the funding playing field. At that rate, the $1 million awarded to the MacArthur genius could have been divided among twenty filmmakers.

The Whicker's World Foundation's 2017 survey revealed an even starker landscape. Nearly half (41 percent) of "documentarians are supporting themselves by living off savings" and only "14% of documentary makers were properly paid for their time." The average amount of money filmmakers applied for was between $30,000 and $65,000, and "roughly half of applicants were unsuccessful in their funding application and others received less than they had applied for."[37]

Although Whicker's World caters mostly to British and European filmmakers, their yearly surveys mirror the terrain for Americans. A 2017 publication from the National

Endowment for the Arts and the International Documentary Association, called "State of the Field: A Report from the Documentary Sustainability Summit,"[38] revealed that only 22 percent of documentary professionals are able to make their primary living from filmmaking, and more than two-thirds make less than 50 percent of their salary, or nothing at all, from their films. Seventy-five percent of filmmakers make their films for less—way less—than $50,000. Even though foundation grants are still the primary source of documentary funding at 33 percent, personal cash is a close second at 24 percent. One must wonder, how much of the available grant funding is going to that 22 percent who can sustain a career in doc filmmaking?

In addition to spreading the available dollars among more filmmakers, major funders could cap the amount one artist can receive in a given two- or three-year period from *all* foundations. Filmmakers are already asked to state on grant applications the money they've received to date, so tracking the total would not be difficult. This would allow more filmmakers—those who actually have to work at other jobs to pay their bills—a slice of the slender funding pie.

The self-doubt that seeps into your soul at this early money-seeking stage of the process is exacerbated if you are also not invited to attend the aforementioned pitch sessions (which are popping up as regular sidebars at many major festivals). These sessions—also attended by festival programmers—are where filmmakers, after yet another grinding qualification process, get a few minutes to pitch or sell their project to potential buyers and broadcasters, where they face a barrage of questions intended to either buoy their confidence or destroy it.

This is Anthony Kaufman's 2015 description of the pitch session at Hot Docs: "For two days, The Forum takes place inside the hothouse Hart House room, where some 200 industry onlookers sit on wooden bleachers surrounding a central table, where nerve-rattled pitchers have approximately seven minutes to hawk their projects. Twenty doc films had their precious chance in the spotlight. Prodded, questioned, encouraged and cajoled by the veteran broadcasters sitting around the table, many doc producers emerged triumphant, with promises of meetings and potential investment, while others were left scraping their wounded egos off the wooden floor."[39]

And this report from John Anderson, writing in 2015 for the media magazine *Current*: "Every year aspiring documentary makers come to Hot Docs to pitch new work, much of it destined for public TV channels around the world. The result is the Circus Maximus of the nonfiction film world: thumbs up or thumbs down, from commissioning editors whose support can mean (financial) life or death"[40] (see Figure 2.6).

Wait. Are we cash-strapped filmmakers looking for a few pennies to make our movie or are we lining up to be waterboarded?

FIGURE 2.6 The international marketing event known as the Hot Docs Forum in Toronto. (Screen capture from the Hot Docs website.)

This kind of intense pressure seems ill-suited to championing new creative voices, and it causes substantial stress for filmmakers. In a 2017 report on the International Documentary Association website entitled "The Risks and Rewards of International Pitch Forums," Christopher Hird, founder of Dartmouth Films, questions the high costs of attending these meetings. "What you have at these things is, on one side of the table, some extremely well-paid TV execs and, on the other side, financially struggling independent filmmakers," Hird observes. "The financial risk is being borne here by the sector of the industry least able to bear it."[41] Filmmakers attending the 2018 Hot Docs conference had to buy a pass costing between $500 and $1,000 simply to be eligible to submit their work for pitching or networking meetings, without any guarantee of being chosen for those meetings, much less receiving funding. The filmmakers who go to these forums often report the experience is worth it for the industry contacts they can make, but they also add that follow-up with these contacts can be frustrating, with emails unanswered and financial support rarely forthcoming.

Granting orgs will also question the social impact bona fides of your project. As the Documentary Core Application states, in order to be considered for funds, filmmakers may have to demonstrate how their films will engage, educate, activate, and target specific audiences.[42] To their credit, grantors are now asking filmmakers to describe their creative approach to material as well as their audience engagement campaigns, but this can sometimes nudge filmmakers to walk a tightrope between expressing a creative vision and satisfying a funder's need for social impact.

For many documentary filmmakers, this hope for impact is the whole point of making a film and will always remain a laudable component of the documentary genre. But sometimes a doc filmmaker simply wants to take us on a journey (J. P. Sniadecki's *The Iron Ministry*) or spend time with an off-the-grid community (Gianfranco Rosi's *Below Sea Level*), study a character (Robert Greene's *Actress*), or seek to humanize the work of a celebrity or artist (Klayman's *Ai WeiWei: Never Sorry*). This can be refreshing for viewers, who are asked by these filmmakers to simply watch, absorb, and appreciate rather than feel that they now must answer the call to action.

You can choose to sidestep some of the fundraising pitfalls if you go the popular crowdfunding route. Create a Kickstarter or Indiegogo campaign, and collect your money a lot quicker than you could sitting through a grant-making cycle. But be aware that the actual month or more you spend begging from your friends is exhausting, potentially dispiriting, and not as lucrative as you might think. Kickstarter takes a cut of your money, you incur expenses delivering the promised rewards, and then the IRS comes sniffing around (you can declare your Kickstarter money as "gift income" to avoid paying tax on it, but then you can't take any business deductions against it; at least that's what my accountant told me).

Crowdfunding is a satisfying way to build an initial audience for your project and to let friends and family know what you're up to. But running a campaign shouldn't be taken lightly. If you're not comfortable asking people for money, it can be grueling and distasteful. You'll need to have a long list of people to whom you must send personalized emails describing your film. You'll need to update your progress with photos and new snippets of video. You'll need to post several updates a day on Facebook.

In effect, you're conducting a personal pledge drive, with no guarantee of success. If you don't succeed, it can read to some people as though you've failed before you've even started. And if you don't think you can or will actually fulfill the rewards you've promised people, then don't take their money. After completing a $30,000 campaign for our film *Zona Intangible*, it took us several more months than we'd planned to send out the rewards, but eventually we did. Don't invalidate the contract you made with your supporters by not providing the rewards you promised.

Another way to rustle up some cash is to find out if any nonprofit organizations are working on the same issues or in the same locations as you. Contact those orgs and ask them if you can make a deal. Perhaps they will pay you to repurpose your B-roll into a short film for them, or if you are flying to a faraway location, perhaps they will pay for your airfare in return for footage about their mission. If you've already bought your plane tickets and paid for lodging, they may hire you to make a film, since you're saving them the cost of travel.

Some filmmakers who work near conflict zones in the Middle East have had success selling their footage to TV stations or production studios, which provides at least a little income to allow them to continue working on their own projects. I have licensed WTO protest footage from *30 Frames a Second* many times in the past eighteen years.

In an article titled "The Messy Truth Behind a Day Job as a Documentarian," written for *Documentary Magazine*'s Spring 2017 edition, the Washington, DC, filmmaker Lance Kramer describes making client-generated films in order to help fund his documentary *City of Trees* (made with his brother, Brandon). He writes about their crowdfunding campaign, the small grants they received, the private money from friends and family, and the debt they incurred on the way to a $400,000-plus budget for their movie. They spent money on a cinematographer and paid interns, an assistant editor to log and organize their 250-plus hours of footage, and then another assistant editor, a composer, a colorist, a sound editor, a designer, postproduction studio services, and several more postproduction crew members, and all of this for a straightforward social agenda documentary. By the end of the process, Kramer admits this kind of funding and filmmaking may be unsustainable.

"If we have the gumption to turn the lens on *ourselves* and tell more honest stories about the underlying financial issues facing the system we work within," writes Kramer, "we can start a different conversation about how to build a new sustainable, diverse and equitable age of documentary. It may seem daunting, but it may also be a necessity, if everyone trying to work in the field today—and the people who should be entering the field in the future—are to survive and thrive."[43]

That "different conversation" could very well start with the filmmakers themselves taking on many of the roles they outsourced to other people, reducing the scope of their project, shooting less footage, exploring inexpensive alternatives to composers and postproduction studios, and hiring extra people only if they can truly afford to pay them a decent fee. Kramer admitted that finishing their film "was often contingent on asking people to work for below-market rates and long hours, which resulted in difficult relationships with our collaborators."

The documentary film industry has created a whole set of expectations around the steps deemed necessary to finish a film, especially in the expensive postproduction world, but are these steps *really* necessary, especially since the majority of films end up online rather than in theaters? *Zona Intangible* played on theater-sized screens at several fests in both the QuickTime movie and Blu-ray formats, and it looked and sounded just as good as the more expensively produced competition. Our postproduction budget for music, color, and sound was less than $10,000. This is not a humblebrag, this is a truth: you simply don't need to spend hundreds of thousands of dollars in order to make your movie look and sound great.

Fundraising is both an expensive and a time-consuming process, which defeats two of the principals of LTDF. It may require you to fatten your team by bringing in producers to make your project appear more professional to potential funders, *and* the start time will be delayed. So when looking for cash, the lean team filmmaker needs to ask these questions: How much money do I really need to finish this film if I do nearly everything myself? How much time am I willing to invest in finding this money? How long am I willing to wait before that money comes through?

TELL ONE STORY

A final note in this chapter about getting close. Sometimes filmmakers can get so emotionally involved in their film they lose sight of the story. They may feel like they need to delve into every aspect of their subject matter—no matter how mundane or beside the point—which results in a rambling, unfocused, overlong film. Or they become obsessed with a single aspect of it, which results in repetition (which often ends up making a film *feel* longer than it really is).

There are often many stories within any given subject. Lean team filmmakers will make the best use of their time and money by picking just one and sticking with it. *The Overnighters* could have been a film about the fracking industry instead of a film about the pastor who housed the workers. *Streetwise* could have focused on the causes of juvenile delinquency rather than on the kids themselves. *Circo* could have diverted its attention to the issues of rural poverty in Mexico rather than simply—and beautifully—telling the story of the circus family at its core.

You will embark on your film project not knowing how things will turn out. You will wonder and fret and be uncertain as to which direction you should take. You will be confronted with many possible stories as you go deeper. My advice is: Pick one. Pick *one* story. Tell *that* story. Shoot that story and don't worry about the others. And when you're deciding how to tell that one story, remember the lean team model: choose your point of view, find your characters, know your B-roll and locations, be confident in your gear, manage your expectations about audience and distribution, and reject the wearying demands of fundraising. Then go out and get started.

/// 3 /// THE LEAN TEAM TOOLKIT

Essential Gear and Supporting Equipment

Every week it seems there is a new camera on the market or a new upgrade for an old camera, or a new lens, gizmo, or gadget that makes your current lens, gizmo, or gadget an antique. There are dozens and dozens of different model numbers and price points for every microphone and tripod, every LED light and wireless system. There are so many tools available to documentary filmmakers that the choices can sometimes induce a kind of tormented paralysis, especially if you're just starting out, and *especially* if you're starting out with a tight budget. Where, exactly, do you begin?

A camera is obviously the first consideration. But do you succumb to the glossy advertisements and YouTube videos touting a camera's alphabet soup of high-octane features? Do you spend $20,000 or more on a camera that will impress high-paid pros who earn a living working on commercials and big-budget corporate videos, or do you buy a camera that works for you, right out of the box, and costs less—way less—than $20,000? And what about everything else you need—the tripod, lights, mics, and batteries—and a case to carry it all in? What if you buy the wrong brand or the wrong size, or too many of one thing and not enough of the other? Stressful, right?

Well, you're in luck. Because you are a lean team documentary filmmaker, you need only the essentials, and the essentials of LTDF haven't changed since D. A. Pennebaker chronicled Bob Dylan's tour of England in 1965. You really only need a camera, a microphone, and a format on which to record. This is all I had when I shot my film *30 Frames a Second: The WTO in Seattle,* and to this day I often film for hours with nothing but a few pieces of equipment. The run-and-gun team known as the Renaud Brothers, Craig and Brent, have made several broadcast documentaries using only limited gear, including HBO's *Dope Sick Love* and *Meth Storm: Arkansas USA*. In an interview with *Filmmaker* magazine, Craig Renaud said, "What is most important is knowing how to use well the gear that you have access to for a given story, no matter how potentially limiting that equipment might be."[1]

In this chapter, I'll lay out what these tools are, breaking them down into categories: the essentials; the supporting essentials; the essential backups; and the optimal additional tools. Nearly everything I discuss here can fit into one or two compact camera bags and can be carried to and from the location by one person (you). If you are already an experienced filmmaker, you'll no doubt have other favorites you consider essential, but these basic tools are all you'll need to make a lean team film.

I won't get bogged down in specific model numbers or explanations of how each piece of equipment works. That's what manuals are for (yes, *manuals*; read them, please!). And when I mention a brand name like Sony or Sachtler, it's only to say that these and other top-notch manufacturers all make excellent, reliable gear that is for the most part interchangeable in terms of quality.

When I consider buying new equipment, I always start with a reputable website like B&H Photo-Video-Pro Audio, the Magic Kingdom of filmmaking gear. I organize my search according to cost or brand. When I find an item I like, I make sure to read the customer reviews, since hearing from other professionals is the best way to find out if an essential tool lives up to its claims. I look for the middle ground in terms of price and quality. I need the equipment that will get the job done without depleting my budget.

There is no excuse anymore for poor quality in either image or sound. Even as an amateur you are expected to have the right tools to do the job. You don't see a documentary these days in which the images look like something from a 1990s TV news broadcast or the sound is so poor all you hear is a noisy room. Some docs with less than ideal pictures and sound enjoy festival or commercial success (*Hooligan Sparrow*), and in some films the raw nature of the footage is intentionally part, if not all, of the content (*Dope Sick Love*). But you owe it to your film, and your viewers, to give them at least a watchable and listenable experience.

To achieve that, you want your gear to be reliable, sturdy, user-friendly, easy to pack, high-quality, and affordable. And you want all of it keyed to the mantra of this book. These tools help to eliminate barriers, not create more of them, so you can *get close* to your characters and your story.

SEVEN ESSENTIALS OF THE LTDF GEAR PACKAGE

Camera with Zoom Lens

It seems like I've always had a camera in my hand, from my first days working for the third-string network news affiliate in Reno, shooting with an Ikegami broadcast camera the size of a suitcase, up through that heady week filming my first documentary with my new fist-sized camcorder, and then cycling through three more cameras and two GoPros while making several more documentaries and short films (see Figure 3.1).

When I worked in local TV news, the station supplied all the gear I needed. When I freelanced for the network news broadcasts, I had to have the same camera as everybody else, so the images would match when there were two-camera shoots. When my wife and I started our own production business, I needed a camera that produced a great picture, recorded professional-level sound, and was built for documentary-style shooting, not for in-studio work. I've had to upgrade this camera over the years, from that initial standard-definition version, which shot 4 × 3 images at 30fps, or frames per second, and recorded

FIGURE 3.1 This Ikegami broadcast camera was widely used by TV stations in the 1980s. (Screen capture from YouTube.)

onto MiniDV tape, to a modified high-definition (HD) camera shooting 16 × 9 images at 24fps onto high-definition video (HDV) tape and then to an HD camera with a 35mm sensor shooting in widescreen 1920 × 1080 resolution directly onto memory cards. I expect that by the time this book goes to print I will have upgraded once again.

The next new thing is 4K, the ultra-high-definition format promising stunning color reproduction and crystal-clear detail, which most new cameras include along with 1920 × 1080 HD. You can buy a palm-sized camera right now that shoots in 4K. But 4K digital files are much bigger than HD files, which means a lot more hard drive space is required to upload and store them, editing render times are longer, and the distribution network has not yet evolved to make it affordable to purchase or screen 4K-based material. More important, if you decide to invest in the additional hard drives and software that enable you to capture and edit in 4K, will you automatically make great movies? No, you won't. I personally hope we're a long way off from 4K replacing the current HD standard format of 1080, simply because it means yet another upgrade and more of our money spent in service of the technology industry rather than in service of better storytelling.

I consider several factors before buying a new camera. I never buy the latest cool camera to hit the market. Or at least I never buy it right away. I always wait several months for the camera to start circulating so I can read the reviews coming in from filmmakers working in real-world situations. I check to see if another camera appears a few weeks or months later that improves on the original. Maybe a few bugs will be worked out. Maybe the price will come down. If at all possible, I try to rent the camera first from a local production rental house. This is harder to do if you live in a small city without production companies. In that case you'll need to watch online demo videos of the camera in action and visualize applying it to the specific type of work you want to do.

For LTDF, the key considerations are cost; size, weight, and ergonomic design; how user-friendly it is right out of the box; and whether the recording media (i.e., memory cards) works seamlessly with your editing software.

Your top priority should be a camera that is comfortable for handheld shooting. You want to be able to hold it for hours and shoot at eye level while standing and also be able to quickly switch positions while still maintaining a steady shot (shooting from the hip, holding the camera at ground level, or raising it high above your head). You want it to feel light but solid. You want to be able to get pictures and sound without having to attach a lot of extra rigging (except perhaps a loupe or Velcro hood for the viewfinder to make it easier to see the picture in bright sunlight). You want to be able to pull it from the box it came in, plug in the shotgun mic, click a charged battery in place, insert a camera card, remove the lens cap, and start rolling.

When DSLR (digital single-lens reflex) cameras became the rage in the 2000s, they were basically 35mm still photo cameras capable of shooting creamy HD video with seductively shallow depth-of-field imagery. I was intrigued at first. But then I saw what you needed in addition to the camera to actually shoot documentary-style footage. You needed camera stabilizers and extra handles and add-on microphones and viewfinder accessories and a tripod. The footage produced by these cameras was gorgeous, when it was in focus. But maintaining focus was impossible when you were shooting handheld, which made them kind of ridiculous for shooting on-the-go docs. They were also *too* light. A camera needs some weight and heft so that you can move it around without ending up with shaky, unusable images. Given these drawbacks, I waited, and waited some more.

I waited until Sony finally introduced a camera that looked like my other cameras—small versions of doc-style broadcast cameras—and also produced creamy HD video with the seductive possibility of shallow depth of field and came ready to shoot with a zoom lens, which enabled you to focus on infinity, move with the action, and keep the pictures looking sharp, while giving you the option of zooming in for close-ups and achieving those soft-focus backgrounds (an effect known among still photographers as *bokeh*).

The camera also came with two channels of XLR audio inputs, a detachable on-board shotgun microphone, two hot shoes or mounting points for attaching a camera-mounted light and wireless receiver, and a viewfinder tube for shooting in bright sunlight. The zoom lens could be operated manually or electronically (servo lens), and it was inter-changeable with other lenses and lens adapters. It was perfect.

Except that it wasn't. The camera didn't perform well in low light (meaning I needed to use the gain controls if I was shooting in available light; more on that in the lighting section in Chapter 4), the servo zoom was quite slow (meaning I did most of my zooming manually), and it lacked built-in neutral density filters (meaning that shooting in bright sunlight required additional screw-in filters to reduce exposure and achieve a decent con-trast in the images). But I decided I could live with these drawbacks because the design, functionality, and price (around $4,500 at the time) were optimal for the type of films we made. The camera still works for me, but it has now been discontinued, which is the camera industry's way of telling you it's time to upgrade (see Figure 3.2).

Nowadays, the prices of even luxury cameras are not beyond the reach of many filmmakers, and those prices seem to keep falling. You can spend between $3,000 and $10,000 for a camera with an interchangeable lens that will produce superlative images and perhaps be more field-ready than the luxury, $10,000-plus models. You can spend as little as $2,500 and still have a fully professional camera that is ready to go out of the box (even less if you're willing to forgo the interchangeable lens).

When shopping for a camera, start in the low range. Read the summaries and examine the specifications. Pay close attention to what accessories you might need to make the

FIGURE 3.2 The lean team camera should be an inexpensive, user-friendly HD documentary-style camera, such as the Sony NXCAM EA-50, used by the author (now discontinued). (Screen capture from B&H Photo and Video.)

camera fully functional (i.e., lenses, microphones, batteries). If the camera has too many limitations, move up in price $1,000 or more. If you've always had success with a particular brand, stick with it. Don't let glossy ads or the documentary industry tastemakers steer you into buying a camera you don't need or that isn't right for the job.

The business my wife and I own has survived for nearly two decades because we follow a few simple budgetary rules: We keep our overhead low and our footprint small; we work from home; and we don't buy bells and whistles we don't need. We work with clients who hire us because we can tell their stories effectively, not for clients who demand a particular type of camera or piece of gear. When we make documentaries, we make them with the gear we have on hand.

Shotgun Microphone

There are literally hundreds of shotgun microphones and microphone kits on the market. They can range from a $6,000 top-of-the-line Schoeps used to record quarterbacks and migrating quail to a $30 Nady that will do an okay job of picking up the excited squeals at your daughter's first birthday party. A good microphone, one that plugs into the XLR inputs on your camera, is a must. But an expensive microphone is unnecessary. Fortunately, the lean team documentary filmmaker has it easy. The mic that ships with whatever camera you buy is probably more than sufficient.

I say probably because there are some of you who cut your filmmaking teeth running sound for a cameraperson, or who are sound engineers, or who play and record music as a hobby. In other words, microphones and how they operate and react are kind of your *thing*. Far be it from me to tell you your business. But if you are in the field working with the LTDF model in mind, if you are getting close to your subject matter, then the microphone that came with your camera (which costs in the $100 to $200 range if you had to buy it separately) will do just fine for picking up the necessary natural sound of any location inside or outdoors. In fact, I'm constantly amazed at how well these microphones work. A longer, fatter, more expensive microphone will do a better job of capturing the nuances of the same audio source, but it may require an adapter for your microphone holder, and its size could make the mic more distracting and your camera heavier, and you'd have less flexibility when shooting in tight spaces.

Field audio recording will be discussed more thoroughly in Chapter 4, but suffice it to say that I've used the on-board shotgun mics to record interviews in a pinch, capture an impromptu musical performance, or pick up the natural sound of a location. These mics are dependable and rugged, and they run off your camera's power supply, so you don't need batteries. All come with their own foam windscreen, or you can upgrade to the fuzzy, furry muffs with names like "deadcat" and "windbuster."

My first documentary, *30 Frames a Second*, was shot entirely with the camera's on-board microphone as the only recording source. It was built in to the camera, so it was not an XLR-grade mic. I couldn't detach it, but it functioned like a shotgun. I just made sure I kept my camera pointed in the direction of the primary audio source and—of course—I *got close*. If you find yourself with nothing more than your camera and your on-board shotgun microphone, you can still make a film.

Wireless Microphone Kit

Remember Pat Craft, the soundperson I worked with when I freelanced for the networks? He and I worked together for ten years, and he taught me a lot about how to place microphones, operate a boom, and rig wireless mics. When we first started shooting for network TV news, we were tethered to each other via a cable that ran from his portable audio transmitter into my camera. Eventually, wireless systems became the pro tool of choice, and it greatly changed the way we worked in the field.

Pat could attach as many as four wireless microphones on the key characters in the story we were shooting or place one or two mics somewhere within the location (on a kitchen table or a desk, next to a speaker). He'd feed the signals to his portable deck and mix them in the field. Usually he'd keep one of his inputs free to record the sound from his boom microphone. At times, he reminded me of a circus juggler, keeping all of his sound balls in the air at one time. He'd then send the mixed audio to one of the XLR audio inputs on my camera. I'd keep the other input connected to my on-board shotgun mic so I could capture sound close to my camera while Pat was across the room capturing everything else.

We'd perfected the method by the time the Tonya Harding story broke in Portland. I'd be scrambling to get close to the perp or the perp's lawyer while Pat would be somewhere in the media scrum trying to point his boom mic closest to whoever was spouting off the loudest. It was a nimble little system that taught me how important a wireless package was to my camera kit.

Today you can buy a high-quality wireless transmitter, receiver, and microphone package for $300 to $600. You can go cheaper, but I wouldn't recommend it. Nothing renders a wireless mic more useless than a limited reach or the possibility of frequency interference, the two drawbacks of cheap systems. You also want to buy a system that allows the receiver to be mounted on the hot shoe of your camera. My camera has two hot shoes on the front and rear, so I can screw in a portable LED light on the front and the receiver on the back. Gone are the days when I had to bungee-cord, strap, or gaffer-tape my wireless receiver to any available real estate on my camera. Buy a package that runs on AA batteries that you can easily change without having to remove either the transmitter from the person wearing it or the receiver from the camera. These three convenient features—direct camera mounting, AA battery power, easy access—are essential for the LTDF wireless microphone kit.

Headphones

Once you have the two necessary pieces of audio gear—a shotgun mic and a wireless—you need to actually listen to what kind of sound they pick up. In my early TV news days, I used a single earbud to check audio, which was crucial when I was a one-man band shooting two to three news stories a day. This was before you could play back video in your camera, so you had no way of checking your footage. If I came back to the station with bad audio or no audio on my interviews or unusable natural sound, the story would be worthless. I upgraded to headphones for my CBS work. I needed to constantly monitor not only the natural sound around me but also the sound coming from whoever was wearing our wireless microphones. Pat also used his boom mic to whisper directions to me if he saw an important moment coming up that I might miss. Without headphones, I'd have been lost.

Headphones are also essential to documentary *storytelling*. In addition to providing an accurate technical reading of sound quality, they force you to *listen*. Listening is a lost art in our sped-up, short-attention-span lives, but it's a necessary skill in doc filmmaking. The voice of someone you're interviewing takes on more narrative weight when coming into your headphones, concentrating your focus, alerting you to a potential change in the emotions of the person wearing your wireless mic, or tuning you to an offhand comment that could provide new weight or direction to an aspect of your story.

While I was filming a crew of union volunteers on their first day rebuilding a church in New Orleans' Upper Ninth Ward after Hurricane Katrina, all sorts of conversations were going on around me. My headphones keyed me into the voice of a plumber talking to another man about the twelve feet of water that had flooded his house. I turned my camera to him, shot a bit of B-roll, fired off a few questions, and then asked if he'd be willing to take us to his ruined home. He became a central character in our film *The Church on Dauphine Street*.

In order to listen, to *really* listen, you need a high-quality set of ear-covering headphones, not earbuds. A popular choice among pros is the Sony MDR-7506 headphone, an industry standard that costs only around a hundred bucks. It features a padded, closed-ear design that helps filter out noise; it's foldable and has a single, springy coiled cable that carries a stereo signal from the headphone jack on your camera. Accept no substitute.

Memory Cards

Easy one, right? You obviously need something on which to record your footage, and nowadays that means memory cards. I'm still in awe of these tiny, indestructible, high-speed wonders. Once I shot for a very long day in dusty, sweaty conditions in that human settlement outside Lima, Peru. I needed to quickly change cards in the field, so I popped out the full card, slid it into its plastic protective case, and dropped it in my zippered shirt pocket. It was only much later when I went looking for the footage that I realized to my horror that I'd tossed my shirt in the washing machine before removing the card. Fending off the rising panic (there would be no way to reshoot the day's work), I fished out the card and checked online to see what I should do next. I immediately found a video demo of someone dropping a card into a glass of water and stirring it up, then accessing the footage without any damage whatsoever. I tenderly inserted the card into my computer and there was the footage, completely unharmed.

This taught me great respect for these memory cards, and I vowed to buy only the best, or *extreme pro* cards, which cost a bit more than ultra or standard cards but are well worth it. The last thing you should scrimp on is your recording media.

Format your cards before going out on a shoot, which means deleting the previous footage on the cards so when you insert a fresh card it's ready to start recording. Formatting on the run in the field involves several camera menu steps and then a few seconds to wait while the card is cleared. This is just enough time to miss forever an important moment in your shoot.

I advise using either 16GB or 32GB memory cards for shooting high-definition video. 16GB cards can hold about ninety minutes of footage; 32GB cards hold three hours (a 32GB card will store only eighty minutes if you're shooting in 4K). You'll change cards more often with 16GB, but if you ever misplaced one before you transferred the footage, you would have lost only ninety minutes of footage. You'd lose twice as much with a 32GB card. But a 32GB (or even a 64GB or 128GB card) is a nice luxury when you're shooting in difficult environments for a long period of time. You have peace of mind knowing you've got plenty of recording space, and you don't have to change cards if your hands are dirty or there is dust flying through the air.

A word of caution, however. The capacity of memory cards makes it so much easier for filmmakers to roll on and on, shooting hours of meaningless footage, all of which will have to be logged or transcribed at some point. Don't let the high capacity of your recording media justify lazy, unfocused gathering of B-roll in the field (a topic I'll address in more detail in Chapter 4).

Batteries

Batteries aren't as sexy as wireless microphones or super-tough memory cards, but they are, of course, essential. *Fully charged batteries* are, uh, even more essential. I try not to go into the field without knowing I have at least two fully charged camera batteries with me (lithium batteries, the industry standard, carry seven to nine hours of shooting time on each). I usually carry three (plus a smaller battery I keep on deep backup that I can also use on my camera-mounted LED light).

In addition to power for my camera, I make sure I have enough AA batteries for my wireless system. If your accessories need AAA or 9-volt batteries, have those on hand as well. Keep in mind that AA batteries run out of steam a lot faster than your lithium batteries do, so carry a lot of them. Thankfully, AA batteries are usually easy to find anywhere in the world.

Even veteran filmmakers have experienced the sinking feeling of that moment when you go to replace your dying camera battery and the replacement is already a cadaver, and you realize the battery sitting back home on your charger is the live, fully charged one. This has happened to me when I've been in a hurry or distracted, so I always try to mark my batteries with white tape that I've numbered one, two, three, and so on. The numbers face up in my camera bag when they are charged; I turn them face down when they are dead. I also try to never leave a battery on a camera I've packed away. One too many times I've kept a battery on my camera and then inadvertently left the camera powered up while I put it back into my bag for the long drive to the next location. The battery, which had a 70 percent charge when we stopped filming, now has a 30 percent charge when we start up again. If you've got more than a couple hours between shoots, remove the battery (unless your next location may require you to leap from your vehicle and start shooting right away).

Remove the battery if you're storing your camera for several days or weeks. It can slowly leach power while keeping your camera's internal clock running.

Bandana

A what? A bandana? Like, to wear around your head or neck when you're shooting in exotic places so you can look fashionable or daring?

No, a bandana isn't a clothing accessory. The reason a bandana is the last of the seven essentials in the LTDF gear package is that it can literally make it possible for you to continue shooting in less than ideal conditions.

A soft, well-worn cotton bandana can be used to wipe water, mud, or blood off your camera lens (it won't scratch or smear). Use it to clean fingerprint smudges from your viewfinder. Drape it over your camera when you have to sprint through a rain shower or a cloud of sawdust. If you're shooting in the developing world and need to wash your hands, use your bandana as a hand towel. And if you ever get tear-gassed, like I did during the WTO protests in Seattle, pull the bandana over your face and run like hell.

I also keep a professional micro-cloth and a small bottle of cleaning solution in my bag, which I use for more thorough lens cleanings. But nothing beats a bandana. I always have one in my back pocket. I'd feel naked, and less stylish, without it. (See Figure 3.3 for a list of the seven essentials.)

FIGURE 3.3 The seven essential pieces of gear needed to make a documentary. The items in this photo are not endorsements of any one brand or model. (Still capture from digital file.)

SEVEN SUPPORTING ESSENTIALS OF THE LTDF GEAR PACKAGE

Tripod

Many of you will argue right away that a tripod should be on the essentials list above. And I would tend to agree. But the point is that if you have the gear in that list, you can shoot an entire documentary anywhere in the world, one that includes interviews and decent ambient sound, without a single other piece of equipment. You can even fool people into thinking you had a tripod for some images by resting the camera on tables or guardrails or boulders or cars, but you won't be able to smoothly pan or tilt. If you're not comfortable with those limitations or your handheld skills are not yet fully developed, then include a tripod on your essential list. For now, we'll consider it a supporting essential, although a very important one!

I am still embarrassed to admit that when I started working as a freelance cameraman, the first tripod I bought was a crummy, used son of a bitch that I could never depend on. The legs would jam so I couldn't extend them, the head was about as fluid as a bag of rocks, I couldn't fully tighten the spreader, and the whole thing was ugly and heavy. Somehow I made it work, until I could afford a brand-new tripod made by one of the top manufacturers, Sachtler. This was when I was shooting with a heavy broadcast camera, so the tripod needed to be strong and steady. It cost me $4,000 and I used it for nearly twenty years, even after I graduated to a smaller camcorder. Finally, deciding to stop the madness (and to give my wife a break, since she ended up carrying the tripod a lot), I bought a much lighter, much cheaper tripod—still a Sachtler, still an excellent piece of equipment, but one that greatly improved our working, and marital, relationship.

The point of this story? Once you've traded in an essential piece of equipment that is basically garbage for a new one that is top of the line, you'll never, ever make the same mistake again. So whether it is a Sachtler, Vinten, Cartoni, Manfrotto, or any other leading brand, get a tripod with these must-have features: a fluid head with several notches of drag (fluid heads use a sealed liquid to create a hydraulic system enabling smooth, steady pans and tilts; drag refers to the level of resistance in panning and tilting), a quick-release mechanism for glitch-free locking and unlocking of the camera, a spreader that connects to the middle of the legs (although some shooters prefer spreaders that connect to the feet for more stability), and two stages of extension. Make sure the legs are made of light-weight, weather-resistant material (carbon fiber or aluminum, light enough to carry on a long hike). You want a tripod you can set up in saltwater if you have to, with legs you can easily adjust to level out on a narrow rocky path (easier done with midleg spreaders) and will keep your camera stable if you walk away from it. It should have an easy to read leveling bubble for the fluid head that allows for quick adjustments to the horizon of your shot.

Don't waste your time on anything less. Don't be a cheapskate (like I was) (see Figure 3.4).

Wide-Angle Converter

As I wrote in Chapter 2, when I was working for the CBS series *48 Hours,* all shooters were expected to have wide-angle capability. When you are close to your subject, the wide angle makes the world look more vigorous, and it draws the viewer immediately into the action. "Why is a wide-angle photo usually better when you are closer to the subject?" asks still photographer Stanley Leary. "Because it gives you the feeling of *being there.*"[2]

A wide-angle lens reduces the amount of shakiness in handheld shooting simply be-cause a wider field of view is more stable. Try shooting a walking, handheld shot while zoomed in to your subject. Then shoot it while zoomed all the way out. You'll see the difference.

Some pros buy expensive wide-angle *lenses* (which cost thousands of dollars), but I like the cheaper and more adaptable *converters* (a few hundred bucks). A wide-angle converter (or conversion lens, as you'll see it sometimes listed in B&H Photo's online catalog) screws directly onto the front of that lens, quickly expanding the field of view.

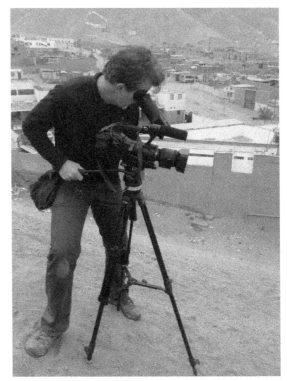

FIGURE 3.4 The author using his lightweight tripod with midleg spreader to shoot on a hillside in Peru. (Photo by Ann Hedreen.)

The glass on the converter is not as refined as the glass on the lens, but the resulting image from this inexpensive substitute is virtually indistinguishable, even to the trained eye, from that produced by the high-priced version and so much easier to attach. A converter is also cheaper to replace if you lose it or break it, an important consideration for the lean team filmmaker.

When researching wide-angle converters, you want to make sure of three things. First, you want a converter you can zoom through. Some don't offer this ability, and you'll be frustrated every time you want to zoom in for a close-up, since you first have to remove the converter. Second, make sure the thread size on the converter—the ridges on the inside of the cylinder—matches the thread size on your camera's zoom lens (62mm, 67mm, 58mm, 77mm . . . the variables are annoyingly endless). Third, check to see if the converter causes vignetting, which means it will reveal the edges of its own rim when zoomed all the way out. Some converters also distort the edges of the image when zoomed *in*, another vignetting effect that can actually lend an interesting, dreamy look to a shot, but one you may not always want.

Neutral Density Filters

Most cameras come with neutral density (ND) filters already built in. These features control the amount of light allowed into the lens, which affects your depth of field (the plane of focus within a shot), and are especially valuable when you're shooting in bright sunlight. They have two to eight ranges of f-stop, and you would activate them when, for example, the iris on your camera is closed down as far as it can go before closing completely (e.g., at f-stop 22), but the scene is still overexposed. It's best to conduct field experiments with ND filters. An ND filter, properly used, will make it possible to shoot in bright sunlight.

Some manufacturers sell cameras without ND filters in order to reduce their price. You can buy screw-on variable ND filters from Tiffen that are designed with a built-in rotating ring to control neutral density ranging over eight f-stops, or you can buy individual ND filters for each stop. Again, check to make sure the thread size is the right one for your lens. The best option, however, is to buy a camera with the ND filters built-in, a more expensive but versatile choice that saves time in the field.

Camera Battery Charger

Batteries today hold their charge much longer than they used to. So, like a Prius owner who forgets to stop at that last Gas-n-Sip before heading out into the desert, you may forget to bring along your battery charger when going out of town on a shoot. Don't.

Even if I know I have full charges on all three (or four) of my batteries and I'm only going to be gone overnight, I always bring the charger. This habit is partly a holdover from my news cameraman days. We never knew when we'd be in one city wrapping up a story, about to head home, and we'd get a call to cover a breaking story in another city. Batteries? Check. Battery charger? Check.

Black Gaffer Tape

When I say "gaffer tape" I don't mean "duct tape." Duct tape is made of plastic or vinyl, the adhesive side is gooey, it too easily sticks to itself (rendering it useless), and it's mainly intended for household repairs or, if you grew up in a rural, redneck county like I did, for attaching a rotting muffler to the underside of a '72 Chevy Malibu. Never take duct tape on a shoot. Don't even think about it.

Gaffer tape is made of heavy cotton cloth with strong adhesive properties. Because it's made of fabric and the sticky side is rubber-based, it's resistant to heat and can be easily removed without damage to the surface it's stuck to. Gaffer tape can hold drapes or a backdrop against a wall (and it won't peel the paint off when removed), it can keep a bulky accessory (like an extra wireless receiver) secure on the back of your camera, it can hold a microphone cable hidden under a subject's shirt or jacket, it can be a temporary fix on a broken piece of gear, and it can reinforce a GoPro attached to a helmet or a car. It can be used in literally dozens of ways.

I suggest you buy a big roll of gaffer tape at a professional camera supply store and keep it with you at all times. Make it black because it will blend more easily with most surfaces that might show up in your shot. If you don't want to carry the whole roll when packing light, pull off a few strips and tape them to your hip belt or knapsack. Strip them off when you need them. They will still retain their stickiness. The one drawback: it doesn't work well when wet, so don't use it on your Malibu's muffler.

LED Camera-Mounted Light

LED technology has revolutionized lighting for the lean team documentary filmmaker. The light I use now is inexpensive, small, and lightweight, runs off AA batteries or a lithium camera battery, and is incredibly versatile. It has two dials on the back—one controls brightness and the other color temperature—so I can go bright or dim, daylight or tungsten. It never gets hot to the touch, is easy to pack, slides quickly onto a camera's hot shoe, and can also be attached to a stand to use as a fill light during interviews or for shooting B-roll. Long gone are the days of the sun gun, a light so garishly bright and hot it made your subjects feel like they were undergoing police questioning. The next generation of that light, a smaller Fresnel version, was only slightly more subtle and required a flip-down filter (called a "dichroic") to change the glaring tungsten into glaring daylight.

These handy, well-designed, but simple to use LED lights can enhance any low-light situation and can, of course, make it possible to shoot in the dark. They should be used as judiciously and subtly as possible, however. They work best to fill in dimly lit faces or to add an accent on close-ups.

Camera Shoulder Strap

As a lean team filmmaker you will be working alone a lot, sometimes on a muddy field or a sandy beach or a sticky wet floor, away from your car or camera bag or any place to set the camera down. You won't have someone carrying and repositioning your tripod for you. You won't have someone to pass your camera up to you after you climb that ladder to get a high-angle shot. You won't have an intern standing by to hold your camera while you dash into a Honey Bucket. That's why you need a shoulder strap. All cameras should come with them. It's not a silly accessory (although it can be a bother if you're shooting interviews and you've already got wireless and headphone cables dangling from your camera).

If I'm heading out to a location by myself to get a few crucial shots and I need to travel light and work quickly, I always make sure I attach the shoulder strap before I leave the car so I can quickly hang the camera across my body when I need to reset my tripod or free up my hands for a climb; I can keep the camera off the floor in a damp public bathroom or hang it from a sturdy hook in the stall. The shoulder strap is nothing fancy, just a supporting essential. Throw it in your bag and keep it there.

SEVEN ESSENTIAL BACKUPS OF THE LTDF GEAR PACKAGE

Camera Manual

I can see your knuckles whitening, the blood vessels throbbing in your neck, the blank look of terror in your eyes. "A m-m-manual? Oh, please, God, *NO!*"

I've been fighting this losing battle for years, but I will never give up. Every camera comes with a manual (either a paper booklet or an online PDF). It's an instruction booklet. It tells you how to operate and get the most out of the most important tool you have. Your creative future, your very livelihood depends on knowing how to make that pricey piece of gear work. It's not junk mail.

But I get it. Manuals are daunting, detailed, long, and boring, the Romanian Slow Cinema of reading material. For that reason, I've always tried to make the process of reading one as "enjoyable" as I can. Here's what I do: I block out two or three hours on a Saturday afternoon. I sit at my desk with music streaming from my computer. I pour myself a tasty microbrew. I set my brand-new camera on my desk and plug in either a freshly charged battery or the camera's AC power cable. I open the manual and start reading, and while I'm reading I play with the camera. I try out all the controls and settings; I scroll through the menu; I shoot a little video, then play it back to see what it looks like when I do something right or do something wrong. If I don't understand something about shutter speeds or depth of field, I Google it.

I make friends with my camera, get to know its idiosyncrasies, its strong points and weak ones. I proceed deliberately and I read the whole manual all the way through at least once, usually twice. It helps to study the manual just before you have your first shoot so you'll remember what you read. And then I put it in my camera bag and keep it there (this is why I prefer the paper version).

The manual can also come in handy on those rare occasions when you get an error reading on your camera. Look up the message, and it will probably be explained. Most errors are temporary and you can easily fix them by rebooting your camera. There will also inevitably be times in the field when you know your camera is capable of doing something but you forgot how to make it happen, or you accidently touched the wrong menu item and can't remember how to undo it. There is no shame is checking the manual as a reminder.

Don't be afraid of the manual. Read it. Learn it. You will be a better cinematographer because of it.

Extra Microphones

A microphone can go on the blink, get touchy, or completely fail. This usually happens when it's old (although I still keep my fully functional, twenty-year-old, industry-standard ME80 microphone on deep backup). Or you can lose it, drop it, or forget to bring it. That's why you carry backups: a backup wireless, lavalier, shotgun. Maybe give your backups an extra touch of versatility. My backup wireless system has an XLR input so I can plug in a shotgun and use it as a boom mic; my backup lavalier will not plug into my wireless, but it works hardwired into my camera, so I can use it for interviews (sometimes your wireless won't work due to radio frequency interference, so your hardwired backup lav will save you). I keep the ME80 mic in the bottom of my bag. I hardly ever use it, but extra mics don't take up a lot of room. Have them for peace of mind.

Audio Cables

Before there were wireless mics there were audio cables. After wireless mics there are still audio cables. Don't rely on a wireless to do all of your work for you. Sometimes you'll encounter a consistent buzz or hum in your wireless due to unexplained frequency issues in buildings. You can try changing the frequencies on your wireless to find a clear channel, or—if you're shooting an interview—you can hardwire your mics with audio cables. (This is not advisable, however, if you're trying to follow your character around; in that case, ditch the wireless and just get close to your character and capture audio with the camera's shotgun mic.) Carry at least one twenty- to twenty-five-foot audio microphone cable and one short five-foot cable. Don't buy them at a chain electronics store; order instead from a professional website. You want tough XLR cables that withstand feet, furniture, mud, and being dropped on concrete. They will last for years. Have a few more on hand to keep at home and bring them with you if the audio needs on your shoot are more complicated.

Prime Lenses

A prime lens is the opposite of a zoom lens. It has a fixed focal length, so you can't zoom in or out. Primes come in many lengths: 14mm, 50mm, 105mm, 600mm, and many numbers in between (in contrast, a zoom lens, for example, can telescope from 18mm to 200mm). A 600mm prime might be used for wildlife shoots. A 14mm would be an ultra-wide lens (like the wide-angle converter mentioned earlier in this chapter, but unable to be zoomed through). Because primes are fixed, they're not a great choice for a constantly changing documentary-like situation, but they can certainly be applied in special situations to achieve a certain look.

A short prime in the 14mm to 90mm range will work well in low-light situations because its f-stop opens to wider maximum apertures, such as 1.4 or 1.8. Primes can be ridiculously expensive, so know what you want to use them for, and ask yourself why a zoom lens isn't sufficient to capture all the focal lengths you may need.

In LTDF, the constant changing of lenses may slow you down, and if something happens requiring a quick change in focal length (a sudden need to zoom in for a close-up or pull wide for an establishing shot), you'll be sunk. I mainly use one prime 60mm lens (priced at around $250) for interviews I shoot off a tripod. The 60mm can shoot at f2.8, which is several stops better than if I pushed my 18–200mm zoom to that same focal length. The resulting soft background, the extra few f-stops, and the sharper focus are an improvement over the zoom lens.

My camera comes with a nifty digital zoom feature, which allows me to attach a prime lens and still zoom in and out within a limited range, meaning that during an interview I can get both a head-and-shoulders close-up and a wider waist-up field of view without any loss in resolution or f-stop. This feature is called *lossless*, and although camera engineers will tell you there actually is a slight loss of resolution in this digital zoom function, it is not perceptible to the naked eye. Without that little bit of zoom capability, I'd have to physically move the tripod closer to or farther away from my interview subject to change the focal length.

I've also used the 60mm to shoot crisp close-ups on faces from a distance in settings where my presence might be distracting, such as when I'm filming kids in a classroom or members of an audience in a theater. It's worth it to have at least one prime lens for this uptick in versatility.

Portable Hard Drive

It's important to have a backup portable hard drive if you'll be working out of town for several days. This gives you two copies of your footage: your memory cards and the drive. If you decide to erase (or *format*) your memory cards while shooting on location, then you should have two backup drives. If you're flying home from this shoot, keep both drives with you on the plane. If you're working with someone, your partner should carry on one of these backups and you should carry on the other. Large-capacity drives (1TB or more) are so cheap, stable, and small that there is no excuse for not having at least one of these with you.

Laptop with Editing Software

If you are bringing along a portable hard drive, you will probably want to have your laptop as well, with your editing software installed in it. It's the easiest way to transfer and then copy your footage, it gives you a head start on the logging process (more on that in Chapter 5), and it allows you to edit a few seconds of your footage if you feel inclined to upload a preview to social media. If you are like me and prefer using both a mouse and an external color-coded editing keyboard, then you'll need to bring along a high-speed USB hub, which provides extra USB ports for easy connection of all your devices.

Additional Camera

One of my earliest fears when I started working in broadcast news was that my camera would break and I'd be expected to know how to repair it in the field. I had no idea how to solder a broken wire or clean a rotating head. Fortunately, my camera has failed on me only twice in my thirty-seven years of shooting. It happened once when I was out of town for NBC News as part of a two-camera team. The other team member took over my part of the assignment. It happened again on a shoot three miles from my house. I ran home and dusted off my old camera so I could continue.

Thankfully, cameras today are extremely well made. They have few moving parts—no more rotating cassette heads or ejection parts to jam up on you—and with their complicated digital circuitry you wouldn't be expected to open them up and fix them anyway.

For years, I rolled the dice when I was out of the country and brought along only one camera. Nowadays, I will bring a GoPro and, of course, a smartphone. Neither of these will replicate your main camera, but it just doesn't make economic sense for the lean team filmmaker to own two of the same camera. What you need is something small and simple that can keep recording pictures and sound while you either get your camera fixed or buy a new one. The latest version of the iPhone will fit the bill, especially with the apps and accessories you can now buy to increase the production value, including sliders, Steadicams, and various lenses.

SEVEN OPTIMAL ADDITIONAL TOOLS OF THE LTDF CAMERA PACKAGE

Up until now, I've been trying to keep the essentials list narrowed down to those things you can keep in a camera bag (except for the tripod, which ships with its own soft case), making it easy for you to leap out of a car or plane (well, not literally out of a plane) and shoot an entire documentary if you have to. But there are a few additional tools that will round out your kit while still keeping your footprint small and your style nimble.

A Compact Key Light for Interviews

I have an LED light from Generay (less than $500) that pumps out around 250 watts of light. I use it as the key light for all of my one-on-one interviews, keeping it close to the subject and usually mixing it with ambient window light, a small amount of fill light, or a reflector. The light head itself is a bit heavy, but the versatility of this handy item is worth it. It can be dimmed from 100 percent to 10 percent, and you can dial in the color temperature from 3,200 K to 5,600 K with the remote or touch screen. It never gets hot, comes with a set of barn doors, and packs up in a briefcase with a shoulder strap. I will get more into the techniques of lighting with this tool in Chapter 4, but it is really all you need for an intimate interview.

Camera Slider

Let's admit it, those alluring tracking shots you see in films, commercials, and corporate videos are hard to resist. But until recently, the tools needed to achieve one of those shots in your low-budget nonprofit video or seat-of-the-pants documentary were way beyond the reach of your budget. You needed to rent a dolly, get your hands on a van to transport the thing, and hire an assistant to push it.

Camera sliders came along in the mid-2000s, making it possible to execute short (three to four feet) tracking shots, as long as you had a heavyweight tripod to support them. They cost over a grand, and they weren't always available to rent. But now, for less than $200, you can buy your own slider, one that weighs less than three pounds, fits on

FIGURE 3.5 This is one of several camera sliders on the market. Many can accept lightweight camcorders in addition to GoPros and smartphones. (Screen capture from YouTube.)

your lightweight LTDF tripod, supports your HD camcorder or your GoPro, and may even be motorized. The slider is easily the coolest—and most improved—toy to come on the market in years.

With a slider range of only twenty-four to thirty-six inches, you'll think at first that this isn't enough length to give you the high-production gloss you crave, but if you use the slider correctly (having elements glide by in the foreground to accentuate the depth of field or using the slider with a slightly extended focal length), you'd be surprised how effective it is. A cool toy indeed (see Figure 3.5).

Extension Cord and Power Strip

Carry at least one extension cord, one power strip, and a three-in-one wall plug. And speaking of plugging stuff in . . .

Ground Lift Adaptor/Three-Prong Adapter/Voltage Adapter Plugs

. . . have a couple of adapters enabling you to plug into those electrical outlets you still find in older homes that take only two prongs. If you travel to another country, research what kind of outlet is used so you know what kind of adapter plugs to bring. Lights, chargers, laptops, etc., all now have built-in voltage converters, so you no longer need to worry about your equipment frying when you plug it in.

Microphone Boom Pole

This is unnecessary if you're working alone, but if you have a partner, you can outfit the boom with a mic and a wireless transmitter, which may come in handy in some situations (although it can be distracting and intrusive in others). You can spend anywhere from fifty to hundreds of dollars on a boom pole, but you can do just fine with a pole that costs around $150. Make sure it's lightweight, sturdy, and comes with at least three telescoping sections. It should be already wired with an XLR cable so you can plug your microphone into one end and either a wireless transmitter or another XLR cable into the other end. Most poles come with a standard ⅜-inch thread on the microphone end and a ⅝-inch adapter that allows you to use a variety of mounts to hold the mic in place.

Light Stand with Adapter for On-Board Camera Light

You can turn your camera-mounted LED light into a standalone light by attaching a simple adapter to a regular light stand and then screwing it into the underside of your camera light. This increases the versatility of this light and decreases its deer-in-the-headlights glare, since you can now move it to the side or the rear of your subject.

Makeup Kit

A basic makeup kit with some face powder and cotton pads can help reduce the glare or hot spots that sometimes appear on a person's face when lit by a bright key light. This usually isn't a problem when you're shooting outdoors where the light is more evenly spread out, and most of the time you won't need it, but it's worth having on you.

ONE LAST THING: A CAMERA BAG

When it comes to your camera, as with any exceptional piece of essential gear, it's important not to scrimp on protecting it. A tough, durable, waterproof, many-pocketed camera bag is the last item I'll mention in this chapter, but it's quite probably the most essential of all the essential items.

Don't cheap out and buy that $39 special from Walmart or the one from Goodwill that smells like cat urine. Instead, plan to spend around $200 for a bag from a top brand like Port-a-Brace with plenty of compartments, heavy-duty zippers, a waterproof bottom, and a padded shoulder strap. Most come with removable dividers. It must fit into an overhead airline bin. Measure the width and length of your camera with the lens attached and then check the dimensions of the bag. You will be happy, so very happy, you spent this money every time you go out on a shoot.

After reading this chapter, some of you may be experiencing a bout of sticker shock. It's true, even a basic LTDF gear package can seem expensive, especially if you are new to documentary filmmaking and are reading this book as a guide to getting your feet wet. There are loans that will help you pay for gear (which is why I recommend avoiding trends and buying tools that will last at least five years, after which they will have paid for themselves), and there is Craigslist, where you can get your hands on used equipment that might do the trick. You can also rent gear, but neither of the latter two options is convenient for long-term documentary filmmaking. You need tools that are dependable, that come with a money-back guarantee if they fail, and that are within arm's reach when you need them. That's why I urge you to make the investment in owning your own gear.

The sample prices I've mentioned in this chapter are already at the low end of what most documentary filmmakers spend. But if the costs still seem too high, you can outfit yourself with a starter package for less than $3,500: an HD camera with large-format sensor, XLR audio inputs, detachable shotgun microphone, and noninterchangeable lens ($1,500); dependable wireless microphone system ($600); headphones ($100); ten 32GB memory cards ($130); two long-life lithium batteries with charger ($350); lightweight two-stage tripod ($650).

And don't forget the bandana (49 cents).

THE SHOOT

Field Production in the Lean Team Style

I learned to shoot documentaries by doing two things over and over again: making them and watching them. I was lucky. I worked at local TV stations that allowed me to shoot and edit on my own time, to experiment with ideas, to try out stuff that sometimes never saw the light of day. I even made a mockumentary, inspired by *This Is Spinal Tap*, in which my colleagues played themselves musing on the whereabouts of a friend who had disappeared abroad (the friend was real, and at the time he was hard to track down, traveling somewhere in Europe). I made it only for myself and my co-workers, but in doing so I learned a lot about narrative, pacing, image, sound—all those elements that need to be finessed to make a film.

You may not work for a local TV station, but that's okay. With today's affordable equipment, you can still practice making a film. Start with a short one. Make a video for free for a small nonprofit you'd like to support or help publicize a friend's art or invention. Maybe there is a real story you want to try telling in a five-minute film. There is even a website for these micro-documentaries, called, of course, Micro Documentaries, dedicated to helping filmmakers distribute their short films. Cinematically engaging micro-docs are popping up everywhere on social media, offering a way for filmmakers to make and share films without the need for large budgets and lengthy production schedules.

If you aren't ready or able to make a practice documentary, then go out and shoot something, anything, and think about how the footage might fit into a narrative or a sequence. The legendary experimental filmmaker Jonas Mekas urged filmmakers to simply get their hands on a camera and start filming as a daily practice. You can go to film school or try the workshop or class listings of your local nonprofit film foundation (if you live in a city large enough to have one). Or buy your own cheap starter camera and a tripod. Shoot something every weekend and then mess around with editing it.

I guarantee you'll be amazed at how rewarding composing and recording your own images can be and then translating those images into meaningful self-expression through editing. You will learn to think visually, not only when you are shooting but also when you go about your day without a camera in your hand.

By becoming a visual thinker, you'll recognize potential images, spotting the area of the frame that demands the focus. You'll learn how to use the verticals and the horizontals of an image to help set the edges of your composition. You'll react intuitively to what to leave in or out of a frame. You'll assess a potential image for how it relates thematically or psychologically to your content. This will help you learn to make editorial choices in the field, rejecting shots that distract from your narrative and including shots that add to it.

In addition to learning to shoot by actually shooting, you can learn by watching. Watch as many documentaries as you can from as many different sources as possible. Peruse your Netflix, HBO, and Sundance documentary channel listings. Flip through the on-demand menu of your cable provider. Explore the more esoteric offerings to be found on websites such as Doc Alliance, MUBI, Filmatique, and Film Struck. Check out what's happening on Vimeo on Demand, where you can often find recent film festival winners for only $5.99 per view before they play at a theater. The Laura Poitras film *Risk* showed up on Vimeo only a couple of weeks after its brief theatrical run. I found a complete version of the Joris Ivens classic short, *Rain*, on YouTube. Many library systems now offer titles from the online services Kanopy and Hoopla, all free with a library membership. Robert Gardner's *Forest of Bliss,* from 1986, is available right now on Kanopy, as are all of Frederick Wiseman's previously hard to find films.

Watch the traditional news-style docs produced by *Frontline* and the more conventional social justice works curated by *POV*. Check out the *New York Times* series of issue-oriented shorts called Op-Docs and the website Field of Vision. Watch the classics, the undersung, the perfunctory, and even the pedestrian; search for the experimental, the edgy, the avant-garde, and the hybrid.

Pay attention to how the camera moves or sits still; how the cameraperson composes, focuses, and lights. Listen to the audio and think about how it was captured. Watch the editing to see how the footage and the sound are used. Examine the camera angles, the cutaways, the B-roll, the talking heads, and the lighting. Think about where the filmmaker is in relation to the action and how they got there. How *close* were they?

Consider how each director confronted the elements of storytelling. Did they approach the story with talking heads, narration, cinema verité, swaths of on-screen text or by relying only on a succession of potent images? Most films employ a combination of these elements; some rigorously adhere to a singular method.

I believe all filmmakers should watch, and revisit every few years, Dziga Vertov's *Man with a Movie Camera*, from 1929, to remind themselves of the dizzying, image-making potential of the camera and how those images can be radically edited into an expression of pure cinema. I also think they should watch the boxed set of Les Blank's short films, *Always for Pleasure*, to see how he ignored the conventions of plot-centric moviemaking by dropping viewers into his immersive regional essays, driven by a love of music, food, and whatever he glimpsed out of the corner of his camera eye.

But there are also dozens of other must-see classics of the genre: *Salesman* (Albert and David Maysles); *Chronicle of a Summer* (Edgar Morin and Jean Rouch); *Dont Look Back* (D. A. Pennebaker); *The War Room* (Pennebaker and Chris Hegedus); *The Thin Blue Line* (Errol Morris); *Sherman's March* (Ross McElwee); *Streetwise* (Martin Bell and Mary Ellen Mark); *Harlan County, U.S.A.* (Barbara Kopple); *The Gleaners and I* and *The Beaches of Agnès* (Agnès Varda); *Hoop Dreams* (Steve James); *Shoah* (Claude Lanzmann); *Primary* (Robert Drew); *Roger & Me* (Michael Moore); *Woodstock* (Michael Wadleigh).

There are many other lesser-known but just as vital films that should be on your radar: Gardner's *Forest of Bliss*, Nina Davenport's *Hello Photo*, Michael Glawogger's *Untitled, Whores' Glory*, and *Workingman's Death*; Philip Gröning's *Into Great Silence*; Nikolaus Geyrhalter's *Our Daily Bread*; Stephanie Spray and Pacho Velez's *Manakamana*; J. P. Sniadecki's *The Iron Ministry*; Lucien Castaing-Taylor and Ilisa Barbash's *Sweetgrass*; Jennifer Baichwal's *Manufactured Landscapes*; Khalik Allah's *Field Niggas*; Aaron Shock's *Circo*; Gianfranco Rosi's *Below Sea Level*; James Longley's *Iraq in Fragments*; Ben Rivers's *Two Years at Sea*; and Leonard Retel Helmrich's *Shape of the Moon*.

Challenge your assumptions about the separation of truth and fiction by watching films that dance along the fine line between the two. *Sans Soleil* (Chris Marker), *I Travel Because I Have To, I Come Back Because I Love You* (Marcelo Gomes and Karim Aïnouz), *Stories We Tell* (Sarah Polley), *The Sky Trembles and the Earth Is Afraid and the Two Eyes Are Not Brothers* (Ben Rivers), and *Homo Sapiens* (Nikolaus Geyrhalter) all question the veracity of image, voice-over, archival footage, or narrative.

Many of the films just mentioned were produced, directed, shot, and maybe even edited by one or at most two people. *Forest of Bliss, Hello Photo, Salesman, Dont Look Back, Sherman's March, The Gleaners and I, Into Great Silence, Manakamana, The Iron Ministry, Sweetgrass, Field Niggas, Circo, Two Years at Sea,* and *Below Sea Level* are exemplary lean team documentary films. Although Robert Drew employed three two-person teams in making *Primary*, it could be considered the very first lean team film, the cameraperson and soundperson enjoying the thrilling mobility of working with new, lightweight, easy-to-handle sync sound equipment.

Many of these films are challenging. Some demand patience. Others qualify as popular entertainment. They all form a necessary foundation for learning the art, purpose, possibilities, and playfulness of documentary filmmaking. If you want to make movies, you have to watch movies. That's the most straightforward advice I can offer.

In this chapter, I'll provide a behind-the-scenes breakdown of tactics, tips, and techniques for working in the field as a lean team filmmaker. I'll cover how you can shoot, record sound, and light, all while keeping a handle on your story and the ultimate goal of your film. Notice how other filmmakers use these strategies in the films you watch, and employ them while making your lean team movie.

I'm assuming that most of you reading this book have some familiarity with cameras in general and your camera in particular (because you've read the manual; see Chapter 3). You know how to accomplish these filmmaking basics:

- getting a crisp focus
- achieving a correct white balance
- properly exposing a shot so it's not too dark or too bright
- manually setting your camera's frames per second (fps), shutter speed, f-stop, focus, and audio levels
- holding the beginning and end of a pan or tilt steady for several seconds to allow for a stable edit
- rolling on each individual shot for at least seven to ten consecutive seconds to give you "handles" on either end of the shot, again for editing
- when shooting handheld, keeping the lens zoomed out and the focus deep; if you or your subject moves, trying to minimize camera shake and loss of focus

In addition to these basics, you may also have experimented with shutter speeds and know to avoid filming at a faster speed than 1/48th when you're shooting with a camera at twenty-four frames per second (fps), which is what most filmmakers use today. This means your shutter is opening for 1/48th of a second to allow light in. Shooting at high shutter speeds of 1/100th or 1/240th creates overly crisp, jagged images that look jittery and unnatural.

If shooting in bright sunlight at 1/48th results in an overexposed image, mitigate this overexposure with neutral density filters rather than by increasing the shutter speed. Shooting a low-lit interior scene at a shutter speed of 1/24th allows more light to enter the shot, but anything lower than 1/24th will give your image a dreamy, blurry appearance (which can be quite interesting if used sparingly and with the right intention).

You also know how to avoid backlighting your subjects (filming them against a bright window or a harsh light), unless that is the specific effect you want.

The perfect resource for learning the technical side of filmmaking is *The Shut Up and Shoot Documentary Guide* by Anthony Q. Artis. It gives you lots of good information, diagrams, charts, and lists. Watch the video tutorials available on YouTube and take a couple of classes. Get the basic skills and then refine them so you can make every second of video you shoot matter. You will end up shooting less footage but better footage, making it easier to sort through and catalog, narrowing down your choices in editing.

FIELD PRODUCTION BASICS

Working with the Camera

The Geography of a Scene

One of the essential differences between you as a lean team filmmaker and you as just one member of a larger team is that the film you are embarking upon is your vision. You are the decision-maker in all areas (story, location, style, pace, script, voice, and editing). And when it comes time to film, you are literally calling the shots. You're already making your first edit of the finished movie. You are deciding what to leave in and what to leave out. This is why beginning your film with a basic sense of story and structure, with that wide-angle-shot list I talked about in Chapter 2, is important as an initial blueprint for your directorial vision. You shoot with editing in mind because you will be the editor of your film.

But where do you start?

Turn on the visual thinking switch in your brain and begin by covering the geography of a scene. Get the basics: wide shot, medium shot, close-up. With these covered, you'll have a starting point for your scenes when you sit down at your computer to begin organizing the footage. When shooting, look for a way to turn any image into three shots: wide, medium, close, and their variations (extreme wide shots and extreme close-ups).

In many situations, you'll have a chance to get only one focal length, and it will most likely be a wide or medium shot. If you are close to your subjects and they are moving, the best you may be able to do is stay with them. That's why you also need to get reverse shots, a variety of angles, and cutaways. You can get these shots while recording continuously as you move fluidly to cover the scene, or you can get what you need in individual shots.

Reverse shots involve a simple repositioning of your body in relation to the person or thing you are shooting. For example, if you are shooting a woman dance instructor conducting a class, you will frame a head-on or slightly angled shot of the instructor watching or talking to her students. To achieve a reverse shot you get behind the instructor and, with her head and shoulder in the foreground edge of the frame, point the camera at the students she is talking to.

To spice things up, get a variety of angles. Show the instructor's face at a distance with the movement of the dancers in the foreground. Shoot through the dancers' legs or hands. Put the camera on the floor behind the instructor and frame the shot with her feet in the foreground. Imagine your camera as the instructor's eyes and get a point-of-view shot of what she sees.

Cutaways are the individual shots of students listening, close-ups of their feet, reflections of their dancing bodies in the mirror, perhaps the clock on the wall, or an extreme close-up of the instructor's notes. Cutaways will save your butt in editing.

You can also opt for a more formalized approach, eschewing cutaways and a variety of angles by mounting the camera on a tripod, walking back away from the action, setting your focal length on a wide shot, and recording the action from a fixed, unmoving field of view. This is what's known as a master shot. Shooting in nothing but master shots will limit your coverage, but the technique is currently in vogue among some cinematographers who prefer a more static, locked-down view (the Austrian filmmaker Nikolaus Geyrhalter makes films composed mostly of master shots).

Other camerapersons may not be comfortable shooting handheld, so they stay in one place. Some may feel that a dynamic, moving camera reflects an old-school, TV-news style of shooting, and they prefer the alternative dynamic of movement within the locked-down frame. I believe this static approach came back into vogue with the introduction of DSLR cameras equipped with HD video capability and sensitive lenses, simply because it was difficult to maintain a sharp, consistent focus while moving those cameras.

There is merit in any and all techniques if used judiciously. The important thing is to capture the quality, quantity, and variety of footage necessary to edit that footage coherently. The lean teamer who works alone without soundperson, lights, extra gear, rigging, etc. can cover the geography of a scene with speed and efficiency. In a later section I'll talk about the importance of sequencing, a rapidly disappearing art of documentary filmmaking.

Continuing with the dance class as an example, you should also look for the establishing shot (an exterior of the building where the dance class takes place) and something that identifies it by name (a plaque in the hallway or a sign on the class door). You may never need those shots, especially if you find a more unique way of conveying this information, but you've got them just in case.

Whenever possible, I try to get the basics recorded right away. If something happens that cuts the episode short—an emergency phone call that takes the instructor away, a fire alarm, or I show up a little too late to get all the shots I wanted—I will at least have the building blocks needed to edit a brief sequence together. Once I know I've got those building blocks, I can zero in on the gestures, sounds, expressions, movements, and textures that add nuance to the story. That's when the fun begins.

Capturing Essential B-Roll

If covering the geography of the scene means making sure you have a variety of angles to work with when editing, a more precise process involves capturing dynamic B-roll that illuminates your character or larger story. When I filmed the priest in our film *Zona Intangible*, the obvious first choice was to show him conducting a service in his church. After recording my wide shots, medium shots, close-ups, reverse shots, and cutaways, all of which established a sense of place and people, I concentrated on the priest himself, who was wearing a wireless microphone I'd attached at the beginning of the service.

When it came time to deliver first communion to a group of children, he lined up the kids to receive the communion wafer and gently placed one on each child's tongue. I'd already decided on the best camera position to capture this scene in one long unbroken take, panning and tilting smoothly between the priest and the kids. I knew I already had the cutaways if this single shot didn't work out as planned, but as it turned out, my angle was perfect, and the field of view remained unobstructed (see Figure 4.1). It's important to understand that I didn't yet know how I was going to use this particular shot in the narrative; I only knew I needed to get it because it established a personal connection between the priest and the kids.

In a subsequent interview, the priest talked about being threatened at gunpoint years before by Shining Path guerrillas (the Sendero Luminoso, a Maoist group that terrorized Peru for more than a decade). He told us the Shining Path didn't want him delivering food to the poor because "if their bellies are full the poor won't think about revolution." I didn't want to use old news footage of the Shining Path for this shot, nor did I want to cut away to a photo of the priest as a younger man. So while he talked about the terrorists threatening to kill him for delivering food to the poor, I used this scene of him delivering communion wafers to his parishioners in the present, thereby making a metaphorical visual connection.

Filming this kind of essential B-roll is the key to enriching your footage. In the movie *Salesman*, Albert and David Maysles established a keen sense of the pressure facing the

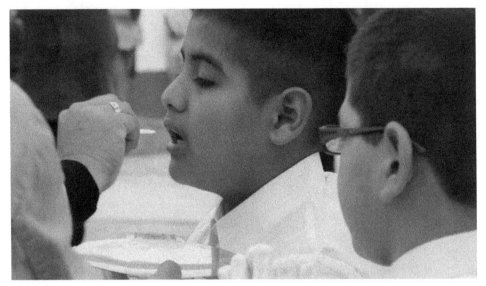

FIGURE 4.1 After surveying the geography of the location and filming supporting B-roll, the author settles on the best spot to capture a key scene in *Zona Intangible* (2017), by Ann Hedreen and Rustin Thompson. (Still capture from digital file.)

door-to-door Bible salesmen they were profiling. After a meeting in which their boss berated the men for not meeting their sales quotas, a scene featuring expert examples of cutaways, the Maysles were free to focus in on the salesman who eventually emerged as their main character. While driving his car to the next address, with the camera nestled next to him on the front seat, he broke into a sardonic rendition of "If I Were a Rich Man," which became a de facto soundtrack for the ensuing sequence of door-knocking and rejection. That's the kind of B-roll that elevates a documentary moment to the sublime (see Chapter 2, Figure 2.1).

In Ross McElwee's first-person film *Sherman's March*, a film constructed from many offhand, randomly gathered moments, the director is shooting at a neighborhood reunion when he decides, almost as if on a whim, to get some footage of an old girlfriend demonstrating a favorite stretching exercise, a series of deep, thrusting squats. While shooting, McElwee accidently shuts off his microphone but keeps on rolling, turning a mistake into a semi-erotic commentary on his lackluster love life. It's a brilliant example of B-roll that McElwee would not have captured if he hadn't been close to his subject and that would have carried little meaning if he hadn't already provided the groundwork of establishing the place, the person, and her context within his unfolding story.

Shooting high-quality B-roll involves staying alert and always listening. It means opening your nonshooting eye regularly to see what's happening around you (if you're using a viewfinder tube, or loupe, in bright sunlight) or looking up now and then from the flip-out viewfinder. Be aware of your periphery. Stay mobile and light on your feet.

There is a delightful scrap of film that plays on a loop at the Fondation Henri Cartier-Bresson in Paris, which preserves the black-and-white documentary work of the renowned still photographer. The silent footage glimpses Cartier-Bresson taking photos of a street performance, and his movement through the crowd—capturing different angles, sizing up compositions, standing on his toes, dashing forward for a change in point of view—is like a dance. Cartier-Bresson's pas de deux reveals an artist synchronized with his camera and the action. "In order to give a 'meaning' to the world," Cartier-Bresson is quoted on the foundation's website, "one has to feel involved in what one frames through the viewfinder. This attitude requires concentration, discipline of mind, sensitivity, and a sense of geometry. It is by economy of means that one arrives at simplicity of expression."[1] Economy and simplicity. This cuts to the core of lean team documentary filmmaking.

I'm a big fan of the camera that travels with subjects, reacting to their movements, gestures, and off-screen glances. It's the way I first learned to work when I was shooting TV news. But I'm also fond of the long static shot, the astutely composed scene that allows a subject to move in and out or within the frame. This is the fly-on-wall idea taken to its extreme: the fly that doesn't move.

The style works perfectly in *Manakamana* (directed, filmed, and edited by Stephanie Spray and Pacho Velez), which consists entirely of long, locked-down takes of people riding a cable car up and then down a mountainside in Nepal. The film exerts a hypnotic pull, precisely because the subjects in the frame are also locked-down, in the sense they can't move beyond the boundaries of the cable car, which enacts a knowing exchange of complicity between them and us (the viewer). The movie is expectant, meditative, and even funny (see Figure 4.2).

Consider whether a more radical approach to image-making will work to your film's advantage. In *Leviathan*, directors Lucien Castaing-Taylor and Véréna Paravel placed several small GoPro cameras in ingenious places aboard a commercial fishing vessel, immersing the viewer completely in the motion, sound, and claustrophobic physicality of the crew and their grinding tasks. The visceral film is composed mostly of footage shot at night, the sea an inky void in the background. At times the movie induces a sensation like seasickness. Both *Leviathan* and *Manakamana* stretch the possibilities of filmmaking and the patience of an audience. The filmmakers know their work is not for everyone.

Nikolaus Geyrhalter's *Homo Sapiens* is made up of an extended series of locked-down wide shots of abandoned buildings and ruined landscapes, without a single human being present. The film expresses a harrowing vision of a postapocalyptic planet, perhaps only a few weeks after all human life has been erased. Much of this

FIGURE 4.2 One of the several long, unbroken shots in *Manakamana* (2013), by Stephanie Spray and Pacho Velez. (Screen capture from film's website.)

destruction is made more vivid by the film's haunting sound design, but also by its rigid refusal to suggest even a presence behind the camera, which never moves or changes focal length.

Homo Sapiens is not a lean team film, although it looks like it could be. It was only after watching the film that I learned Geyrhalter worked with a crew that included lighting technicians and grips, sometimes enhancing the dramatic images with additional light or by flooding a location with water. Although the scouting and securing of permissions took up a lot of preproduction time, I was astonished at the thematic power communicated by the film's simple visual conception.

Homo Sapiens is shot consistently at a standing eye level. One way to introduce visual flair in your film is to liberate the camera from this viewpoint. Place it extremely close to the action, mount it on things that move (vehicles, conveyor belts, animals), put it underwater, revolve it in 360-degree pans, use a slider or drone, or adopt a completely kinetic, always-moving style.

Check out the Oscar-nominated *Cartel Land*, directed and shot (mostly) by Matthew Heineman. The camera is a whirligig in the film, hugging the characters, constantly in motion in the middle or near the edges of the action. The images explode off the screen like firecrackers (unfortunately, a relentless and unnecessary music score dilutes some of the power of the movie).

Dynamic B-roll of a scene is far more important to the construction of your film than perfectly lit interiors or interviews, and far more important than a single dolly or tracking shot that takes an hour to set up, during which time you missed dozens of other potential shots. The lean team filmmaker's fast, stripped-down style makes it possible to get complete coverage of a scene expertly and efficiently.

Shooting Texture or Metaphor

Whenever possible, I try to break away from the main action and record what I've come to call *texture*. This refers to shots that may be used later in editing to add metaphorical, emotional, or cultural meaning to the story. They can also be handy as transitional elements in editing, to issue a change in mood, location, character, or narrative arc. An example of texture is the too common image of sunlight flashing through trees shot from the window of a moving car. Other oft-used examples include close-ups of rippling water in a lake or stream, the rising moon, and flying insects dancing in silhouette against a sunset.

Be alert to them and try to avoid the clichéd, easy choices, but don't reject them only because they've been used before. You won't know what works until you're making your film, until you know what materials are at hand, what elements make sense. Sometimes an image that might seem trite can be inserted in a sequence at just the right moment and a whole new meaning emerges, or a series of images seemingly unconnected to your storyline will powerfully underscore an emotional moment. The last shot in *Spend It All*, Les Blank's wander through Cajun culture, is a pan across the back porch of a rural shack, the camera coming to rest on a few rows of muddy boots.

Ross McElwee, in his autobiographical films, is often entranced by the dance of light on a seemingly generic background and may even comment on it in his voice-over, owning up to being momentarily unsure as to what to film next, therefore passing the time by filming this lovely cutaway.

Leonard Retel Helmrich captured many isolated moments of geese, bats, lizards, and ants during the making of *Shape of the Moon* and then inserted these shots to amplify or underscore narrative points. A stunning shot of a brigade of ants carrying a dead praying mantis acts as a metaphor to an ensuing scene where dozens of villagers hoist a bamboo house onto a new foundation (see Figure 4.3).

For our film *Quick Brown Fox: An Alzheimer's Story*, a friend suggested we check out the visual possibilities of an old communications museum in an industrial part of Seattle. The place turned out to be a treasure trove of powerful metaphors for the tangled clutter of a brain succumbing to the scourge of Alzheimer's: an avalanche of twisted phone wires cascading down a wall; a bank of greasy, clanking, industrial-sized switches; and an old teletype machine that could be set to print the test sentence "A quick brown fox jumped over the lazy dog" over and over again. The repetition itself suggested a symptom of Alzheimer's, but then we asked the technician to cause the machine to malfunction,

FIGURE 4.3 A team of ants (*left*) and a team of volunteers (*right*) illustrate the use of metaphorical imagery in Leonard Retel Helmrich's *Shape of the Moon* (2004). (Still capture from DVD.)

resulting in jammed gears and mistyped words. We walked out of the museum with not only the title of our film but also a collection of metaphorical images that we used—sparingly—while editing the film.

These textural elements can also supply your story with an impressionistic, historical weight. A short film called *The Black Belt* by the director Margaret Brown (*Be Here to Love Me: A Film about Townes Van Zandt, The Great Invisible*) offers a glimpse into the suppression of minority voting rights in Alabama in 2016. The film begins and ends with several static images of a cotton field. At no point in the movie do we see people or machines picking cotton, nor does anyone talk about it. But the metaphorical implication of the imagery registers the deep legacy of racism and oppression in that southern state.

Another, less abstract way to use a textural element is to include foreground in your shots and sequences, which adds both literal depth to your image and layers of subtext to a scene. Examples are the dance instructor's feet framing the background action of the dancers mentioned earlier; a clutter of paint brushes partially obscuring the motions of an artist working on a canvas in the background; the side mirror of a car, positioned to the left of the frame, reflecting simultaneously the landscape that has passed by and, beyond the mirror, the landscape still to come.

I often see textural possibilities during a shoot, make a mental note of them, and go back later when I have more time to compose my shot and consider the meaning. The decision to film foreground elements usually has to be made on the spot, while the background action you are foregrounding is in process. This requires an intuitive sense of framing, an arrangement of the elements of a shot that comments on or expresses tension between them. You have to make sure that neither the foreground nor background elements are too cluttered or busy, and you should try to reduce the empty space between elements (unless that emptiness is important to the meaning of the shot). Throw either the background or foreground out of focus, or employ your wide-angle converter to boldly accentuate the foreground element.

Practice Sequencing

It's time now to talk about that lost art I mentioned earlier: sequencing. While the jump cut has become a shortcut in editing that can cover a multitude of missed shots, it has also made it easier for camerapersons to simply disregard the practice of sequencing altogether.

Sequencing means breaking down an activity into a series of individual shots that, when edited together, will present a seamless chronicle of that activity without any need for abrupt cuts, light jumps, and distracting angles or the breaking of the 180-degree rule. This rule refers to the screen space between a character and another character or object within a scene. An imaginary line called the axis connects the characters, and if you keep the camera on one side of this axis for every shot in the scene, the first character will remain frame right and the second will remain frame left. The viewer has a logical sense of their placement in a scene. If the camera passes over that axis, called *crossing the line*, the viewer could become disoriented. If disorientation is your goal, then deliberately crossing the line can help achieve it.

By shooting an action scene in sequence, you capture the necessary images for editing a coherent scene later. It's good practice to get those basic building block images even if you plan on reordering their chronology later in editing. Great examples of sequencing can be found in any number of early industrial and educational films, especially in episodes endearingly referred to as IOP, or "industry on parade." These are sequences featuring bottling plants or newspaper printing facilities or dam construction. They were shot by professionally trained union camerapersons and they are wonderful learning tools: you see the basic building blocks of coverage, perfectly panned or tilted cameras, the use of foreground, etc. Many of the great cinematographers of fictional films from the 1970s (Vilmos Zsigmond, László Kovács, Haskell Wexler) got their start shooting industrials.

A photographer shooting a sequence is like a builder turning an architectural blueprint into an actual house, with a foundation and rooms, and doorways, halls, and staircases connecting them all together into a logical space.

My boss at KIRO-TV in Seattle once pointed out a critical flaw in a sequence I was quite proud of. It was for a profile of an athlete now confined to a wheelchair who agreed to let me film her rolling down the sidewalk. I had my wide shots and close-ups, my cutaways of her hands pushing the wheels, a silhouette of her crossing the frame against the bright sun, an eye-level, head-on shot I captured walking backward with her down the sidewalk, and then a reverse shot walking behind her down the same sidewalk. However,

I neglected to get the eye-level, head-on shot in the same direction as all my previous shots, so the sun was shining against the wrong side of her face. Many casual viewers probably never noticed, but I now understood I'd made a potentially distracting mistake. In the eyes of a pro, the sequence was compromised.

You can sequence a scene handheld, on a tripod, or with a combination of the two, but the great advantage for the lean teamer, working with a handheld camera, is the ability to move into position quickly, get the shot, then anticipate and move on to the next position. I don't want to interfere, manipulate, or coach, so I try not to make any of my subjects wait for me to get in position before they move on to the next step of the sequence. But sometimes I ask them to pause for a few seconds if their next action is too critical to risk missing, or I ask them to repeat an action if it's easy to do.

Figure 4.4 shows a series of numbered still frames from the sequence I shot in Peru of the doctor and nurse on their way to pay a house call in the squatter city, Manchay, outside of Lima. I shot the entire sequence without turning off the camera, looking ahead to see where the next good angle was and then running to get in position. My subjects began the sequence walking right to left through the frame. At one critical point, they crossed the 180-degree line when they climbed through a fence (image 4) and then proceeded to walk left to right.

Sometimes while watching a documentary in which sequencing barely plays a part, you may ask yourself if a few well-shot and edited sequences would have served the film

FIGURE 4.4 Nine sequenced shots and edits from *Zona Intangible* (2017), by Ann Hedreen and Rustin Thompson. (Still capture from digital file.)

better. Hubert Sauper's *We Come as Friends* uses striking, disconnected, disorienting images, some only barely related to each other, to create a portrait of the new nation of South Sudan falling into chaos. Sauper's method works in theory, but the scattered effect of the imagery is wearying.

In Crystal Moselle's Sundance award-winning *The Wolfpack*, a family of teenage boys and their sister are kept virtual prisoners by their father in their small New York apartment. While the publicity for the film promised a strange, one-of-a-kind tale, it felt more superficial and desultory, simply because the footage Moselle shot lacked focus and direction. None of the kids, who all resembled each other, emerged as a central character, and the space they lived in—arguably a character in itself—was never clearly delineated by the camera. The movie lacked strong, directed sequences to help clarify its narrative.

One of director Frederick Wiseman's rare shorter films, *Boxing Gym*, is a virtual textbook on both sequencing and covering the geography of a scene. The clean, direct cinematography paints a brief but evocative portrait of a diverse neighborhood gym in Austin (most of Wiseman's later-career films lack this same crisp brevity). Another director who included carefully constructed scenes in his globetrotting exposés was Michael Glawogger. Watch his staggering film, *Workingman's Death*, to see his portraits of human beings engaged in some of the most horrific labor on the planet, all clearly illustrated by the expertly sequenced cinematography of his cameraman, Wolfgang Thaler.

Director-cinematographer-editor Jon Alpert's docs attest to his skill in efficiently capturing hard-hitting sequences in volatile, perpetually changing conditions. *Cuba and the Cameraman* displays the veteran's light-on-his-feet ability to get closer to Fidel Castro than most other American journalists over many decades.

Inexperienced camerapersons who may never have learned the basics of sequencing can often fixate on simply collecting enough footage to link their sound bites or to provide basic coverage of a character, without considering how a well-constructed sequence can actually carry a story forward while their characters talk in voice-over. There's a tendency to string together a series of artfully composed images that look pretty but do very little to enhance a viewer's understanding of character. I attribute this trend to the fact that nearly all cameras these days produce beautiful pictures that can lull cinematographers into relying on gorgeously rendered video postcards to fill their film's running time.

Whenever you have an opportunity to get your characters engaged in an activity, take the time to cover your sequencing shot list: master shots, reverse shots, point-of-view shots, close-ups, cutaways, and over-the-shoulder shots following your characters as they move through a space. The sequence, which may seem like filler while you're shooting it, could become a vital link in your finished film.

Resist Overshooting

One of the reasons I wrote this book is that I was hearing from more and more filmmakers about the number of years they spent and the amount of footage they shot in order to complete just one documentary. Not only is overshooting expensive and time-consuming, but it also complicates the process of finding a story. It turns editing into a chaotic search for meaningful images hiding among the detritus of way too much unnecessary footage.

"The idea of finding the story in the edit is a false one," says Werner Herzog in the on-line Masterclass series. "My heart sinks when I see young filmmakers who come excitedly at me and they say, 'Oh I shot 450 hours for my documentary and it took me three years to shoot this and one-and-a-half years to edit.' If you shot 350 or 600 hours of footage then these people didn't know what they were doing. They were just rolling the camera."[2]

The veteran Kim Longinotto agrees. "I don't shape my films in the editing room, I try to find the shape during shooting . . . Twenty-five hours (of footage)—that would be a lot for me . . . I wouldn't want my editor to have to watch two hundred hours of raw film, I want his life to be pleasurable in the editing room and I want his energy to be spent on editing, not looking through hours of useless material."[3]

Yet many filmmakers work this way, sitting down to hundreds of hours of footage to begin rooting out narrative through lines. If you have the money, the time, the assistants, and the patience, then this method could work for you. But still, too many filmmakers today simply shoot way too much.

Digital cameras have made this easy and inexpensive. You can insert a memory card, shoot for three hours before it fills up, pop it out and pop in another one, and eventually download all of your footage to inexpensive 5TB hard drives. The technology has obviated the need to be specific or judicious while shooting in the field. "The danger in the new formats," Michael Glawogger once said, "is that because filming doesn't cost anything, you can film everything. Through the older process of filmmaking we learned to reduce what we shot, and that sharpened our vision."[4]

Filmmakers who overshoot aren't sharpening their vision. They shoot everything going on in front of them because they're unsure how to zero in on what material will work well in editing or what will make a watchable sequence. "Since it cost virtually nothing to let the camera run, why turn it off?" writes Betsy McLane, director emerita of the International Documentary Association. In her view, the arrival of low-cost digital cameras "led to the capture of wonderful, previously unavailable moments; in others it led to overlong navel gazing of the most boring sort."[5]

"We are not garbage collectors," Herzog declares. "We are filmmakers." Herzog says he never shoots more than thirty hours of footage for his documentaries. For his film about death row inmates, *Into the Abyss*, he shot only eight hours. Many classic documentaries—*Sherman's March, Salesman, The War Room*—were shot on film with shooting ratios of 40, 50, or 70 to 1 (shooting ratio refers to the number of hours shot compared with one hour in the final running time of the edited film). *The Babuskas of Chernobyl*, with a seventy-minute running time, was completed in just a few weeks with as little as forty hours of original video shot by Holly Morris and her cinematographer, Japhet Weeks. The movie tells a brief but engaging story in concise, well-crafted strokes. Morris and her cameraman realized they didn't need to spend months (and thousands more dollars) to make their film.

I shot the seventy-three-minute *30 Frames a Second* in one week on 32 one-hour MiniDVD tapes. I never once questioned if I had enough footage to work with. If I'd decided to make a different film, spending many more weeks or months traveling around interviewing experts, cops, and activists, conducting a wide-ranging examination of the issues and fallout from that week's protests, it would have complicated the defined narrative punch of the material I already had.

The observational filmmaker Maise Crow spent three years shooting seven hundred hours of footage for her documentary *Jackson*, about the last remaining abortion clinic in Mississippi.[6] A worthy subject and an award-winning film on the festival circuit, but I shudder to think of the hours and hours of unused footage captured in its making.

"We are not flies on the wall," exhorts Herzog, who rejects what he calls a "bank camera" approach to getting B-roll and advocates a more poetic regard for a film's purpose and power. Instead of waiting for something to happen within your camera's frame that might be interesting, learn to edit in the camera. Know the narrative thrust of your film, and question whether the footage you're shooting is essential. Always be mindful of your directorial vision.

Quite often, the central characters in your film and their actions can be illuminated with a modest amount of B-roll. A quiet slice-of-life film called *Uncertain* by Ewan McNicol and Anna Sandilands (which the directors first distributed themselves on Vimeo on Demand) paints a gently contoured picture of a few characters in a tiny Louisiana hamlet with a series of images that unfold as if from a scrapbook, just enough to reveal a few truths of their existence.

How do you know when you've shot enough footage? Or whether you're shooting too much? The answer usually comes from trial and error. Screen your own footage (rather than leaving the task to assistants), and see if you can detect patterns in how and what you shoot. When in the field, look for a definitive moment in a scene that explains what is going on and, once you have it, move on. Be confident in the material you do have rather than anxious about the material you may miss.

What if you turn off the camera, pack it away, and then something really dramatic and important unfolds? Yes, that could happen, and if it is something truly valuable to your film, you can include the moment with a little creative narrative restructuring.

In some cases, you can ask the person to recreate an action (although recreating an *emotion* will often feel false, not to mention unethical). You can interview the person about what you just missed and then film something else that can visually comment on the missing scene, using the imagery as metaphor or analogy. You can describe the moment with on-screen text (intertitles) or, if you're already narrating your film, with your own voice.

My philosophy is: if I didn't shoot it, it didn't happen. I realize that's a bit glib, but it's better than beating yourself up for missing a crucial moment. When shooting *30 Frames a Second* on those chaotic Seattle streets, I had to quickly let go of the fact that I couldn't be everywhere at once. Wherever I was, that's the footage that would be in my movie. I also knew that if I really, truly missed something spectacular (a death, a stampede, a raging fire), I could borrow or buy the footage. But when I started editing months later, I made the decision to use only my own footage because I wanted to keep the film confined to my point of view.

"If I didn't shoot it, it didn't happen." This frees you from the tyranny of insecurity and indecisiveness. It forces you to concentrate on what's happening right now in front of your camera.

One way to reduce the sheer volume of material is by giving yourself a time limit before you even begin. If your focus is only one character, like the disgraced politician Anthony Weiner and his mayoral bid in the documentary *Weiner*, then the time frame is already dictated by the length of the campaign. When making our post–Hurricane Katrina documentary, *The Church on Dauphine Street*, we committed ourselves to ending our field shooting when the rebuilding of the church was completed. In our more open-ended documentary about my mother-in-law's Alzheimer's disease, we decided from the outset to film for no more than a year rather than allow the project to continue until her death.

"Shoot in a few days, edit in a few days," is Herzog's philosophy, and his run of films in the past few years attests to this way of working (*Encounters at the End of the World* was shot in just seven weeks). Not all of his films are masterpieces, but Herzog's speed and curiosity are inspiring examples of how to sustain your energy and output in the world of documentary filmmaking.

Experience counts for a lot. As your skills improve, you'll become more selective about what you shoot. By applying the shooting tips and techniques I've written about here, you'll learn to work faster and more efficiently, so you can move on from your first film and apply everything you've learned to making your next one, and the one after that, and the one after that. You'll become a constant filmmaker.

Filming Interviews

Interviews will always be one of the signature components of documentaries. There is no getting around the fact that eventually you'll have to shoot one. However, the early direct-cinema pioneers never did. You won't find a conventional interview in any of Frederick Wiseman's films. You won't see one in Robert Drew's *Primary*, in D. A. Pennebaker's *Dont Look Back*, in the Maysles's *Gimme Shelter*.

Nikolaus Geyrhalter eschews nearly all human communication in his films *Homo Sapiens, Our Daily Bread*, and *Abendland* (except for overheard conversations). The Italian filmmaker Gianfranco Rosi also avoids talking-head interviews in his films *Fire at Sea, Below Sea Level*, and *Sacro GRA*, even though those docs are impressionistically human. The Chinese filmmaker Wang Bing makes epic-length movies without a single interview. Mary Ellen Mark and Martin Bell's *Streetwise* is told with the audio of conventional interviews, but you don't see the characters speaking the words; the narrative of the film is constructed from their voices and actions, but not their talking heads. Several of the films produced by members of the Harvard collective known as the Sensory Ethnography Lab—*Leviathan, Sweetgrass, Manakamana*—are rigorously immune to sit-down interviews. *Foreign Parts*, by J. P. Sniadecki and Véréna Paravel, includes many people talking, but they are talking to one another, not the filmmakers. Zhao Liang's *Behemoth*, a searing indictment of ecological destruction in rural Mongolia, is accomplished with a poetic voice-over and a formidable juxtaposition of images, completely without interviews. It's no surprise the directors shooting in this style today have a harder time finding audiences for their work.

Viewers expect to see talking heads and sometimes feel adrift if they hear someone talking without seeing the person's face. This explains why the majority of docs today rely on interviews as their central expositional component. If you decide to include them in your film, ask yourself how many is too many. Do you need five experts commenting on your issue, or will one do the trick? Do you need experts at all? In fact, how many people do you need to see talking on-screen if they are basically giving the same information?

Colin Hanks's film about the rise and fall of Tower Records, *All Things Must Pass*, is a veritable talking-head salad of seemingly everyone who ever received a paycheck from the company, turning a film about music into a film about talking. A doc I mentioned in Chapter 2, *Promised Land*, is a textbook example of too many talking heads repeating themselves in a verbal potluck of words, with hardly a cutaway or illuminating visual image in sight. The movie's message of indigenous rights is undercut by its tedium. Compare it with a film whose message is similar, the Canadian documentary *Haida Gwaii: On the Edge of the World*, which combines the selective use of a few interviews with B-roll (fishing for kelp, carving a totem pole) and most of the audio spoken over lovely shots of the town and landscape.

Perhaps the most powerful use of the interview can be seen in *Shoah*. The interplay of testimony and image achieves its intensity precisely because the architecture of the film is decluttered. There is no narration, little on-screen text, and only one expert, a historian, in the film's entire nine-hour running time.

Look at all the techniques available to you in documentary filmmaking and ask yourself which are the best ways to tell your story. And then use them sparingly but definitively. If you have many interviews, or only a few, is there a way your B-roll, your visual evidence, can cover them?

I will explore how to record audio and light interviews in the next section, but for shooting interviews in the lean team mode, the requirements are quite simple. If you are shooting an interview handheld, you'll want to get close, zoom in to the subject's face to get a focus, then zoom out to the widest focal length possible to reduce camera movement, and frame the interview with the surroundings, background, and thematic needs of your story in mind. If you are shooting the interview on a tripod, you can choose to be close or far away, depending on the demands of your story. By setting up farther away and zooming in to your interviewee, you will throw the background out of focus (a shallow depth of field), which is desirable for keeping the viewer's attention focused not only on what is being said but what the interviewee's expression may be communicating as well.

Or you can try the opposite approach. Get close with your tripod but shoot wide. This brings everything into focus, including the deep background and the surroundings. Another method is to shoot the interview handheld while the subject is driving or walking or while engaged in an activity that illuminates the person's character.

The traditional rule in composition is to divide the frame into thirds, with the subject's eyes at the line dividing the top third from the middle third, positioned with the correct "look space." This means that if the subject is answering questions asked by someone off-screen to the left of the frame, their head will be positioned in the right side of the frame, and vice versa. But this is only a starting point.

For more dramatic effect, position the camera at or near ground level and shoot up at them. Frame them to the extreme right or extreme left. Shoot them in profile. Expose more of the area above their head than you normally would. Take the time to consider how the environment surrounding your interview subject can underscore what they're saying. Does it convey something nonverbal about the character or setting?

The spare lighting and blacked-out background in David Sington's *The Fear of 13* intensifies the lone interview subject's mesmerizing story. Werner Herzog's interview of an Alaskan bush pilot encircled by a swarm of mosquitos in *Grizzly Man* illustrates the unforgiving wildness of the landscape. The generous framing of a subject in Cecilia Aldarondo's *POV* film *Memories of a Penitent Heart* offers vivid commentary on the character's religious beliefs (see Figure 4.5).

I try not to have the person interviewed look directly into the camera. This is awkward for your subject and for your film. The only filmmaker who can pull this off is Errol Morris, and that's because he invented a special device called the Interrotron. His wife named it that because "it combined two important concepts—terror and interview."[7] The Interrotron inputs a live video image of Morris asking questions directly onto a screen that hangs on the front of the camera like a teleprompter. The person interviewed is actually looking at a live person. The eye contact is real rather than pretend. But you won't have an Interrotron in the field (although you can rent something like it, if you must), so don't have your subject try to look into the lens.

Always keep in mind that the ultimate effect of any alternative framing approaches should be to enhance what the interviewee is saying, not distract from it. Ask yourself if the camera angle is thematically helpful or merely self-indulgent.

When I shoot a sit-down interview, I sometimes exchange my camera's zoom lens for that prime (fixed) lens I mentioned in Chapter 3, a 60mm lens that provides shallow depth of field and a couple of extra f-stops for better shooting in low light. With my

FIGURE 4.5 A generous amount of headspace fills in illuminating details about a character in Cecilia Aldarondo's *Memories of a Penitent Heart* (2016). (Screen capture from digital file).

camera's digital zoom capability, I eliminated the need to physically move the camera to get a closer or wider view of the interviewee.

I try to avoid the cliché of slowly zooming in to a subject who gets emotional during an interview or starts to reveal something especially dramatic. This was a standard practice in broadcast news, but I think it cheapens rather than enhances an honest emotion captured during an interview. If you want to zoom closer just to change the focal length, do it when a subject is being asked a question rather than answering it.

If you ever feel the urge to shoot an interview with two cameras, then turn in your lean team documentary filmmaking card. Herzog calls this two-camera method not just "stupid" but "brainless, devastatingly stupid."[8] It is unnecessarily expensive and overcomplicated.

A colleague of mine was hired as an assistant editor on a series of short films about water crises in the developing world. The films were generously funded by an international beer company, which hired a Sundance-winning documentary film director to produce them. Every field interview was shot with two full crews consisting of a cameraperson, soundperson, and producer, and even the B-roll was covered with two cameras. The result was a logjam of duplicate video and audio requiring several assistants to untangle. The B-roll often consisted of similar angles shot by both crews, who mainly worked to avoid getting in each other's frame. This is a perfect example of the burden of having too much money to spend and having to spend even more money to fix the problems this surplus created.

Most distressingly, using two cameras often results in a phony, distracting interview when the two angles are edited together. This was an annoying, seizure-inducing tactic in *All Things Must Pass*, where the convoy of talking heads constantly switched back and forth between varying angles and depths of field. The content of the interviews seemed far down on the filmmakers' list of priorities. Switching between angles dilutes the human connection between the filmmaker and the subject, as well as between the viewer and what the character is saying.

Interviewing is an art in itself, but don't be intimidated by it. Think of interviews as conversations. My wife, Ann, doesn't come to an interview with a legal pad full of questions at the ready. She knows her questions ahead of time and asks them casually. She then refers to her notes at the end of the interview, telling the subject she wants to check to make sure she didn't miss anything.

Respect the persons you interview, but also remember that you need something from them to make your film work. Some people will start telling you their story before you've had a chance to get your camera and microphone set up. Don't be rude by interrupting them, but try to get them to pause until you're ready to film. Say something like, "Wait. Let me stop you there. I know you've got a great story to tell so I want to make sure I'm ready. Give me a few minutes to get my camera out and put a microphone on you." Nearly every interview comes off more naturally if someone is telling their story to you for the first time.

Use a disarming approach when you ask questions, keeping them open-ended and reflective. Ask your subjects, "Do you mind if I talk to you on camera for a few minutes?" Ann uses these phrases: "describe for me" or "tell me about" or "give me an idea." If she needs them to tell her something she already knows, she'll say, "I know I'm stating the obvious, but . . ." in order to get the information on camera. She'll share her own personal experiences as a way to bond with them. To loosen up nervous interviewees, she'll ask them to "imagine we're meeting for coffee and just getting to know each other."

Try to avoid yes or no questions, other than to get basic information, such as "Were you living here when Hurricane Katrina struck?"

"Yes."

"Can you describe for me what that was like?"

If during the course of an interview your subject says something vital to the story but mispronounces a key word or misstates an essential fact, have them repeat it. When appropriate, at the end of the interview, ask if your subject has anything to say that you forgot to ask. Never turn the camera off immediately at the end of an interview. After you say, "Thank you for talking to me," many people will let down their guard and say something revealing or repeat something in a more conversational or personal way. As long as you're not deceiving them into thinking that you've turned off the camera, there is nothing underhanded about this.

Sometimes during an interview, people may pause for a long time before they answer. Resist the urge to say anything. Let the silence fill the space. These silences come in handy during editing to lead in or out of an especially dramatic or moving sound bite.

And finally, if you need to move furniture or background objects around to get the best framing for the interview, remember to put everything back the way it was. If you turned something off because it was emitting a background noise, remember to turn it back on. Once while working for CBS News we shot an interview in a house where the occupants were on vacation but they let us use their place as a makeshift studio. The refrigerator was making a loud hum, so we turned it off for the duration of the interview and forgot to turn it back on before we packed up and left. Two weeks later, CBS wrote the homeowners a large check for all of the spoiled food.

Filming Photographs

You may want to include photographs in your documentary. This offers a wonderful opportunity to creatively rethink what is often a dry, noncinematic exercise, a box you tick off your shot list. It's all too easy to simply insert a modern-day digital photo in your film and call it good.

Ken Burns set a new standard of working with photos, inspiring the "Ken Burns Effect" that you see on slideshow prompts from your computer's photo application. Don't avoid this effect simply because Burns's name is attached to it. A slow zoom in to a photo can still have dramatic power. But before succumbing to this easy choice, try some other methods.

If I need digital photos as part of my B-roll, I usually print them out, place them in a contextual setting, and shoot them as though they are analog, not digital. This can be as simple as sliding a photo into a frame, placing it on a bureau among other photos or personal items, and slowly panning or tracking across them. Other times I take photos into the field with me and, where appropriate, place them in a natural setting that underscores their content (see Figure 4.6).

In *Zona Intangible*, I placed a 1950s photo of three kids on a Lima beach directly among the pebbles of that same beach, with the waves crashing in soft focus behind it. For the opening sequence of our Katrina film, *The Church on Dauphine Street*, I needed something that reminded everyone of the devastating floods without resorting to the cliché of using TV news footage. I printed out freeze-frames of some of the people and places we shot, placed these snapshots on my asphalt driveway back in Seattle, and allowed a stream

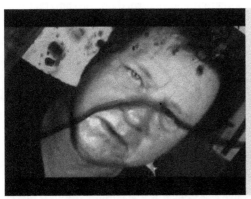

FIGURE 4.6 *Left*: Water flows over photos to suggest post-Katrina flooding in *The Church on Dauphine Street* (2008), by Ann Hedreen and Rustin Thompson. *Right*: A photo connects past to present in Lima, Peru. From *Zona Intangible* (2017), by Ann Hedreen and Rustin Thompson. (Still captures from digital file.)

of water from a hose to ooze over them. Not only was the sequence a fresh metaphor, it also saved me from paying $100 per second of news footage of the disaster. It was a cinematically playful solution, accomplished with only the tools filmmaking (and gardening) can provide.

In Yance Ford's *Strong Island*, the director made extensive use of family photos in sequences where his hands are shown in the frame neatly arranging the pictures on a pale, papery background, as if he were trying to regain control over a past event (the murder of his brother) that was decidedly out of his control.

Practice, Practice, Practice

One last word in this section on shooting. That word is "practice." I'm not going to get on my high horse and tell you the only way to become a competent cameraperson is to spend years, like I did, shooting television news day in and day out (although that is one way to do it). Many people become technically proficient as filmmakers because they are already skilled still photographers, painters, animators, graphic designers, etc. Some are preternaturally gifted (damn them!). Most of us, though, get better only by practicing.

We can all learn how to operate the buttons on a digital video camera, how to hold it and focus, how to get an exposure and a white balance, etc. in just a few hours. But getting truly comfortable with shooting takes time and practice.

One way to get better at handling a camera in dynamic situations is to film sporting events, where the players are always on the move. Take your camera to the nearest playfield and shoot the soccer, football, or Ultimate Frisbee game. Start by putting the camera on a tripod, isolate one player, and try to follow them. Practice keeping the person in focus and in the frame. Learn to anticipate their movement. Then take the camera off the tripod and film them handheld. As a beginning news photographer, I was often assigned to shoot the Friday night football game or Saturday's college hoops action. I had to walk the sidelines or sit under the basket where tripods weren't allowed. It was great training for shooting off the shoulder in all types of situations.

It can be difficult to replicate the conditions you'll experience working on a real documentary, but as I said at the beginning of this chapter, try shooting a few short films for practice: fundraising films, music videos for musician friends, how-to videos on cooking or assembling cabinets (also great training for sequencing). Shoot these in the lean team style, with plenty of mobile, handheld camerawork. Learn to think on your feet, get coverage, sequence your shots, and—as I'll explain in the next section—record your own sound.

Recording Audio

Be Your Own Soundperson

The part of in-the-field filmmaking that seems to cause the most anxiety for the inexperienced cameraperson is recording audio. Even many veteran filmmakers don't like to bother getting their own sound. Instead, they hire a professional soundperson, immediately doubling their one-person lean team. A good soundperson is often worth the money; a bad or inexperienced soundperson can end up hurting your film. Either can sometimes distract from the intimacy and unobtrusiveness you seek. Many filmmakers hire a soundperson for shooting interviews, but in the LTDF model even this additional cost is unnecessary.

In Chapter 3, I listed the microphones you need for recording nearly all of your sound: a wireless system with a lavalier mic and a camera-mounted shotgun microphone. Keep the wireless receiver mounted on your camera and plugged into one of your two audio channels. I usually plug it into channel one, because then I can quickly switch my input on my camera to record that audio onto both channels, which is handy for recording interviews (I keep my shotgun mic plugged into channel two when using it along with a wireless). Keep the transmitter with attached microphone in a pocket, backpack, or waist belt, ready to attach it to your subject when necessary. Make sure you have fresh batteries and backup batteries, and make sure you have the windscreen that came with the microphone if you are shooting outdoors.

Attach the lav to your subject's shirt, a few inches below the chin. The closer the mic, the less extraneous noise you'll hear, but if you get it too close, the sound may be muffled and the mic may appear too distracting in the shot. Run the wire under the subject's clothing if possible or under their hair and behind the neck. Use a bit of gaffer's tape to keep it in place. Try to camouflage the wire as best you can, but don't worry about disguising the mic itself. Overly fussy filmmakers care about hiding the mic, but viewers don't. Hiding the mic can also result in muffled sound or clothing brushing against it. Just make sure a person's hair or necklace or anything else doesn't rub against it. The cosmetic purity of hiding the microphone is not worth the scratchy audio.

Set your audio levels to bounce between a range of –20 dB and –6 dB, with –10 dB to –12 dB the optimum ("dB" refers to decibels, a measure of sound pressure or volume levels). Audio levels that push continuously to –0 dB and beyond should be avoided. If your volume level peaks into the red zone on your camera's VU meter, the audio will be distorted. Audio that is recorded too low can generally be boosted in the editing suite, while audio recorded too high is more difficult to fix. Put on your headphones, listen, and look at the VU meters on your viewfinder screen while testing the audio in any environment.

If for some reason you can't use your wireless and the sound is too important to pass up, *get close* to your subject so your camera-mounted shotgun mic points toward them. Position your subject so they face *toward* whatever the ambient sound source might be (wind noise, an air vent, refrigerator hum), which means your mic will be pointing *away from it* (your fuzzy windscreen should already be cocooning the mic). If you are recording the subject with a lav attached to their shirt, reverse their position so the ambient source is *behind* them and blocked by their body.

While working with my wife, I sometimes bring along a boom pole; I connect my wireless transmitter to a shotgun microphone on the boom, and Ann operates the boom mic for quick, on-the-fly interviews. But I prefer using the wireless lav whenever possible, and I try to remember to dedicate both of my camera's audio channels to the lav when I'm shooting an interview with this mic, temporarily disabling my shotgun mic. This means that when I transfer the footage to my hard drive, and eventually my editing system, the interview audio will be all I'll hear. I won't be confused by extraneous audio picked up from my shotgun mic. I also like to have two full channels of the interview sound when editing. To my ear, this yields a richer sound. But you can achieve the same richness if you record on only one channel in the field and then duplicate the sound on two tracks in editing (and further enrich the audio in postproduction).

At times the background noise during an interview will be inescapable. If the noise is audible and its source is visible in your B-roll before the interview, after it, or while it's going on, then it won't be too distracting, as long as it remains low in the background. But if it's something like a plane or a lawnmower and you're not making a documentary about planes or lawnmowers, either you have to wait until the noise subsides or you can try incorporating a shot of a plane or lawnmower in the footage before or just after the interview. Working that into the flow of your edit, however, can be more trouble than it's worth. The important thing here is to be listening, to be aware of all sounds that may cause you trouble later.

At times, your wireless microphone will be attached to your main character while you capture B-roll of someone else. This is when it's a good idea to have your shotgun plugged into channel two so you can grab a quick interview or ambient sound. When you transfer that audio later, you'll hear audio from both channels, but as long as you transfer that audio in stereo rather than mono, the two distinct channels will be easy to separate in editing. Make sure the automatic gain control switch (AGC) in your camera's audio settings is turned off, since you will want manual control over audio levels. You may also be tempted to use the trim settings for your mic. Turning these on will reduce handling noise your mic might pick up, but they can sometimes lower the volume range on other sounds.

If you are working with a soundperson, they will no doubt be sending you the audio they are capturing into one of your two channels, preferably channel one. That leaves channel two free for your camera-mounted shotgun, allowing you to get your own sound when you get close to your subject.

Now that you have your microphones properly set up, you are ready to respond to any situation.

Recording Natural or Ambient Sound

This is a vital element of any film, short or long, independent or client-driven. It helps lure viewers into the emotional fabric of a scene. It amplifies and enlivens a character. It fills out dead spaces. It can act as a transitional element from one scene to another, one location to another, one mood to another. There is no excuse for not recording ambient sound while you're shooting in the field. You can decide in editing whether or not to use it, as long as that decision is a defensible aesthetic choice.

In my paid work as a filmmaker for nonprofits, I've noticed a distressing lack of ambient audio in the films made by our competitors. Children play happily on the floor of a daycare, but I can't hear their giggles. A group of volunteers clears the brush from trails in a city park, but I can't hear the sounds of shovels, axes, and saws. What is going on? Either the cameraperson failed to get sound, the editor is not confident enough to include it subtly in a sequence, or the director is making an aesthetic decision not to include it in order to enhance another aspect of the scene.

I once watched three short films that were shot in Nicaragua and El Salvador for a microlending group. The filmmakers traveled to those countries with a crew of five, including a soundperson, yet the only sounds in the finished films were the voices of the talking heads, the narration, and the music. If this was an aesthetic choice, it was unsuccessful. When you have B-roll of people doing things with their hands that clearly make noise, it is more distracting not to be able to hear it.

In the earlier camera section, I talked about surveying the geography of a scene for potential images and sequences. Here, you survey the geography for potential sound and consider how you can use your two main tools, the wireless and the camera mic, to get what you need. Open your ears and listen. Start thinking of how you can use audio to help propel the sequence forward. Where can you place your wireless? How can you get closer to the sound source? What are the possibilities for using that sound in the finished film? Again, you are thinking like an editor while in the field, aware of how sound will help you tell your story when you sit down and start cutting your film.

For his experimental film *Field Niggas*, Khalik Allah shot B-roll and slow-motion, portrait-like images of people on the corner of 125th and Lexington in Harlem. He interviewed the regulars, passersby, cops, and business owners, captured the sounds of the street, and then, in editing, disassociated much of the audio from the person speaking. The result is a free-form collage that shreds standard documentary practice. Allah's movie feels like a floating nocturnal dream—culturally aware, political, raw—that he created by the simple manipulation of the two necessities of doc filmmaking: image and sound.

Use your wireless to do more than record interviews. Keep it affixed to your main subjects while they go about their activities. Set it on a table in the middle of a group of schoolkids to record their voices; hide it among an artist's jars of paint to capture the sound of a dipping brush; conceal it in the kitchen to get the audio of breakfast being prepared. These small bits of ambient sound will enhance your sequences.

Use your on-board microphone in the same way. Suppose you are profiling a specific character on that volunteer trail crew I mentioned earlier. You've got the wide shot of them using a chainsaw to cut a downed tree in half, but the sound was too faint to use. Move in for a medium shot or close-up of them sawing the next tree, making sure to get the sound, and then, when you edit, use that audio first over the wide shot before you cut to the close-up.

A more imaginative way to use the chainsaw audio is to alert viewers to an impending edit. Follow the trail crew in a wide shot as they walk along a path carrying their equipment. Slowly fade in the sound of the chainsaw, and then make an abrupt cut to a close-up of the saw cutting through the tree. The sound has evolved from mere background presence to a powerful editorial tool, cueing viewers' ears to a change before their eyes see it. You tuned into the sound's potential in the field to help move the scene along later in the edit suite.

Watch fictional feature films and listen to how they employ even the most minor audio elements to enhance a scene. Footsteps, clothing noise, traffic sounds—most of this sound comes from the Foley process and is added later. The documentary filmmaker has access to these sounds as well (there are very affordable music libraries stocked with Foley sounds for the cash-strapped doc editor), but why not try to capture as many of these sounds live in the field as you can?

When filming the doctor and nurse in *Zona Intangible* trekking up the path for their house call, I began shooting the sequence by following close behind them at ground level for at least thirty seconds, my camera-mounted mic pointed directly at their feet. I also had a wireless attached to the doctor, picking up his breathing. Later, when I edited the sequence, I combined these two elements at varying volume levels and rhythms to supply the audio track for the entire sequence, including wide shots of the doctor and nurse walking across the frame. Yes, I could have searched through Foley libraries to maybe find a match for these sounds, but it was more authentic (and simpler) to capture the real sound as it happened. I did, however, use a Foley library for the sounds of barking dogs, faraway background traffic noise, and the flapping wings of a crow that appeared in one of the shots.

One element I often neglect to record is called "room tone," the ambient hum of a heater or the soft whirr of an air conditioner you can hear in the background while recording an interview. You may need a continuous bed of that sound to seamlessly cut in and out of the interview. To record room tone properly in the field, you often have to stop everyone from talking or wait for a specific, nonrecurring sound, such as that of an airplane or a garbage truck, to pass before recording thirty to sixty seconds of nothing but the continuous sound of your location. This can be difficult when conditions are dynamic. In those instances, I instead create a background ambience in editing, either using sound I captured at a different point in the shoot or by relying on sound effects libraries, which carry a vast selection of room tones.

The films of the Sensory Ethnography Lab are known for their overall sound designs, sophisticated aural landscapes that punctuate the imagery in compelling ways. One of the most mesmerizing elements of *Manakamana* is the repetitive, but not unpleasant sound of the moving cable car as it clacks across the stanchions supporting it, lulling the viewer into a kind of hypnotic appreciation of the rhythm of the journey.

You don't necessarily need to hire a sound designer to achieve similar results for your film. Keep costs low by recording decent sound in the field, buying tracks from libraries, recording specific audio effects later, and experimenting with layering or rearranging these sounds in the editing process.

Recording Performances or Speeches

When filming an important character giving a long speech, delivering a lecture, or leading a business meeting, rely on your wireless to record the sound. While continuing to roll the camera, pan away to get cutaways of the audience, an establishing shot of the room, etc. Because you're always listening on headphones, you'll be able to quickly pan back to the character talking if they say something you want to have on camera.

Use the same technique for recording a musical performance. Find a place to mount or set down the wireless to record all or a part of the performance at a consistent audio level, and then work the room to get your supporting B-roll. Remember to keep rolling. You'll want an unbroken piece of music in case you decide to use it as part of the soundtrack in your edited film. I'll admit that a single wireless microphone is not the best device for recording the high-quality performance audio we hear in music-centric docs such as

nusicians happen to have a sophisticated
cable from your wireless transmitter di-
nal of their performance. Or you can rig
best you can do is record a general feel
t. Your audio will at least be faithful to

deo footage: a shot of the sun flaring
lo the same with audio. The sounds
ream gently flowing over rocks—
ject matter or the sequence you're
ater, while you're editing, a piece
evoke an emotion or a memory.
those moments when you wish
tself. These effects are accom-
should be to listen, react, and
it later.

tc
ph
rec

Light

Natur

In the _____ a movie without pulling a single light from your
gear ba _____ .plained in Chapter 3, the only essential light, the camera-mounted LED, is
a supporting essential. And since nearly all professional camcorders now have excellent
built-in low-light capabilities, you don't even need that. But you still have to assess your
locations to understand how to use the light that is there. This is called natural or ambient
light, and if used properly it can add a lovely naturalism to your scene.

Again, start by surveying the geography of a scene's available light. It should be the
very first thing you notice, even before you start making a mental list of images. For
interiors, notice the windows, or lack of them. Will the windows allow enough daylight
in to illuminate the location? Is the quality of the light harsh, bright, soft, dim? Are there
artificial lights such as fluorescents hanging from the ceiling? Maybe floor lamps or desk
lamps? Candles or computer screens?

For exteriors, is the sun shining or is it cloudy? Maybe it's lightly overcast. What time
of day is it? Morning and afternoon light are better than the light around midday. Where
are you in relation to the equator? The sun rises earlier and sets later in the northern and

southern reaches of the planet (and vice versa in the winter). Is there shade from trees or buildings? Will that shade go away as the sun moves across the sky? Where will you stand or move with your subjects so you don't cast your own shadow on them? Maybe it's night-time. Is there enough available light or do you need that LED light after all?

Once you know where your light is coming from, you can determine if it is a single source or a mix of natural daylight, fluorescent, or incandescent light. This is when white-balancing your camera is most important. Even though many cameras have sophisticated auto white balance systems that respond quickly to light changes, sometimes it's better to set your own white balance and compare the two. Many cameras now allow you to dial in a specific color temperature, using your flip-out screen as a monitor. If competing light sources make it difficult to get an accurate representation of the same color you see with the naked eye, turn off or obscure one of the sources or add your own light. Overhead lights can often be a problem. They can compete with a more desirable source such as the natural window light or your own lights. Turn off the overheads if possible, but only if the resulting image stills looks natural and realistic.

Think about how you can use the available light to your advantage. Window light can provide a pleasing back or rim light to a face, or it can turn it into a silhouette. You can move or rotate a desk lamp to light up an object for a close-up, provide instant fill light on an interview, or add depth to a shot by illuminating an object in the background (these lights, which already exist in your location, are called *practicals*).

A slightly overcast sky is often the best light for shooting exterior interviews. Flat, even shade can also be lovely, especially on a sunny day when glints of sparkling light filter through a background screen of trees. For interviews shot indoors, use window light, if possible, as the key or main light, turning your subject at a 75-degree angle toward the light so it will have a soft, modeling effect on the subject's face.

The point is to find the main source of light, determine if you can work with it, and be aware of how it may change during the course of your shoot.

Adding Light

Working without additional artificial light is the fastest, cheapest, and least distracting op-tion, but adding your own lighting will improve an image that looks flat or dim. When appropriate, keep your portable LED light mounted on your camera while you're shooting B-roll, and use the dimming and color temperature controls to fill in faces that are a tad dark or to light a close-up when other options aren't handy. Even the faintest hint of extra light will add a pleasing contrast. You can also use this light for outdoor interviews to fill in dark eye shadows or provide fill light, making sure to dial in the daylight color temperature.

Maybe your interior scene will look better with a touch of side- or back-light. Remove the light from your camera and attach it to a light stand using the adapter listed in Chapter 3. Position the stand just outside the frame, with the light illuminating the object or person you are filming. The use of this light in any capacity can be distracting, announcing you and your camera's presence when you are actually trying to blend in. I'm often surprised, however, by the way subjects become fairly comfortable with this spotlight. The ability to manually lower the intensity helps considerably.

Sometimes, though, there is just no denying that you need to bring up the overall light level of a room with a more powerful tool. This is when you can bring one or two 500- or 1,000-watt lights out of your camera bag, place them in the corners of the room—camouflaging the stands as best you can—raise and point them at the ceiling, turn them on, and notice how this creates a flat spread of bounced light throughout the room, bringing the available light up to an acceptable level for shooting your B-roll. If the ceilings are too high, try bouncing lights off a wall or pointing them at the main action in the room, dimming them so they don't create a harsh, studio lighting effect. If you suspect you may need these more powerful lights on a particular shoot, expand your lean team gear package to include them.

To light interviews, I rely on two basic tools: a 250-watt, AC-powered rectangular LED key light with touchscreen controls for intensity and color temperature, placed on a stand within three to five feet of the subject and angled at 75 degrees, and an additional light used as fill. This light is either a 400-watt LED or my 100-watt on-board camera light, removed and attached to a stand. Both have controls allowing me to adjust the intensity and color output. Whether I use them depends on how much available light is already in the room. I position the LED to light the side of the person's face not illuminated by the key light, providing a subtle fill.

Sometimes I'll bring in a collapsible reflector to provide reflected fill light. I'll put it on a stand or ask someone to hold it. I may also decide to use the 400-watt light as the key if I need the extra punch, but this light does not have the same broad face as my 250-watt light, which creates softer, naturalistic shadows (you can certainly buy higher-wattage broad-faced LED key lights, which you may need if your camera doesn't perform well in lower light). Sometimes I use only one of these lights to either complement or provide a soft fill to existing window light.

There is nothing fancy about this lighting package, but it offers just enough tools to create an agreeable image. They aren't too cumbersome to haul around. I can set them up quickly. Once up, they don't take over the room and intimidate an interviewee. More lights, properly modulated, can enhance any digitally created image, but more lights mean more time, more money, and maybe more people to manage them.

I'm personally not fond of the overly fussy and expensive-looking mood lighting you often see in big-budget documentaries, usually on display in interviews. These extensive lighting schemes are used to make celebrities look good but are often at odds with the B-roll, which tends to look more naturalistic. Ask yourself how important it is to have this kind of lighting in your film, especially if it means a huge uptick in your budget. Maybe celebrities would prefer to be lit like regular people, perched on the edge of a desk, illuminated by the ambient light of an off-screen window.

You should, wherever possible, make sure the source of your light is "motivated." That is, it should look like it is coming from a realistic, already existing place. If you can see a window in the background of your subject, consider making your key light on the person's face match that color temperature, as if lit from a window we can't see just out of the frame (see Figure 4.7).

You may see both a window and an incandescent practical light in the background. Consider lighting your interview with a key light whose color temperature matches the practical light, as if a similar type of lamp is just out of frame. In that case, the window light in the background will likely have a blue tint to it, which can look rather nice.

FIGURE 4.7 The author uses an off-screen window as the key light to match the background window light in an interview with his mother in *My Mother Was Here* (in production, 2018). (Still capture from digital file.)

Turning Up the Gain

If all else fails and you find yourself with inadequate natural light, without a practical in sight, nowhere to plug in your AC-powered key light, and you forgot your camera-mounted LED, there is one option left: turn up the gain switch on your camera.

The gain switch accomplishes the same thing as the ISO reading in still photography. It electronically increases the sensitivity of the camera to existing light levels, allowing you to shoot in dark places with enough exposure to register an image. Using the gain reduces image quality because it adds noise to the picture, meaning it can look electronically grainy. More gain equals more grain. You can preset your camera to different gain levels, measured in a signal-to-noise ratio denoted by the same abbreviation, "dB," that is used for sound levels (although the meaning is obviously different). Settings such as +6, +9, and +18 dB are common. The higher the number, the grainier the image will be, and there will also be a slight dulling of the color. That's all you really need to know, except for this: cameras these days have greatly improved their gain settings, expanding a camera's capacity to brighten a dark image with less apparent grain and less apparent color loss, even at what was once a prohibitively high setting like +18 dB.

I discovered this while filming one day in a dark hut off a dusty road in rural Peru. The only daylight in the room came from a narrow doorway, partially blocked by the doctor and nurse attending to a bedridden elderly man. I hadn't anticipated ending up there, so I didn't have my camera-mounted LED with me (a rookie move on my part). I filmed a close-up of the patient's face by following the doctor's penlight shining in his eyes. When he turned that off, I was forced to kick the gain to 18 dB, then 24 dB, which didn't look too bad in my viewfinder. Later, when I examined the image on my computer monitor, I was amazed at how clean the shot looked, how much richness the color retained. The slight graininess only added to the gritty, rural texture of the hut's interior.

The point here, one that gets at the essence of the lean team filmmaking style, is that the immediate power of the content should override technical considerations. A grainy, rough shot of a moment that is about to disappear is more important than no shot at all. As long as you have the essentials of the moment covered—a solid, crisply focused image and clean audible sound—that's all that matters.

Continuing to Find Your Story

I wrote in detail in Chapter 2 about story and structure when you are evaluating the viability of your lean team film. But you never actually stop thinking about story, even while dealing with all the technical stuff involved in capturing your footage. Your story is always with you, guiding your choices, evolving while you work.

While making my memoir documentary, *My Mother Was Here*, I've been continually confronted with choices about the story I want to tell and the way I want to tell it. I'm making a doc about the challenges of growing old in America, while avoiding as much as possible the clichés and predictable arcs typical of such films. I'm also making a film about my difficult relationship with my mom and how her history of loss turned her into a somewhat stubborn and defensive hoarder. My focus is on two people: her and me. This is the spine of my film, my anchor, if you will. Even when the story dips and swells and sways, the anchor keeps me from drifting.

Throughout the many years I've been working sporadically on *My Mother Was Here* (Ann and I made another feature documentary and several dozen of our short advocacy films during this time), I've constantly questioned my intensely personal focus. I wonder if I should hunt down relatives and interview them; I think about the broad issues of caring for the elderly in our culture and consider whether I should talk to experts about Medicare and Death With Dignity; I wonder if I should dispense with the idea of a first-person approach and make a more strictly observational film; I question my desire to use old-time cowboy songs on the soundtrack and to risk losing less adventurous viewers with some abstract images or daring sound edits. These questions have dogged me all the way through the editing process. But I remain determined not to alter my original vision of the film. Documentary filmmaking involves a fair amount of exploration, especially in the early stages, until you find the hard ground of the narrative through line. If you've begun your film with a sense of the story you want to tell, then the anchor that grounds that story will soon become clear.

A strong sense of story will help you focus your efforts and eliminate distractions. In the beginning, this could be only an outline or a rough blueprint, with themes, ideas, characters, and locations plotted out to help guide you while in the field. When you actually start filming, elements of that story will likely change, forcing you to adapt to new challenges or developments. This is when a sturdy anchor will see you through and keep you focused. And it will act as a positive limiting force as you work toward the completion of your film.

"The enemy of art is the absence of limitations." This phrase, reportedly attributed to Orson Welles, has always inspired me.[9] I believe it to be especially applicable to the lean team filmmaker. This less-is-more philosophy is now actively taught in media studies programs. Students work more creatively and imaginatively when limits are imposed on funding, gear, crew size, and the scope and arc of a story. EDIT Media (Equity, Diversity, and Inclusion in Teaching Media), a consortium of media faculty members from around the United States, encourages this approach: "Creating boundaries on student work discourages problematic content while students are still developing theoretical and conceptual skills . . . a way of directing student work to encourage deeper engagement with specific skills. Such constraints can include limiting the length of projects, allowing only specific equipment to be used, focusing on conceptual approaches like a theme, or emphasizing stylistic approaches like the use of color."[10]

Self-imposed limitations are not just for students. In Ross McElwee's *Sherman's March*, the director-narrator traded in his dry historical documentary for a wry and rueful personal approach. Once he made that switch, everything in his film kept returning to that narrative. His doc became a meta-rumination on the difficulty of completing his academic film while dealing with lovelorn distractions.

In Aaron Shock's *Circo*, the photographer-turned-filmmaker elides his own presence in favor of observation, working completely alone to concentrate solely on the circus family in front of his lens. He resists the urge to take on a wider view of rural poverty or the history of itinerant performers in Mexico. The harmonious, firsthand feel of the film is delightfully unforced because Shock remains anchored to an organic, small-scale story, yet the family dynamics at the core of the film are universal (see Figure 4.8).

Don't be afraid of experimenting with an odd or oblique approach to your story. Perhaps you will begin your film with a more conventional vision in mind, but that will

FIGURE 4.8 Filmmaker Aaron Shock rides in the back of a pickup with one of the members of the family circus in *Circo* (2010). (Still capture from DVD.)

change as you start delving into it. Your narrative goal will stay the same, but the way in which you tell it will evolve into something more elliptical. If you go down this path, stick with it. Have the confidence to adhere to this new vision, no matter how unconventional.

In his thoughtful 2016 essay entitled *Pretentiousness: Why It Matters*, art critic, musician, and filmmaker Dan Fox writes, "Pretentiousness keeps life interesting. Without the permission it gives—the license to try new experiences, to experiment with ideas, to see if you want to live your life another way—people from all kinds of backgrounds will not be exposed to difference, to new ideas or the histories of their chosen field."[11]

In other words, pretension (not a pejorative term in Fox's view) is a perfect fit for the lean team filmmaker, free to apply a creative twist to a standard filmmaking challenge. Without artists willing to embrace pretension, Fox continues, "the doors to imagination would be locked tight in fear of finding behind them something that violates the consensus over what is an acceptable creative act." This is why you as a filmmaker would be best served by seeking out and studying all kinds of films, by being skeptical of trends and absolutes, by rejecting consensus and taking risks.

Without a healthy embrace of pretension, I doubt if Errol Morris would have made *The Thin Blue Line*. Without an inquisitive imagination, Chris Marker would not have made *Sans Soleil*. Without an obsession with *The Shining*, Rodney Ascher would not have made *Room 237*. And certainly, the Portuguese directors Marcelo Gomes and Karim Aïnouz would not have made the hypnotic, confounding *I Travel Because I Have To, I Come Back Because I Love You* if they had adhered to rules governing the separation of fiction and documentary.

Remember, there is no one right way to make a documentary. In the 2008 film *Capturing Reality*, director Pepita Ferrari interviews thirty-three documentary filmmakers engaged in all aspects of the craft. Watching it you soon realize they all have firm but different opinions on how best to shoot B-roll, record sound, interview, light, and deal with ethical concerns. They clearly learned to cultivate and embrace the style that works best for them.

As a lean team filmmaker, you may find managing all of these details in the field at the same time daunting. Thinking visually. Capturing images. Recording sound. Paying attention to lighting. Moving the camera. Responding to the changing nature of your subject matter. And doing all of these things while remaining aesthetically engaged. In addition, you've got a story to tell, so you're making a series of narrative decisions on top of everything else.

If you're a beginner, go slow. Get comfortable with your camera's image-making capabilities first. Take your time framing and focusing. Keep inching closer to your subjects. Capture basic audio via your on-board camera mic, then graduate to a wireless.

Separate the two incoming audio sources into your camera's two distinct channels. Use your headphones. Maybe even ask for a little help in the field from someone with more experience. Learn from them, and then take over.

If you've been shooting for a couple of years as part of a three- or four-person team but feel fairly confident that you can handle all the technical demands yourself, then trim the fat, slim down, reduce.

If you're a grizzled veteran who is used to working only as a cog in a laborious hierarchy, you're probably beyond hope. *Kidding*! You are actually in a great position to be truly independent, because you've already got the skills and the experience. Try working as a lean team filmmaker, calling your own aesthetic shots, learning to get the most out of the fewest pieces of equipment, experiencing a new intimacy, a fresh emotional honesty, with the people and places you encounter. Your life as a filmmaker is about to get way more exciting.

/// 5 /// THE EDIT

Cutting as a Lean Team Filmmaker

I finally had my own editing suite. In a spare basement room of our house, I'd installed a desk and a lamp, put my poster of Michelangelo Antonioni's *Blow Up* on the wall, and bought a luxury-model leather desk chair. Expensive, but comfortable. It was 2001, and I planned on spending many hours that year crafting masterpieces with my brand new nonlinear editing system, Final Cut Pro, and all the computer hardware needed to make it work. The day the boxes arrived I put them in my editing suite and there they sat, unopened, for *two months*. I was simply too overwhelmed by the task of assembling the gear, turning it on, and figuring out how to make it all work. What if I lacked the brainpower, the patience, or the talent to tackle this new world of nonlinear editing?

My wife and I were betting our new business on my being able to edit our scripts and footage into coherent videos for clients who were paying us with their precious non-profit dollars. I had no choice. I had to cut open those boxes and see what was inside. Once I'd got rid of the Styrofoam packaging, plugged everything in, and turned on the computer, I timidly double-clicked the FCP icon. Yes, there it was, the program I'd seen demonstrated at a conference I'd attended, the one that I'd fiddled around with for a few hours at a workshop (there were no YouTube tutorials to watch because YouTube hadn't been invented yet). I confirmed that everything seemed to be functioning properly and then I turned it off.

The next day I cleared my schedule, restarted the program, and went to work learning how to edit with this creatively powerful new tool. It didn't take long before I'd edited my first sequence, and in the next month we finished our first client video, keeping the portion of our fee that we used to pay for an editor and suite at a downtown production studio. Within a year I'd edited my second feature-length documentary, one that I also produced, filmed, and wrote. Since then, I've edited nearly every frame of video I've shot.

In this chapter, I'm going to urge you to reconsider the conventional wisdom about needing another pair of eyes to edit your movie. While this is a reasonable next step, especially for filmmakers who may lack the technical skills or the confidence to edit, I personally feel that the crafts of shooting and editing are linked; they are a singular creative act. A painter doesn't mix the colors and then hand the brush to an assistant, watching over their shoulder as they paint the canvas. An author doesn't write a first draft and then let another writer finish the job.

You researched, planned, and shot your film. You understand the footage; you know better than anyone what you were thinking in the field, how one image connects to another, where to insert a piece of texture, what the meaning and intent are behind a transitional image or sequence you filmed. This familiarity with your own work means you are logically poised to become your own editor.

After all, editing is the ultimate lean team experience, right? One person alone in a dark room with keyboard and monitor? In theory, yes, that's what it should look like. But the reality has become something different. The lean team field crew of one or two people starts putting on weight as soon as the last frame of video is shot. There are interviews to transcribe, footage to log, video to edit, color to correct, sound to mix, final cuts to be mastered, DCPs (digital cinema packages) to process, and H.264 digital files to upload. No wonder the postproduction process can stretch on for months (or years!) and get very expensive.

You've rustled up interns (paid, I hope) to log and transcribe; you've hired a couple of assistant editors to organize your footage into select bins; you've managed to get on that sought-after editor's schedule; you've received a grant that will pay for half of the expensive color-grading session at that sleek downtown studio and maybe half of the rate for the best audio engineer in town. You've convinced executive producers, supposedly with connections to the industry, to join the team, and they—along with everyone else who has come on-board—are giving you advice about your film. By the time the picture is locked, your scrappy, small-footprint film has tripled in budget, your labor force has quadrupled, and it may not even feel like your film anymore. *Your film*. The film you spent all those days and nights planning and shooting.

There is a chance—a small one—that your expensive, no longer lean movie may get an early buzz that will propel it onward to the best film festivals and worldwide distribution. But it's more likely that your rewards will be modest, that you'll achieve a relatively satisfying level of success dependent largely on your own efforts. You may look back at the money and time you spent on editors and assistants and wonder if you should have edited the film, color-corrected footage, and built a soundtrack all on your own and then uploaded the final product to your Vimeo on Demand page.

I first learned to edit by splicing and gluing 16mm film in college. The next year I learned to edit three-quarter-inch tape in a broadcasting class; then it was half-inch Betacam a few years later. In the late 1990s I was introduced to AVID, before I purchased those boxes containing my new Mac and the first version of Final Cut Pro. I've been cutting for nearly forty years, so yes, maybe it's easy for me to say, "Edit your own film." But the thing is, by learning to edit, I became a better shooter, a better producer, a better writer and director, and, of course, a better editor. Without the promise of editing my own material, I would lose my passion for capturing images, since an image that is not linked—emotionally, thematically, narratively, physically—to another image has little meaning for me.

It is absolutely never too late to learn how to edit. The software was specifically *designed* for you to learn it. Filmmakers who edit (and produce, write, shoot, and record sound) remain the true author of their film from start to finish. This philosophy was the original intent of Robert Drew's pioneering outfit Drew Associates, which in 1960 sent out squads of lean team filmmakers working with newly invented lightweight equipment to make the film *Primary*.

"This was the year I decided that photographers and correspondents must also edit,"[1] Drew said. "This would give them responsibility for paying off on what they shot and help each one of them develop as a 'filmmaker'—a person capable of going beyond his or her specialty to also produce and manage the editing of films." Drew eventually realized, however, that many of his camerapersons had no interest in editing, so he never forced the idea. But he also had the luxury of broadcast budgets that could pay for both shooters and editors (see Figure 5.1).

You can learn the basics of editing in a few hours. Start by exploring the drop-down menus of your editing system. Watch online tutorials. Consult the help manual when you are stumped. If a key task in editing trips you up and the manual doesn't provide the answer, Google it. I couldn't wrap my head around the differences in Final Cut Pro X between the terms "events," "projects," and "library" until I found a brief, clarifying video on YouTube.

Play and experiment. You're just getting started. It may be helpful to take a short introductory class to demystify the process and ask the instructor questions. If you are in film school, your college probably offers hands-on classes in the latest technology.

You don't need to learn everything your nonlinear editing system is capable of. You don't need to learn all the shortcuts. You don't need to buy all the fancy plug-ins, scopes, and X-ray glasses that gear-focused editors love to nerd out about. You just

FIGURE 5.1 One of Robert Drew's camerapersons stays close to JFK as he walks on a stage in *Primary* (1960). (Screen capture from digital file.)

want to cut your documentary, and the mechanics of documentary editing are pretty straightforward. It's the *aesthetics* of editing that take more time to learn.

Many high-profile docs these days are cut by experienced editors based in New York or Los Angeles. Directors ship their footage to them, along with instructions and notes, and then wait to see what the editor comes up with. These sequences are then uploaded to Vimeo, WeTransfer, Dropbox, or other file-sharing sites for review. If you live in the same city as your editor, you'll usually meet in person to discuss the work as it progresses.

There is nothing at all inherently wrong with this method. Many filmmakers not only enjoy the collaborative aspect of the process and truly believe the extra pair of eyes is essential to making their film better, but also are simply not interested in editing their own work. For them, an editor is a must.

Let me be perfectly clear here: I have nothing but respect for editors. Their patience, skill, organizational talents, and perceptiveness have rescued many documentaries from the scrapheap of mediocrity. They've turned clanking jalopies into smooth-purring machines. They deserve every penny they can get for their work. But in the LTDF world, the fee a competent editor requires may simply be beyond your budget. If you can learn to cut your own films, you'll save money *and* retain complete creative control of your work.

In addition to the cost, there is another caveat to consider. Professional editors bring their own style, conventions, and prejudices to a project. They take pride in the seamlessness and invisibility of their work. Pay close attention to the popular documentaries you see in theaters or on cable TV or Netflix, and you'll notice an efficient predictability in the way these films are cut: the pro forma biography *What Happened, Miss Simone?*, the sensationalized *City of Ghosts*, the talking-head-laden *We Steal Secrets: The Story of WikiLeaks*.

Alex Gibney made *We Steal Secrets*, one of twenty-one features he's directed in thirteen years. "Gibney's investigative documentaries tend to share a structure and a tone," writes Boris Kachka for Vulture. "Binge-watch them and they start to bleed into each other—one long, smoothly segued cascade of talking heads, found footage, and astonishing revelations."[2] Gibney makes no apologies for his assembly-line approach to doc filmmaking, and his films are dependably researched, entertaining, and relatively profitable. But there is little that is unpredictable or daring in the way they're constructed.

Compare those films with the vibrant, risk-taking, at times abstract cutting of *The Iron Ministry* and *El Mar La Mar*, the unhurried rhythms of *Sweetgrass*, the contemplative unfolding of images and sound of *Into Great Silence*, the dialectical mash-up of *Man with a Movie Camera*. It's no surprise that in all of these examples, the directors edited their own work.

Recently I watched the first ten minutes of about a dozen films from both the Sundance Channel and Netflix. Many of the films began with a sequence *in medias res*, which is Latin for "in the middle of things." They started with a single heightened dramatic moment, followed by the quiet swell of the music score, then a scene-setting montage overlaid with opening credits, which transitioned to a sequence set in the present day, with either on-screen text or more sound bites providing expository information.

These were all pretty good opening scenes in terms of compelling you to keep watching, but what stuck with me was how they all looked and sounded alike. The slick professionalism on display certainly helped these films to achieve at least some commercial success, but they seemed to be designed by a committee rather than organically arising from a director's singular vision.

Cultivate your singular vision by learning to edit. You will gradually see how satisfying it is to become the top-to-bottom creator of your own work. You'll realize that editing will make you a more astute cinematographer, and vice versa. You'll have a firsthand look at how your footage translates to storytelling: what you needed more of, what you could have left out. While in the field, you'll begin to recognize how the images and sequences and textures you're shooting might fit together on an editing timeline. You'll realize that good editing is not simply stapling images together to fill space. Creating a montage set to music is a fine way to get used to the simple process of putting one image after another, but it's not necessarily good editing, nor is the breathless barrage of quick-cut images many editors think they need in order maintain a viewer's attention.

I was once nominated for a regional Emmy Award for the editing of my documentary *False Promises: The Lost Land of the Wenatchi*, which I'd spent months working on. I was up against several other projects, none of them long-form docs. I lost to a fast-paced sports highlight package. When the producer stepped up to the podium to collect his Emmy he admitted, rather sheepishly, that he had cut this award-winning piece in a few hours on his laptop during the flight from New York to Seattle. I was more amused than appalled.

Good editing is a matter of pacing and tone, of subtle shifts in rhythm, of well-placed transitions, of the application of sound, silence, pauses, and music. Good editing is good storytelling. Good editing involves seeing your film through the eyes of an audience, but also judging what kind of audience you want your film to have.

Documentary style is often molded in the editing suite. The cutting rhythm of the film—fast, slow, staccato, measured, hurried, patient, choppy, fluid—will affect different viewers in different ways. One viewer may appreciate the contemplative, composed pace of your film; another may be bored to death. The contemplative viewer might get restless and hit fast forward while watching fast-paced sequences. The bored viewer might prefer films that leap off the screen with lots of quick shots. I put myself in the former camp. I'm more impressed by editing that creates a mood through the slow build of imagery, sound, and transitions rather than a surplus of frantic energy. I like the single bold cut that draws attention to itself or a meld of images and sound that challenges me to keep up. Sometimes I want to see the seams between scenes. I want to connect to the imaginative, intelligent presence of the director-editor at work. It's really no surprise that these types of films have a hard time finding an audience and making money.

The point is: If you edit your film in an attempt to appeal to the widest audience possible, you may make compromises that you never intended. Make the film you want to make. Edit the film the way you want to edit it. As long as it gets the central job done—telling your story—and you haven't sacrificed your artistic integrity, you can be proud of it.

When editing, you will make decisions about exposition and structure. Exposition is about what information you will deliver, and structure is about how you deliver it. In this chapter, I break down these two decisions into steps, methods, strategies, elements, and aesthetics to consider when you're editing your film. Entire books have been written about both the practical and artistic components of editing, so what follows is far from comprehensive and can only begin to suggest the intuitive, creative possibilities of the craft. For a more detailed examination of all the stages of editing, read Jacob Bricca's *Documentary Editing: Principles and Practice* (Routledge, 2018), which takes you from organizing raw footage through to the fine cut and final export.

IN THE EDITING SUITE

The Paper Edit

Way back in the days of the Yellow Pages and grunge rock, when I was editing video on analog tape decks, I learned to always work with an actual paper script or written structural outline. This is how I created a blueprint for telling my story, the first rule of efficient lean team editing. But before you get to this outline or script stage, it can be helpful to use three-by-five cards.

This method is very old school. It involves writing down, on an index card, each scene in your movie, adding a few details about characters, location, potential sound bites, etc. and then either arranging the cards on a large bulletin board, attaching them to a whiteboard with magnets, or spreading them across the floor (color-coding the cards is an additional option). You can easily move scenes around to get a sense of flow and story arc. Some editors like to print out freeze-frames of key scenes in their movie and use those as reference points. It's a handy way to visualize the whole film and see what might be missing from your story (as you would expect, there is now software that replicates this process). Once you've got an overview of your film that might work, you can organize a script.

A script without voice-over narration is still a script. Your interviews, on-screen text, images, other sound elements—these can be the "words" of your script. I've used two different formats for scripting. One is the classic two-column format for an editing script, with the left side of the page containing the markers that push the story forward (references to both interviews and B-roll, names of characters, suggested transitions, music cues, etc.) and the right side containing the actual words spoken by characters or the narrator and on-screen text, if any (with time code included). The other is the standard movie script format, with scene descriptions, blocks of dialogue (i.e., interviews), and transitions in a continuous flow down the page. If your film is perhaps more experimental, containing very little interview sound and relying mostly on visuals, then a basic outline could be all you need.

Your first step is to transcribe your interviews with time code references (one of the few times I hire an assistant is when I have hours of interviews to listen to). Study these transcriptions and develop a system for selecting potential sound bites, bolding or color-coding the best ones and sorting them into their own folder. Begin to add these into your script, a sort of jigsaw puzzle approach whereby you move blocks of dialogue around on the page to see how they flow and fit. If you are working without narration, your sound bites form the narrative voice of your film. Before you commit to using any sound bite, go back and look at the actual video of the interview. There may be a problem with the inflection or delivery that renders the bite, which looked good on paper, not so good for the actual film. If your film is driven less by interview sound than by images, sequences, or the course of events, these become your signposts for organizing your footage.

In any case, a paper script is an important organizational tool. You can scribble notes on it, which is hard to do on a computer screen; you can spread out the pages to get a sense of how your story moves forward; you can easily mark starting points for scenes, sequences, and transitions. The script or outline is an important second edit in the process (the first being those editorial decisions you made in the field). I shudder when I hear of editors who sit down to piles of footage without at least some form of written guide to organize their approach. This method is time-consuming and inefficient, and often results in a meandering film.

It's at this script or outline phase of the edit where you confront one of the more steadfast truisms of storytelling: the three-act structure. I'm not advocating this structure for your film; I'm only describing it.

The model breaks down into the setup, the confrontation, and the resolution, and in both narrative and documentary filmmaking, it follows a fairly predictable progression. The setup lasts about twenty minutes, at which point the dramatic confrontation occurs, followed by the bulk of the film, forty to sixty minutes of characters developing and events unfolding. As the tension heightens, it builds toward a climactic resolution, the final ten to fifteen minutes, in which the characters have been transformed and the issue solved, at which point the ending delivers a satisfying conclusion. In documentaries, endings are often more brooding and ambiguous than in fictional films, since that's what real life is like.

Artists tend to balk at the predictability of the three-act structure. Yet it has remained the sturdy model for coherent storytelling for so long precisely because it gets the job done. Most of the work in both literature and film that *appears* to upend this structure still contains the three essential ingredients—setup, confrontation, and resolution—they may just be rearranged or disguised behind abstract methods. Even *Homo Sapiens,* an experimental work, has a (barely) detectable three-act structure: the images seem farther and farther removed from human presence before they circle back to the same location we saw at the beginning of the film, now more ruined than before.

As the lean team author of your film, you have complete freedom to experiment with these elements, to challenge an audience's ritualized assumptions, to be playful, unique, and surprising. You may have opted for a more avant-garde approach while shooting in the field, avoiding the three-act structure early on. Or you made sure to gather the footage you needed to conform to this structure, knowing that in editing you were going to turn it on its head.

I'm drawn to films that blow up expectations, as long as they are true to a coherent and consistent vision. *Room 237* is a film I thoroughly enjoyed watching because its construction and rule breaking were energizing, even though much of the actual content was pretty nutty. A film called *Eldorado XXI* by Salomé Lamas pulled me in mainly due to its opening fresco-like images of a snowbound Andean town, followed by a locked-down, unbroken shot of miners ascending and descending a hillside as the light faded from the sky, with the disembodied audio of interviews and radio announcements playing underneath. That single shot lasted nearly *one hour*! Lamas knew her one-hour shot had a home in the final narrative, but where it was placed in the film, the audio that supported it, and what came after—in other words, the structure—were decided in editing.

Using three-by-five cards, a script, or an outline for your paper edit, you are able to map out a blueprint of a film's structure. Not only will this guide you through the next several phases of editing, but it will represent your story. You should be able to see the spine of your story remain consistent throughout the many pages of the script or outline. You should be able to see characters come to the forefront. You should be able to identify points where exposition or clarity is called for. You should get an early sense of the rhythm and pace of your film. Is information, whether visual or aural, coming too soon or too slow? Is it being expressed didactically or organically? Is the film beginning to veer off into tangents? Are those tangents distractions or are they worth exploring?

You shouldn't have to answer all these questions before you start editing. Remember, the edit is as much of a journey as the shoot was. But it's a journey of intent rather than discovery. This is where you take all of the material you gathered from the expedition and try to make sense of it.

Organizing Your Footage

The second rule of efficient lean team editing is to clearly, cleanly organize your footage in your editing software. This is the third edit of the movie, after the first (capturing footage in the field) and the second (the paper edit). This is when you determine which pictures and sound may have a chance to make it into your final cut.

I always begin by dedicating a folder on an external hard drive to my project. I never expect my laptop, which holds all of the applications, photos, music, emails, etc. from my daily life, to function as the primary hard drive for my editing projects. My Final Cut Pro or Premiere program lives on my laptop, but not the raw footage or edited files. I always keep those separate.

Study your editing program's manual to understand the best preferences for ingesting your video and audio. Your audio preferences should always be set to capture or transfer in *stereo*, but your video can be set at different resolution levels depending on the final output of your project. With HD footage, a lower resolution can be hard to distinguish with the naked eye from a higher resolution. A lower setting also means your footage will take up far less hard drive space (4K video takes up way more space). However, in nonlinear editing platforms today, the editing timeline can work with many different resolutions without having to render them first. When you get to the final stage, you want to export your film at the best settings possible.

A quick admission here. Like many documentary editors, I still use Final Cut Pro (FCP), even though we all know time has run out on this faithful friend of the editor. The old version of FCP was discontinued in 2011, when Apple introduced the much-maligned FCP X, a restructuring of the software that angered legions of professional editors and studios and forced many to switch to Adobe's Premiere editing system, which had an architecture similar to that of the original Final Cut Pro. Late in 2017, I finally bought the most recent version of Final Cut Pro X, called 10.3 (while keeping my old version, FCP 7.0.3, intact on a separate computer). This recent upgrade of FCP actually bears some resemblance to the old system and may lure many editors back. While many of the references I make to nonlinear editing systems (NLEs) in this section are to the classic interfaces of FCP and Premiere, the basic elements of editing will always be the same, no matter how many upgrades or disruptions these companies want to throw at us.

Okay, let's get back to organizing your footage.

Once I start transferring raw footage into my project, I label each shot as I go, with references to relevant camera movement (pan, tilt, zoom, etc.), and I number the shots in consecutive order if I have several takes of the same image. I make note of wide shots (WS), medium shots (MS), and close-ups (CU), rack focuses, soft focuses, tracking shots, telephoto shots, shots with strong foreground (FG) or background (BG) elements, etc. If I have long, unbroken takes made up of several potentially smaller takes, I create subclips and label those. I make notes of pertinent audio that I may use later for transitions or narrative information. Right away I cull footage that is unusable, choosing not to clutter up my bins with throwaway stuff.

During the transfer, I'm creating and labeling bins or folders in my NLE browser to sort the footage (these can also be called events, projects, libraries, or other terms depending on your editing software). I label the bins in ways that make sense to me. I want to be able to access the shots I put in those bins with one or two clicks instead of endlessly scrolling through my browser. I always start off by creating bins marked "interviews," "music," "SFX" (for sound effects), and "sequences"; then I create the other bins according to themes, locations, people, etc. Using the dance studio example from Chapter 4, I might create one bin called "dance studio B-roll." If I have several shots of one dancer, I'll create a new bin just for that person.

Consistent, concise, and clearly labeled bins and footage are the keys to editing creatively. It is here where my choices in the field make editing easier and more focused. Instead of having spent hours and hours shooting vague footage, I'm happy to see that nearly all of my shots have potential. Because I began telling my story in the field, I don't have to hope that the editing process will figure it out for me, or wait until editing to realize I don't have a story, just a bunch of undirected footage. I can sit down to edit with my concentration focused on storytelling.

Practice these organizational tips (or devise your own) on every single film project. Develop habits that streamline the process, that unclutter the visual thinking part of your brain.

Building the Timeline

This is where you begin the critical fourth edit of your movie, the assembling of images and audio. Your timeline is where all of your elements come together, where the magic begins to happen. Again, for the sake of clarity, I'll assume most editors are using Premiere Pro or the older Final Cut Pro, but note that FCP 10.3 actually employs a rather nifty automatic method of arranging and layering your video and audio.

I recommend starting out with three video tracks and ten audio tracks. Organize similar footage on its own dedicated track. For example, put B-roll and interviews on the first video track and any graphics or on-screen text on tracks two and three. Or you can place B-roll on one track, interviews on the second, and text on the third. With audio, drop interview audio on tracks one and two and ambient or natural sound on tracks three and four, usually synced with the video. On tracks five and six put additional audio, such as sound pulled from other images but not synced to the specific image on the timeline. Add sound effects or Foley effects on these tracks. Drop music or additional audio effects on tracks seven and eight. Use tracks nine and ten for narration if necessary. You can always move elements to different tracks at any time

When you get more comfortable with editing, add as many tracks as you desire, but keep in mind that even unconventional documentaries make an impact with fewer tracks, which means a cleaner, more easily manageable timeline.

Avoid fancy transitions, superimpositions, strange fonts, etc. You'll see that hard edits, a spare use of on-screen text, and an uncluttered sound mix make the images and story more potent.

When you're working on a feature-length film (sixty minutes or longer), it can be helpful to build several shorter timeline sequences and then combine them all when you're finished. I always make copies of every sequence, sometimes retaining earlier versions, since I may want to go back and grab a shot or sequence or block of sound to insert into the most recent sequence. It is very important to clearly label your sequences so you are always working on the most up-to-date version. You will learn this lesson quickly if you ever make the mistake, as I have, of spending hours working on the wrong sequence.

There are several approaches you can take to building the timeline. You may start with a defining sequence you shot in the field and then fill in around it. You may decide to start out by stringing together a series of extended scenes and then shape them according to the structure you've come up with. Some experienced editors like to edit the end of their film first, so that's the first scene they put on the timeline. If the information is driven mainly by interviews, other editors will lay down all of their sound bites in order first, just to get a feel for the expository thrust of their story. They will then trim the sound and begin filling in with visuals. I like to work from the very beginning of the story, building it from the first shot onward, advancing the story scene by scene, meticulously cutting every scene to a polished first cut. I'll go back and trim or move whole chunks around later after I have a sense of whether the story is working or not.

Editing B-roll and Finding Your Story

Remember what I said in Chapter 2 about shooting B-roll? It should advance your story, express your ideas, and make a metaphorical or symbolic point. It should never function as mere filler. To be fair, we will all, at some point, have to use an image we don't really want to simply because none of our other options quite work. If this happens, don't berate yourself. Viewers won't remember your film for one or two weak pictures, as long as the rest of the imagery is as strong as you can make it.

Adding B-roll into your NLE timeline is the most creative part of editing. This is where you bring the visual thinking strategies you employed in the field into the creation of your story, giving your images heft and focus by connecting them to other shots. Sometimes you'll already know—because you thought about it when shooting—exactly where an image will be placed in your story. Other times you'll need to try a variety of images to see what works. "There is no greater joy in the life of an editor," writes Jacob Bricca, "than to see a scene moved to a new spot in the cut (or a shot moved to a new spot in a scene) and suddenly see it take on new life. The content remained the same, but the alchemical mix of the ordering produced something new."[3]

This is where good organization comes into play, because you must be able to try out several different shots quickly to keep the momentum of a sequence going. Will the shot you've selected make sense when connected to the next shot? Having a paper outline next to your computer helps you keep the big picture in mind. You may be enthralled by the dynamic sequence you just edited, but if its rhythm, pace, or intentions are at odds with what came before or what's coming next, its effect may be jarring or atonal, causing your film to veer off-track.

In order to maintain a consistent, organic pace, always review the last two or three minutes you've cut several times during an editing session. After working intensely on a single sequence for one, two, or three hours, you may have lost your feel for the rhythm and pace and mood you previously established. Go back and replay the scenes before this sequence to make sure your flow is intact, that you haven't broken the spell. If you step away from your edit for a day or two or longer, go back even further in your piece when you return.

When beginning your film, make your first image count. Use a bold, extreme close-up or a gorgeous beauty shot, an expressive face or a mysterious landscape. Choose an image that forces the audience to pay attention and then hold on it for several seconds. Don't rush. Lingering on the first series of images in your movie allows a viewer time to settle down and lock in to your film. Too many documentaries cut away from their first images too quickly. I find watching foreign-made documentaries helpful; their pace tends to be more patient, their style less hurried.

Try using an important piece of sound over a black screen to draw viewers in, forcing them to pay attention with their ears first so their eyes can follow. Use this method if you need to start on an image or series of images that may not be especially compelling by themselves but have sound that *is* compelling enough to grab a viewer's interest. The effort to make an impact in those first couple of minutes can lead to regrettable choices, such as overly sensationalized material or a lengthy prologue that gives away too much information too soon. Sometimes a film will have three different beginnings because the director couldn't decide which was the best.

The importance of your opening scene or scenes can't be overstated. The first few minutes tell your audience what kind of film they can expect, how it is paced, what relevant issues may be raised, what kinds of characters they may meet, whose "voice" is being represented: the filmmaker's or the characters or an interaction between them. It can be a bit nerve-wracking to figure out how to sufficiently grab a viewer's attention, especially in today's documentary world, with so many films competing for film festival slots and so many digital distractions on a laptop screen. Be mindful that the beginning of your film "teaches" your audience what kind of film they will be watching.

In *My Mother Was Here,* I open on a single, locked-down, thirty-second shot of my mom sitting alone in an empty living room with bits of debris scattered on the floor. We hear traffic from the busy highway. She stares silently into space. After several seconds, I fade in three short pieces of on-screen text, one at a time and written in the second person, that hint at the story to come:

Mom,
(*4 seconds elapse*)
You always told me you didn't want to end up in a nursing home.
(*5 seconds elapse*)
I can't promise that won't happen.

The text fades. The shot on my mother holds. Then the scratchy sound of an old 78-rpm record and the voice of a country-and-western crooner fade up on the soundtrack. The shot cuts to black, followed by a brief series of scene-setting vistas from the rural area of Washington State where my mom lived, and then I return to her in that living room. I speak to her off-screen, and then, on camera, she describes where we are: the house I grew up in, cleared of the clutter she accumulated over sixty years, now on the real estate market.

This opening sequence tells the viewer many things about the movie: it will have an unhurried pace, some information will be delivered via text, it takes place in a farmland setting in the Pacific Northwest, there will be music, my mom will be the central character, I will be a presence in the storytelling, and the tension in the story will involve keeping my mom out of a nursing home. This opening sequence establishes the film's overall mood. It may not be a mood that fits the desires of all viewers, but at least they know what they're in for.

Every filmmaker or editor has grappled with the process of "finding the film in the edit." Werner Herzog believes this strategy results in mountains of footage, waiting for a miraculous rescue. Disciplined veterans like Ross McElwee and D. A. Pennebaker feel that shooting less footage makes finding the story easier. Others, like Joe Berlinger and Bruce Sinofsky, believe that the process of cutting reveals a structure or storytelling angle that you may have missed while shooting. This is part of the organic process of storytelling I talked about earlier. There isn't a single method that works across the board. "We're talking about incubating and massaging and struggling," says Ken Burns, "and crying and taking out things that are great because they slow down something later on."[4]

Editing is a process of rewriting the paper script you started with. After we finish a film, my wife will rewrite our original script while watching the final, locked film. Huge chunks of our original idea will have been radically altered, moved to different places, or deleted. Did we find a different story in the editing or refine the story we started out with? "That is the second thing," says Burns, "when story and moment and art coalesce in the editing room seemingly out of nothing, and you feel a great deal of satisfaction and excitement about that."[5]

For her offbeat, surprisingly charming documentary-fiction road movie, *Before Summer Ends*, director-cinematographer Maryam Goormaghtigh had been filming three of her Iranian friends, expats living in Paris, for several years. "I started like a documentary filmmaker just observing," she says, "but for the final movie, I had 70 hours of footage captured in two-and-a-half weeks on the road, and didn't use any of the older footage."[6] This is perhaps an extreme example of the adage "kill your darlings," but Goormaghtigh realized the discarded footage provided her with the backstories necessary to "direct" her nonfiction characters in a new setting with all new footage. (see Figure 5.2).

FIGURE 5.2 The three main characters in Maryam Goormaghtigh's *Before Summer Ends* (2017). (Screen capture from digital file).

Cutting on Action

When you're editing your B-roll, one rule of thumb to follow that has been around as long as thumbs is to *cut on action*, which means matching the movement in one shot with the movement of the next shot. A common example is a short sequence of a person getting out of a car and walking into a house. This concept was first associated almost solely with fictional moviemaking. But you can use it too, especially if you've sequenced your footage in the field. Cutting on action also means simply starting and ending any shot in the middle of an action, which helps maintain momentum. Cutting on action is a way to engage the viewer in the kinetic energy of a shot, scene, or sequence.

Take a chaotic emergency room scene. While shooting, you may not have time to sequence one individual's action, but you'll have a lot of shots of general activity to work with. When cutting that scene, make each edit an action edit: Something moves into or out of or within the frame. You cut into each shot just as an action begins and out of each shot a split second before the action ends. If a nurse enters the shot, you cut at the moment the nurse can be glimpsed at the edge of the frame. If a doctor picks up a syringe from a tray, you cut into the shot just as the syringe is lifted.

On the other hand, if your film is more meditative, composed mainly of wide tableaus, stillness may be what you're going for, and the sudden intrusion of a quickly edited sequence will spoil the mood. Even in these types of shots and sequences, however, you can use movement within the frame to cue the next shot or to bring life to a static shot. The single, locked-down frames in *Homo Sapiens* are alive with movement: birds, wind, water (see Figure 5.3).

In the emergency room example, you could opt for a single wide shot of the room, held for a length of time well beyond what is normally expected, where the viewer's eyes dart from one activity to the next. Perhaps the edit that ends this sequence is a cut to a nearly empty hallway, where the patient's wife waits alone, or a cut from that frenetic wide shot of the emergency room to a silent close-up of the wife's wringing hands, then to a wide shot revealing her and the hallway.

Understanding Transitions

Transitions require the most important creative decisions you'll make while editing. They determine the flow and pace and narrative thrust of your film. The great sound and film editor Walter Murch (*Apocalypse Now, The Conversation*) has described editing as similar to creating a piece of music. Listen to music and you'll hear how the rhythm and momentum of the song are established right away, how the rest of the song flows from

FIGURE 5.3 The long static shots in Nikolaus Geyrhalter's *Homo Sapiens* (2016) are often quite active with moving water, blowing debris, birds, and other animals. (Still download from film's website.)

that starting point. You'll feel the beats, the pacing, the trajectory, the narrative arc, and especially the transitions as the music envelops you emotionally.

A well-edited film has a similar structure with a similar emotional effect. The editing has beats, an inherent timing that dictates when to cut and what to cut to. Sometimes these beats are determined most obviously by a soundtrack, but try to avoid cutting a sequence timed to recognizable music beats. This is the sports montage method that renders footage and any idea behind it generic or trite. Instead, look for the beats as they arise organically from the emotional tenor of your story and the actions of your characters. In his book *In the Blink of an Eye*, Murch suggests that the most important edit is the one that remains "true to the *emotion* of the moment" and that the next two most important factors in motivating an edit are story and rhythm.[7]

Allow the emotion, when possible, to determine the timing and length of the edits. This can entail something as simple as cutting to a shot of someone reacting emotionally, or it can mean cutting a sequence that is driven by the weight or feeling of an emotion. *Into Great Silence*, which takes place entirely in a rural monastery, is patient, reverent, and slowed-down, but thoughtfully so, its rhythms determined entirely by the subtle rituals of prayer, reflection, and labor.

In a short film I made for the International Rescue Committee, which helps refugee families settle in the United States, I filmed a gathering of Syrian family members at an airport, waiting for their loved ones to arrive. I allowed the emotion of the jubilant, chaotic moment of the reunion to direct both my camera in the field and my cutting in the editing studio. The reunion occurred at the end of the five-minute film, in which we'd already met or at least identified most of the family members. When the time came, I captured an image of each member reacting to the reunion. Things then calmed down and the crowd began to thin while the local TV stations interviewed the Syrian parents. The father spoke movingly of the dream of freedom in America, and I used this sound bite to end the film. But the image I chose to place over his words was one I'd captured several minutes earlier of his daughter crying with happiness. My choices were not driven by chronology, screen space, or continuity of action, but by continuity of emotion.

Since you are the one who shot the B-roll for your film and you know best the story and the people and the locations, you are the best judge of how you want your movie to flow. Having experienced the mood and feel of your story in the field, you're in the best position to recreate that mood and feel in editing.

When shooting our post–Hurricane Katrina film *The Church on Dauphine Street*, Ann and I were struck by the friendly, tranquil pace of life in New Orleans, an openness and resilience tempered by a heaviness of heart as the city went about the hard work of rebuilding. I shot footage of an Upper Ninth Ward neighborhood that reflected this mood—nearly still images of people, sidewalks, trains, the sun cresting a spire. We wanted to impress upon viewers the residents' determined response to their fate and how they came together in a spirit of cooperation, and we wanted to convey how the languorous momentum of a given day defined this most unique of American cities. Our film ended up playing for nearly a year in steady rotation on the New Orleans PBS affiliate station, and the local movie critic for the *New Orleans Times-Picayune* praised us and our movie for taking the time to "get our city right."[8] I'm not sure if a third-party editor, especially one who'd never set foot in New Orleans, would have understood the emotional resonance of our experience or appreciated the special ebb and flow of life there.

Transitions are the crucial narrative traffic signs of your film. These are the moments when certain elements you gathered in the field can be employed to move your story ahead. I'm not talking here about effects (dissolves, wipes, fades to black); I'm talking about a transition's vital role in creating a contrast or enhancing a relationship between the images it connects. Use sound, silence, texture, music, or simply a dramatic compositional difference between one image and the next to key the viewer into a change of location, character, time frame, or mood. Often all you need to bring the audience along with you is a second or two of natural sound or a perfectly placed hard cut from an extreme wide shot to an extreme close-up. Always try to give your sequences time to breathe: an extra beat or two to linger on an exquisite shot, a moment's rest to allow the viewer to think more deeply about a scene or character.

The other night I happened to watch a segment about fossils on the PBS show *Nova*. I was amused but mostly horrified to see that nearly every edit in the piece was accompanied by a digitally inserted whip pan and sound effect (*whoosh, boom, clang*). These were decisions made by an editor and no doubt an executive producer who were unable to trust the images and arc of their story without bludgeoning the viewer with tacky transitions. *Nova*, whose weekly audience is probably ten times bigger than the audience of an average independent doc throughout its lifetime, was teaching the world what bad editing looks like.

Audio as Character

Think of audio as a separate element of your film, with its own character, its own creative potential, that adds a fascinating richness to your work.

Begin by laying in natural sounds and adjusting the audio to correct levels as you go. If there is a shot of a fast-flowing river, I want to hear the sound of rushing water; if people are talking in the background, I want to hear at least the faint sound of their voices. Sound helps sequences feel fully formed, feel lived in. Adding a bit of appropriate sound can help a sequence that feels flat come alive. Once you're deep into editing, you may find that taking out a piece of audio is also effective. Silence, when used intentionally, conveys its own emotional weight.

Use sound to energize or comment on an image or series of images that may not seem that compelling on the surface. In *My Mother Was Here,* I use the continual audio of daytime TV, with its commercials for prescription drugs and its big-money game shows to amplify the loneliness of my mom in her cluttered house. I use TV news reports as time stamps: we hear sound bites from President Obama on immigration and healthcare and, later, pundits discussing President-elect Trump.

Learn how to use a consistent stretch of audio to supply the rhythm to an entire sequence, as director Robert Stone did in his excellent film *Guerrilla,* about the allegedly brainwashed revolutionary Patty Hearst. He used a simple but dynamic ticking time bomb effect over surveillance-camera footage of a bank robbery, which greatly enhanced the tension inherent in the jerky, jittery, low-tech quality of the video.

Experiment with how you can use a piece of sound to alert an audience to an impending change in location or mood by bringing in the audio of the next shot before cutting to it. Many films begin this way, with unspecified audio over a black screen. I had one of my earliest revelations about the artful use of sound while watching Sergio Leone's *Once upon a Time in the West,* in the opening gunfight sequence at a train station. There is a lot going on audibly in that sequence, but it's the slow *drip, drip, drip* sound in the background that caught my attention. Many shots play out before the source of that audio—which gets subtly louder on the soundtrack—is revealed: drops of water landing on the brim of a gunslinger's cowboy hat, which he finally removes, then slurps the water pooled there.

If the audio under the image or sequence you shot is simply not workable—it's ruined by airplane or construction noise or people jabbering off-screen—then replace it with audio pulled from somewhere else in your film. You want audio that enhances or complements your images, not distracts from them.

Don't hesitate to purchase audio from online production libraries. You can buy tiny bits of sound like the click of a computer mouse or a car door closing for only a few dollars each. You may need a consistent source of traffic noise to smooth out a scene of passing cars. Buy a minute's worth of this audio and you can use it over and over again. Maybe you need to fill in the sound of footsteps on a dirt path or the brief rustle of clothing. This is when you turn to Foley archives, which have a vast supply of nearly every sound a human can make. You can also buy folders stocked with room tone to mask abrupt dropouts when you cut between sound bites. It isn't cheating to use these sound effects, but they aren't substitutes for recording clean sound in the field, either.

Jenni Olson's film *The Joy of Life*, shot on 16mm film, consists of three main elements: a voice-over, static long-shot exteriors of San Francisco streets, and a continual, just-audible hush of ambient street noise, the audio level never wavering. The narrator ruminates on the history of the Golden Gate Bridge as a site for suicide attempts and muses about her search for a meaningful lesbian relationship. Although simple and, to some, monotonous, the film has a low-grade hypnotic effect, complementing the strictly composed, stripped-down images and the matter-of-fact intonations of the narrator.

Director Jane Gillooly's fascinating experiment, *Suitcase of Love and Shame*, could be called a "found-sound" film, as it relies exclusively on audiotapes of phone calls, conversations, and lovemaking between two people having an illicit affair. Gillooly bought a suitcase on eBay that contained the tapes and photographs of the lovers and recreated their ultimately doomed relationship by using the tapes to form the narrative, the audio playing over recreated shots of hotel room beds and office hallways.

Whose Streets? by Sabaah Folayan and Damon Davis, is another kind of found-sound film. The soundtrack is constructed from cell phone audio, court testimonials, overheard conversations, and the chants of protesters, all gathered during the aftermath of the police killing of Michael Brown in Ferguson, Missouri. The film's anguished immediacy springs from the director's use of unvarnished audio and video (see Figure 5.4).

When working with sound, remember that it's important to have good speakers (or a high-quality pair of headphones, if you're editing in a space where the sound can

FIGURE 5.4 *Whose Streets?* (2017) by Sabaah Folayan and Damon Davis, captures the sound and feel of outrage during protests in Ferguson, Missouri. (Still download from film's website.)

distract others). To gauge the consistency of your audio levels, pay attention to two guidelines: your audio meters, which should range between –10 and –20 dB, and your ears, which will tell you how everyone else will experience your film. I'm always working without the luxury of a postproduction budget, so I treat my audio mix as if it has to be audience-ready. After I've watched the film several times, I make a final pass where all I do is stare at the audio meters while listening, making minor, last-minute adjustments if need be.

Learning to master the inherent glitches and interruptions in sound recorded in the field can be time-consuming if you're just starting to learn. Working with imperfect interview audio can be especially frustrating. One of the most common issues is the frequent "you know's," "hmmm's," "like's," and false starts peppering a person's conversation. If these tics are distractions and not essential to a character's personality, then learn to take them out. You can edit to the precise frame before and after a "you know," and lift it out. Of course, then you'll have a jump cut. One or two jump cuts in an on-camera interview is acceptable nowadays, but for the most part you'll want to cover it with B-roll (FCP 10.3 has a new fix for this problem called a "flow transition" that magically removes the jump cut; I have no idea how they do this).

The other common issue with audio edits, especially in interviews, is what is known as an audio *upcut*. It occurs when you've cut out the first several frames of a piece of audio, but the audio you want after that is too close to the section you cut, resulting in a jarring audio effect. A simple fix for this is to add a short one- or two-frame audio dissolve to the beginning of the sound bite, which smoothly and quickly fades into the bite.

Editing your audio can seem just as forbidding as recording your audio. But as a lean team filmmaker, as the editor of your own work, you'll come to view audio as another essential and exciting part of the entire creative process. Editors (and shooters) who explore the power of audio become better all-around filmmakers.

Adding Music

If you plan on using music in your film, start with a scratch (or temp) track. A scratch track is a piece of music that you probably won't use in the final cut but that conveys the mood you're going for. It can be something you pull from a favorite CD or off iTunes, and it will no doubt be too expensive to copyright, but use it to get a feel for what the music might sound like in your movie. You will need to think about how much music you can actually afford to include in your film. A song by Kendrick Lamar is beyond the reach of a lean team filmmaker, but an original score may not be.

My preference is to edit to a piece of music that is not structured to fit the edited "beats" of a scene, as in a Hollywood movie. Ken Burns commissions music before he edits, working with session musicians who provide him several versions of the same tune. This way he can start editing with a rich soundtrack, which helps to inform the mood and rhythm of his sequences.[9] A precomposed piece of music allows for greater freedom in editing and is much less expensive.

I try to work with composers I know, and I book recording time at a local nonprofit sound studio, where the rates are low but the equipment is just as sophisticated as a for-profit studio's. I try to simplify the whole process by booking only two or three musicians and having them record unbroken takes of the tracks, which cuts down on time spent in the studio remixing. I walk away with digital files on a thumb drive, which I immediately transfer to my music bin in my editing browser.

If an original score is beyond your means, there are dozens of music production libraries offering inexpensive licensing on tracks you can use in your film. Some filmmakers may scoff at this low-end solution, but the music available in these libraries has grown more and more sophisticated and varied in the past decade. These are not computer-generated synthesizer tracks, but film-ready scores written and performed by actual composers.

As with any tool, music should be used sparingly and specifically. It should function, like all audio, as a character, a presence that accompanies a scene, leads it somewhere, or enhances an emotion. Godfrey Reggio's intense ruminations on our unbalanced world in the *Qatsi Trilogy* are fueled by Phillip Glass's driving score playing over otherwise soundless, epic scenes of humanity, the music functioning as an aesthetic, primal force. Glass also provides the music for Morris's *The Thin Blue Line*, the repetitive fugues plunging us ever deeper into the conflicting mysteries of the film. This is documentary soundtrack music as character, coming and going as the film's dramatics unfold.

In contrast, more and more commercially released docs these days seem to be relying on a kind of dramatic Muzak, a wall-to-wall, uninterrupted flow of soundtracky-ness. The relentless music score driving *Cartel Land* worked against rather than with the dramatic visuals, and in the winner of the Sundance World Cinema Audience Award, *Joshua: Teenager vs. Superpower,* the story drowns in a bath of melodramatic mood music. An overuse of music also marred the Oscar-winning short-subject doc *The White Helmets,* the story of a civil defense squad of Syrian volunteers who rescue survivors from the rubble of bombed-out buildings. The filmmakers captured gripping sound by *getting close* to the volunteers, but allowed a lush music score to overwhelm many scenes. Bill Morrison's *Dawson City: Frozen Time* also suffers from an overinsistent soundtrack.

I'm not sure what's driving the music choices in these docs. Does the director or executive producer think audiences will be unable to follow the emotional arc of a story without the prodding of music cues?

Other documentaries adopt a different strategy of methodically avoiding music altogether, which can be rewarding if the ambient sound of the film is compelling enough to help drive the story. But this formal approach can become a rigid signpost of self-serious documentaries, a style filmmakers may fear departing from. Any film that categorically rejects music "presents the possibility of an embarrassing insufficiency of meaningfulness," writes John Corner in *New Challenges for Documentary.* "One very basic function of music is to reduce the risk of the attention frame slipping towards too much self-consciousness and loss of focus."[10]

Corner suggests that music can add both "aesthetic satisfaction" and "directed thoughtfulness," a perfect description of music's power to shape the viewer's experience. Music, used with restraint and as a character (but not as Muzak), is one of those essential ingredients elevating film to its unique place in the world of art.

Another musical element I always look for when I'm shooting is what's known as *diegetic music,* music whose source is visible on the screen or implied by the action of the film. In other words, diegetic music comes from people singing and playing instruments or from music heard on a radio or TV in the footage you're shooting. You have to be careful if the music is popular, easily recognizable, and copyrighted, since the presence of even a few seconds of such music could lead to expensive licensing headaches. I tend to stay away from recording well-known music in the field, opting instead for obscure, indigenous, or original music performed by street musicians.

I recorded a man playing a scratchy violin in the streets of the Andean city of Ayacucho for *Zona Intangible*, using his tune as a de facto soundtrack, not revealing the music as diegetic until later in the scene when I cut to a passerby dropping coins in the man's tip jar. While it's perfectly legal to record street musicians in a public space, be respectful and take a moment to explain to them what you're working on.

The Upside of Narration

The once-standard voice-of-God narrator is rarely used in documentaries anymore, except in films by Ken Burns and Lynn Novick (where God is most often played by Peter Coyote) or on the long-running PBS series *Frontline* (still an excellent example, by the way, of journalistically sound, informative documentary filmmaking). But this doesn't mean that narration should be condemned outright. Filmmakers who work in the style of memoir or essay believe narration to be an essential way to state the honesty and subjectivity of their work. In fact, many believe that objectivity is a feint, since the very presence of a camera alters the reality of what viewers see. "I don't think a mass audience gives a damn about whether or not there's a narrator," says filmmaker Josh Hanig. "If it works for that particular film, it works. The only people who look down on narration are effete film theoreticians and people who think their film is not art if it's narrated."[11]

Unfortunately, narration continues to be a bit of a whipping boy in today's documentary world.

Toronto *Globe and Mail* critic Kate Taylor decries the fact that "the film world has made a fetish of not using voice-over, equating it with poor storytelling and false authority."[12] The internationally renowned documentary "doctor" Fernanda Rossi adds that "the unfounded myth of narration as intrinsically bad might have had its origin in some ideological and technological turn of events . . . Yet, there is more to voiceover than meets the ear."[13]

Some directors, afraid of the stigma of voice-over, have adopted the novel but unnecessary device of appearing as an interviewee in their own film (John Maloof in *Finding Vivian Maier*, Sebastian Junger in *Which Way Is the Front Line from Here? The Life and Time of Tim Hetherington*).

If used sparingly and artfully, narration can add depth and character to a film, as well as increase viewers' understanding of what is going on. Watch the incisive films of director Charles Ferguson (*No End in Sight, Inside Job,* and *Time to Choose*) to see how he employs the mellifluous vocals of actors Campbell Scott, Matt Damon, and Oscar Isaac in service of his expertly crafted exposés. Delve into the first-person works of Doug Block (*51 Birch Street, 112 Weddings*), Pamela Yates (*Granito: How to Nail a Dictator, State of Fear*), Patricio Guzmán (*Nostalgia for the Light, The Pearl Button*), Agnès Varda (*The Beaches of Agnès, The Gleaners and I*), and all the films of Ross McElwee (*Sherman's March, Photographic Memory,* et al.) to hear how filmmakers can deepen viewers' connections to their stories by narrating their own documentaries.

Watch the groundbreaking 1972 first-person short *Joyce at 34*, by a young Joyce Chopra, who made what some critics consider the first autobiographical film of its kind. Decipher the meaning and intent of the ever-puzzling seminal doc–fiction hybrid *Sans Soleil* by Chris Marker, in which a woman reads aloud the letters sent to her from a globetrotting cameraman. Listen to Werner Herzog's distinctive, idiosyncratic story-telling voice in *Grizzly Man* and *Cave of Forgotten Dreams*. Get lost in the diaristic voice-over of Joachim Pinto in his 164-minute film *What Now? Remind Me.* Enjoy the dry wit in the hard-charging films of director, soundman, and narrator Nick Broomfield and the quizzical, first-person snark in Michael Moore's liberal screeds.

An unabashed proponent of voice-over is aforementioned San Francisco filmmaker Jenni Olson. In *The Royal Road*, she delivers a narrative, autobiographical, and histor-ical commentary over images of houses, alleys, freeways, and road signs, her intentionally flat delivery both complementing and contrasting with the quotidian details inside the frames.

Many filmmakers today decide against this poetic storytelling device, arguing that it disrupts the purity of their vision. An Oscar-nominated director once told me that directors should "never insert themselves into their films." I think the late Claude Lanzmann would have objected. The director of *Shoah* appeared frequently on camera during his interviews with survivors and witnesses of the Holocaust, acting as a kind of moral inquisitor, obsessively interrogating his subjects about the banal horrors and terrifying minutiae of what transpired in the death camps.

Ross McElwee, who may have single-handedly popularized the first-person documen-tary, realized long ago that "I identified a documentary filmmaking stance in which I was not at all comfortable—that of the invisible voyeur hiding behind a camera, pretending not to be present among his living, breathing subjects"[14] (see Figure 5.5).

Chronicle of a Summer, a 1961 film by Edgar Morin and Jean Rouch about life in Paris in 1960, considered by critics and film historians to be the first true cinema verité documentary, begins with the filmmakers on camera discussing the intent of their film with one of their assistants. That assistant then becomes a character in the movie. Other characters are introduced, their stories deepening as they become part of the filmmakers' widening circle of collaborators.

FIGURE 5.5 Ross McElwee, with camera in this scene from *Sherman's March* (1985), did not want to be an invisible voyeur as a documentary filmmaker. (Still capture from DVD.)

Morin, a sociologist, is frequently seen on camera interacting with these characters, his friends, and even his own children. Near the end of the film, the lights come up in a screening room where many of the film's participants discuss the movie they and we have been watching. They disagree over meanings of truthful representation, what felt authentic and what felt phony. The film has moved ever farther away from its initial conceit as a series of "person-on-the-street" interviews about happiness to a meta-critique of how people act and comment on their lives when asked to do so for a film. It's a movie about performance and truth and moviemaking. Nearly sixty years after it was made, *Chronicle of a Summer* stands not only as a contribution to the Nouvelle Vague of its era, but as a bracing corrective for today's generation of narration-averse filmmakers.

Whenever another filmmaker—or critic, or programmer, or funder—tells you never to do something, such as put your voice in your film, question the hierarchy of unwritten rules behind such a statement. Journalists and other nonfiction writers frequently write in the first person. Musicians use the "I" pronoun all the time in their songs about love, heartbreak, struggle, and hard traveling. Nearly all visual art springs from a deep, private need to publicly express thoughts and emotions.

The *New Yorker* film critic Richard Brody has written about the "documentary-industrial conventions that reduce the complex and personal experiences that go into documentary films into impersonal, processed audiovisual fodder."[15] These conventions can prohibit, or at least dilute, true personal expression in documentaries today. Avoiding voice-over at all costs is one of these conventions, and it has a limiting effect on a film's power. This edict results in too many films cluttering up their narrative with on-screen expository text or ignoring fascinating details of a story because directors decide against delivering relevant information in their own voice.

Brody's observation appears in a review of the documentary *Cameraperson*, which is composed of leftover B-roll from cinematographer Kirsten Johnson's career of shooting footage for other films (disclosure: Johnson borrowed my camera to shoot a few seconds of family footage for her movie). In *Cameraperson*, we don't hear Johnson in a voice-over, only in bits of audio from behind the camera as she interacts with subjects and discusses framing, lighting, and safety issues with her producers. Both the audio and images might seem unremarkable to veteran filmmakers who have wrestled with similar concerns, but the movie is exemplary in revealing the enviable breadth of a cameraperson's experience.

Brody, however, felt something was missing. "The very point of *Cameraperson* is to evoke Johnson's personal connection to the films on which she has worked," he continues, "yet the film reveals little of Johnson herself, despite the presence of scenes involving her parents and her children. Only a few of the connections made in the film . . . evoke any personal implication at all."[16]

Johnson's decision to eliminate her voice-over from a previous cut of the film made the movie less about her and more about exploring the ethics of camerawork, an exploration the film mostly implies and is best understood if the viewer has read her director's statement on the film's website before watching the movie.

This insistence on an invisible directorial presence can limit narrative depth. The 2014 film *Rich Hill*, which I reviewed for *Crosscut*, an online Seattle-based magazine,[17] was made by Andrew Droz Palermo and Tracy Droz Tragos, cousins who have family roots in the small Missouri town of the title. This familiarity made it easier for them to engage with the three very poor teenage boys at the heart of the film, but it may also have blinded them to the way their portrait of these kids and their incredibly dysfunctional family lives adopts a muted, mildly exploitive point of view. The review website *Slant* called *Rich Hill* "poverty porn, examining lower-class spaces with pity as its operative mode and engendering little more than a means for viewers to leave the film acknowledging its sadness."[18]

The film was tenderly crafted, but perhaps the directors' approach would have been more precise and honest had they grappled with their own feelings and personal histories in relation to their subjects through voice-over and on-camera engagement.

Fernanda Rossi believes that "voice-over is the most malleable, flexible and possibly creative element a filmmaker can use in the otherwise outwardly regulated world of doc filmmaking. Why not put it to good use when it's called for?" Rossi urges us to shut out the voices of decision-makers who think they know better and "clear your mind of prejudices regarding narration. Forget what people (read: your judgmental colleagues) will say. People rarely condemn a film well done or a story well told no matter the device used."

Narration should be avoided when your images can tell the story better than words. There is no need for you or your narrator to repeat something you've already told us through your characters or previous images. Narration should also not crowd out a viewer's participation in the flow of your film. If your audience is being constantly talked at, especially if all you're doing is providing practical or statistical information, ask why you're making a film instead of just giving a lecture or writing a magazine article. Looking back at some of our own first-person films, I wince at our occasional overuse of narration. Sometimes the images really do say it all.

As an alternative to straightforward narration, filmmakers can audibly ask questions from behind the camera, intentionally including expositional prompts for their character to respond to. In *My Mother Was Here*, you can hear me off-camera asking my mom questions that move the narrative along without the need for conventional voice-over, such as: "This is the town you grew up in, Mom. Tell me what that was like." And "What are you going to take with you to your new apartment?"

You could also have your central character act as a de facto narrator for your film, probing other characters to respond to their questions. Joshua Oppenheimer used this approach in *The Look of Silence*, a powerful follow-up to his controversial *The Act of Killing*, in which an optician calmly interrogates the men who murdered his brother during the Indonesian genocide of the 1960s.

As with music, you can use a voice-over scratch track (also called a temp track) while editing. Record your own voice (which may or may not be the voice you use in the final film) to get a sense of how the delivery will fit the timing of scenes. This gives you a chance to refine your script before you commit your narration to a final, locked picture. You may find that when you start adding words to your film, the images stop speaking for themselves. This is the time to pare down your narration.

Scratch tracks also save you money, especially if you plan to use a professional narrator who expects to be paid union rates for their time. Since narrators charge by the hour, you want to bring them into a recording studio only once. Most likely, though, your lean team film will (and should) be narrated by you or someone who has a connection to the making of the film. Use a professional, disembodied narrating voice only if it will be applied in a creative way, such as when an actor reads from a character's diary, or if your story is so complex and its issues so broad that a commanding, authorial voice is truly the best way to keep your viewer engaged. One of the best examples of the diaristic voice is Samuel L. Jackson's reincarnation of the words of James Baldwin in the spellbinding *I Am Not Your Negro.*

One final word about narration. If you're going to use it, commit to it. Make it an organic component of the film. Avoid dropping it in your movie randomly to fill in holes in the narrative. I think it's odd when we hear voice-over at the beginning of a film and then it disappears, as it does in Marshall Curry's *Point and Shoot,* or when it arises intermittently and unconvincingly, as it does in the otherwise excellent *Hell on Earth,* or when it feels obviously tacked on, as in *The Eagle Huntress,* in which the celebrity narration was added after the film was completed and a Hollywood studio picked it up for distribution.

On-Screen Text

The use of words on the screen (or intertitles) to deliver information has become a fairly standard device in nearly all documentary films these days. This is due to several factors: an unwillingness to use voice-over narration to advance a story (as described earlier); an increase in films focused on complex issues instead of characters; filmmakers who struggle to find their story in the field and then resort to plugging holes in the narrative with text; and the easy ability to add text on the screen during the editing process.

Like any creative element at a filmmaker's disposal, on-screen text should be used only when absolutely necessary, with as few words as possible, and in a way that adds richness to a film. How can you use the text poetically, in terms of both the words chosen and how they appear on screen? Can you use text as a transition or in the form of a quote to underscore a narrative or thematic point?

In *Concerning Violence,* Swedish director Göran Olsson employs bold swatches of on-screen text in his dense, formidable interpretation of the first chapter of revolutionary writer Frantz Fanon's book *The Wretched of the Earth.* These intertitles, which read like agitprop banners, are repeated aloud by narrator Lauryn Hill (formerly of the music group the Fugees), and Olsson weaves these elements through archival footage to drive home Fanon's anticolonial arguments. Clearly, Olsson is unconcerned with rule breaking, and part of his film's power comes from his audacious blend of text and image.

In the epic and moving *The Human Flow,* a film about the worldwide refugee crisis, the Chinese artist Ai Weiwei combined three strands of text—statistics, poetry, and a kind of CNN-style news crawl—to deliver both information and depth to his sweeping odyssey. By contrast, in *Dawson City: Frozen Time,* director Bill Morrison includes bits of descriptive text over nearly every historical photograph and film clip in his movie, making for an exhaustive watching, and reading, experience.

On-screen text has become an all too convenient way of wallpapering exposition into a film. "Their essential function is to fill in the blanks," writes Luke Moody of intertitles in the online journal *11Polaroids*, "but are these blanks that could not be otherwise audio-visually represented or is this deployment and reliance a result of lazy or desperate editorial glue?"[19]

On the other hand, many strictly observational documentaries could benefit from a few well-chosen words on screen. Christopher LaMarca's *Boone*, a film about goat farmers, is commendable for its earthy visual and audio textures, but it grows monotonous because the viewer is denied any context for understanding the economic struggles of the nameless individuals on screen. After the film ends, a single paragraph of on-screen text tells us a few vague details about the imperiled future of goat farming.

Critic Godfrey Cheshire is more pointedly upset about the utter lack of orienting information in the stubbornly observational movie *Machines* by Rahul Jain. Referring to the film's "stylistic puritanism," Cheshire writes on RogerEbert.com that "*Machines* is one of those fashion-conscious docs that ends up being mildly infuriating for not supplying the basic information about its subject that most viewers will want."[20] In fact, much of the film's informative content is to be found on its website.

These web-only directors' statements are a documentary filmmaker's version of art gallery wall text, necessary to explain the murky narrative and emotional intent of the work on display. Before you head down this path, ask if you are withholding information because of an adherence to this "stylistic puritanism" or because it is the best way to tell your story.

Words are also used in the form of the lower-third "chyron" (from the Chyron Corporation, which manufactured on-screen graphics in the 1970s) or the "super" (as in superimposition) that you see on TV news reports. Nothing announces a standard talking-head documentary more emphatically than these diehard identifiers. You can avoid using them by having people introduce themselves on camera, or you, the narrator of your lean team film, can introduce them to us through voice-over. Perhaps you don't need to identify your characters at all. I rejected the use of onscreen IDs for *30 Frames a Second* out of necessity and a sense of fairness. Some of my sound bites were quick snippets that I caught on the fly while in the streets; others were impromptu sit-down interviews with trade officials. What these people had to say was equally valid and more memorable than their names and affiliations.

If you must use these lower-third titles, think of unobtrusive ways to place them in the frame or have them appear over a shot of something the interviewee is talking about. But keep their visual appearance subtle and classy. Stay away from distracting wipes and fades and background colors. They are performing one simple function: to identify your talking heads, nothing more.

Another possibility is to wait and identify all of your interviewees during the closing credits, a method that might frustrate some viewers but will at least reduce the amount of text they're asked to read during the film. As we all know, most viewers leave the theater or click to something else on their computer screen when the credits roll, so if you want to use this method, reprise images of the people in the credits along with their names to help keep viewers watching.

In the stimulating and strange *Room 237*, director Rodney Ascher used only the voices of his interviewees. He didn't identify a single one of his talking heads, or even show their heads talking. This method added to the conspiratorial, cultlike nature of their musings on the hidden meanings of Stanley Kubrick's *The Shining*.

Animation, Graphics, and Gimmicks

The use of computer animation has been on the upswing in recent years, as filmmakers turn to this visually unique medium to illustrate moments for which they may lack live footage. I'm not a big fan of its use in documentary films. Animation exists as its own expressive, standalone genre. Whenever I see an animated sequence pop up in a documentary, my mind is instantly torn away from the "realness" of the footage I was watching and instead forced to admire the skills and technique of the animator. I stop seeing real life. Rather than functioning as a tool to enhance a film's narrative, animation more often serves as a substitute for more visually concrete and organic footage, footage that functions as metaphor or comments on the absence of supporting visuals.

Imagine if animation had been used to replace the railroad tracks and empty barracks in *Shoah*, the vivid reenactments of the cop shooting in *The Thin Blue Line*, or the barren battlefields in Ken Burns's *The Civil War*. Two consistently sober films of recent years, *Watchers of the Sky* and *Jim: The James Foley Story*, used animation to dramatize places and events from the past that were difficult to recreate with video, and they did so with admirable inventiveness. *Tower* animated actors who recreated the mass sniper shooting at the University of Texas fifty years ago, resulting in a fresh way of bringing history to life, although the most memorable section of the film occurs toward the end when the real-life survivors appear on-screen.

But in too many films, computer animation has become a convenient new go-to device for filmmakers, made easier by computer software. Before employing it, ask yourself if it fits within the carefully constructed tone and style of your movie. Is there another way to say what needs to be said that matches the consistency of your vision without resorting to animation?

The overuse of graphics—numbers, statistics, maps, diagrams, etc.—is not a huge problem, thankfully, among independent documentary filmmakers. Most recognize these sometimes cheesy effects as a device best reserved for television docs, propaganda, or broad-based social issue films with urgent agendas. Like animation, graphics take over a film's visual flow and force part of your brain to process the digital magic of these effects, distracting you from the grounded reality of your documentary images. Be careful before you turn to graphics to represent information better expressed through images, character, voice-over, or simple text.

The dictionary definition of gimmick—a "trick or device used to attract business or attention"—is really all you need to know to avoid using them. In filmmaking, gimmicks usually spring from technology that offers an ability to manipulate imagery that was previously unavailable. The list of offending gimmicks in documentary filmmaking is long, growing, and ever changing. Most techniques become gimmicks only through overuse.

Both slow motion and fast motion fall into this category. Slow motion can have a beautiful and transfixing effect, and it seems especially useful in sports documentaries, but when it shows up unnecessarily in a film it can be a showstopper, and not in a good way. Fast-motion scenes, or time lapses—those speeded-up shots of crowds filling and emptying a plaza; the locked-down montage of a building being constructed; traffic rushing along a freeway at night—have become ubiquitous to the point of meaninglessness. The reason we're seeing more and more of these gimmicks is that today's digital cameras are capable of producing these effects in the field, or they're easily achieved in editing.

Drones are marvelous tools that were previously available only to big-budget productions. Now that they are more accessible, many filmmakers are inserting unnecessary drone shots haphazardly into their films, distracting viewers from the content.

This is on annoying display in the crowd-pleasing doc *The Eagle Huntress*. The film came under fire from critics suspicious of the obvious staging and meticulous recreations of scenes in the film. The director, Otto Bell, claims to not have staged but "restaged" events, filming ostensibly real behavior in Hollywood-style setups. This quasi-documentary tips its hand in the first several minutes. An unstoppable display of drone flyovers and soaring crane shots brands the movie not as a gritty real-life story, but as a prettified Disneyesque fable. The simplistic, script-ready interviews only add to the feel of the movie as more fantasy than documentary.

One of the most effective examples of drone cinematography can be seen in *The Human Flow*, in which the vast swells of refugee camps are revealed in sweeping aerial shots and then contrasted with close-in smartphone video footage. The drone seems to have been invented specifically to make palpable this film's heart-rending vision of human cruelty, but will it be necessary for your film?

One of the more tiresome editing effects popularized in the past several years is actually named for the documentary that gave birth to it, *The Kid Stays in the Picture*, a profile of the iconic movie producer Robert Evans, composed mostly of photographs from the producer's life. The directors, Nanette Burstein and Brett Morgen, chose to "animate" these photos by having elements within them, such as the foreground and background, magically separate before our eyes into a kind of poor person's 3D effect. Most viewers had never seen this before. It was eye-catching, and in some ways, it alleviated the monotony of looking at so many photographs. But by the end of the film, you never wanted to see the gimmick used again. Unfortunately, that was in 2002, and the use of "The Kid Stays in the Picture Effect," made accessible through Adobe After Effects, multiplied in documentaries over the next decade. However, the question of how the effect enhances the impact of a photograph or the telling of a story hasn't been answered.

The Kid Stays in the Picture Effect finally seems to be on the wane, which is the one good thing about gimmicks: they come and go. Of course, gimmicks can have a place in your documentary if your film has elements of comedy, satire, or absurdity, a certain style in which a schlocky graphic or a sudden swerve into slow motion acts as a comment or accent on your subject matter.

Feedback

Your lean team film is your DIY path to creative freedom, a way to avoid the potentially crushing imperatives of the industry. But that doesn't mean you should avoid seeking feedback. Intelligent, thoughtful feedback can help you correct mistakes in narrative logic and force you to reconsider choices that may have looked good at the time but actually may come across as heavy-handed or unnecessary.

This is different than getting advice from all of the people—associate producers, investors, assistant editors—who can't help but put their paw prints all over your work before you even get started. First, edit in solitude, working through the difficulties of a story that only you know intimately. Make sure the audio is mixed well and any on-screen text is free of misspellings. Make your film as polished as it can be, then test-run it for an audience.

Proceed with caution, however.

Work-in-progress screenings can be ego-crushing, momentum-killing, anxiety-inducing experiences, especially when they're done in front of a group of people who may have only the slightest idea of what you're trying to do with your film. These sessions invite a cascade of criticism, advice, suggestions, and maybe a little praise. They can feel more like public eviscerations than helpful brainstorming platforms.

Instead, gather a handful of trusted colleagues or friends (but not family members, unless you have relatives who will pay attention and provide an honest and fair appraisal), show them a refined cut of your whole movie, or at least a significant portion of it. Listen to their feedback and quiz them about potential trouble points. If more than two or three people repeat the same criticism, it's worth looking at a fix. After getting this initial feedback, make adjustments to your film and then ask another core group of trusted colleagues or friends to watch it. Ask two or three from the original group to join. During this session, I always point out what I'm willing to change and what I'm not willing to change. For example, I'll stress that no more interviews or B-roll will be shot and that I'm not going to dramatically alter the arc of the story but that I am willing to fix or rearrange the structure, clarify important points, bring a character more to the forefront, and tweak or excise some of the footage.

Don't feel that you must show your film to a large group of people who don't know you. You are not a focus-group filmmaker, bullied by a production studio into tailoring your film to fit the generic desires of the masses. You are an artist expressing a personal vision with your film. Do not make changes to your work based on the ephemeral whims of random viewers or pressure from executive producers, changes that could render your film mediocre.

For a little inspiration, I refer you to the eccentric, beautifully constructed 1989 documentary *Vincent: The Life and Death of Vincent Van Gogh* (directed by the late Paul Cox and "narrated" by actor John Hurt speaking as Van Gogh). In a letter from the artist to his brother, Van Gogh asks and answers the question, "How does one become mediocre? By making compromises and concessions." This is where you, dear reader, remind me that Van Gogh sold only one painting in his lifetime and eventually went insane. But mediocrity, in my opinion, is a much more ignominious fate.

Postproduction

This aspect of filmmaking requires the kinds of technical editing skill and expensive equipment that are beyond many filmmakers. The cost of services such as color correction and audio sweetening alone can rapidly deplete your meager funds. This is why it's important to do whatever you can in the field to get clean, crisp audio and properly exposed and color-balanced images. With the tools already packaged into most NLE systems, you can even do a reasonably good job of balancing audio and correcting color on your own. But there is noticeable value in passing your finished film on to a postproduction audio professional who can smooth out levels, accentuate certain sounds, fix annoying issues like wind noise or distortion, and present you with a polished, perfectly balanced soundtrack.

The same goes for an expert colorist, who can adjust color schemes and correct exposures, refining the overall palette of your movie. But there is no need to raise $25,000 or more to fund this final step of your production. I advocate searching for a freelancer, a person who, like you, works from a home studio, has built their gear and experience from the ground up, piece by piece, and who is just as capable as the folks at the fancy corporate studio with their bowls of mini M&Ms and bottled artesian spring water. Develop a relationship with these freelance pros; tell them about your film and your expectations (theatrical release? maybe; film festivals? hopefully; online streaming? definitely) and ask them what they can do for you. More often than not, they will offer you a friendly rate for their services simply because they don't carry the high overhead of gear, employees, and expensively bottled tap water. Be wary—very wary—of an offer of pro bono postproduction from one of the corporate joints. This means charity work to them, and your film will be the last item on their to-do list.

Common Mistakes in Rough Cuts and Finished Films

Most documentaries are too long. There are some very good films that are epic in length (*The Corporation* runs 145 minutes; *Into Great Silence* is 162 minutes; *Shoah* runs 9 hours), but many movies try viewers' patience at the 90-minute mark. "It's a truism among programmers that all documentaries are 10 minutes too long,"[21] says David Wilson, co-director of the True/False Film Festival. He believes that the best documentaries run between 70 and 85 minutes.

Many producers advise filmmakers to make their movie "as long as it needs to be." But I think it's better to have a TRT (total running time) in mind and aim for that when shooting and editing the documentary. This will force you to make creative decisions within set parameters. The languorous documentary *Uncertain* came in at 82 minutes, just at the point before it ran out of new things to say. *Kedi*, a lovely and surprisingly nonsaccharine film about wild cats in Istanbul, ran for a perfect 79 minutes. The filmmakers felt instinctively they could carry the kitty thing only so far.

Repetition is the culprit in films that are too long, but it also shows up in films of any length, and it's easy to spot. When several talking heads appear in a row, each reinforcing the same point but in a slightly different way, this is repetition. When the subject matter or main thematic point of your film comes across in the first fifteen minutes and you spend the rest of the film illustrating it rather than telling a story that reveals new ideas or directions, this is a truly agonizing form of repetition. And then there is this complaint by Nancy Buirski, the former artistic director of the Full Frame Film Festival: "I see films with three different endings. The film ends and then comes back with more and then it ends again and comes back again. I can't tell you how often that happens."[22]

Some docs simply don't have a clear message, story, or vision; the film is muddled, tentative, or structurally clumsy. It could be attempting to do too many things at once, or the one thing it is trying to do is simply not compelling enough.

A complaint often heard from decision-makers, especially those in the United States, is that the stakes don't seem high enough. A movie lacks conflict, tension, a climax, or a gripping journey. This is a complaint I often take issue with. If pushed too far, it will turn documentaries into superhero films, with an emphasis on contrived plots, sensationalism, and hype, often delivered through fast-paced editing, overly dramatic pauses and transitions, and that wall-to-wall music score I wrote about earlier.

I believe that if a movie has a distinct point of view and is well crafted, it can be about almost anything, and it can engage an audience without resorting to tactics that artificially up the ante. The amiable, travelogue vibe of *Before Summer Ends*, which built its narrative through casual conversations about identity and a longing for home, was memorable precisely because it avoided hyperbole. And Wang Bing's *Three Sisters*, which takes place entirely in the dung-strewn, fogbound village of a young peasant girl, maintains an absorbing hold on a viewer's gaze because it avoids dramatics, accurately depicting the uneventful rituals of her day-to-day life.

The lean team documentary filmmaking philosophy is all about authorship and creative control, about returning the complete aesthetic design of your film back to you, the filmmaker. Editing is the crucial final step in this process. Be true to yourself and your vision. Be confident you've made the film *you* want to make. This attitude will help steel you for the next part of the journey, which is sometimes the most difficult of all: getting your film out to the world and finding an audience. This is where self-expression meets self-doubt. But pushing beyond that doubt is an essential step in discovering your own voice. If you give in to doubt, that's when your film is endangered. It may end up looking, sounding, and *feeling* like every other film.

/// 6 /// FILM FESTIVALS AND DISTRIBUTION

Keep Your Lean Team Soul and Find an Audience

My wife and I enjoyed a modest run of no-buzz film festival success with our film *Zona Intangible*. We screened at seven festivals in large and small cities, we saw many other fine and not so fine films, and we watched our movie play on large theater-sized screens and other screens the size of a living-room wall. In most cases our movie looked and sounded beautiful, in one case the audio was out of sync, and in another the theater's speakers emitted a constant deep rumble for the duration of the film. I took it all in stride. Our expectations for the doc were humble to begin with, and we still managed to secure a nonexclusive deal in the educational market with the veteran distributor Alexander Street Press. We made the film because there was a story we were curious about, because we wanted to go to Peru, because we enjoy making documentaries, and because it had been ten years since we'd made one.

However, when the time came to plunge back into the funding and festival world, the experience turned out to be more frustrating—and eye-opening—than I'd anticipated. I was surprised to see that these two interlocking parts of the documentary industry, whose success and very existence rely completely on the work of independent artists, were now often treating those artists so rudely. A funder or festival will happily take filmmakers' limited cash, pass judgment on their art, provide zero feedback on that art, and then dismiss them with a form-letter email (if at all). The organizers point to the tsunami of content drowning them as their rationale for favoring established directors or executive producers over unknown filmmakers. They play it safe with proven subject matter and continue to exploit a system that many filmmakers say is broken.

These gatekeepers need to fix it. They need to make the system work better for themselves and for filmmakers. Here are a few ideas for improvement: stem the tide of blind submissions; encourage a code of respect for filmmakers' hard work and feelings; establish parity in the doling out of money and coveted film festival slots; and offer more transparency, honesty, and feedback. A few regional funding organizations and neighborhood film festivals do a good job of respecting the artists behind the work, but too many simply take filmmakers' application and entry fee and never even bother to send an email saying their film was rejected. Perhaps that is the strategy. If enough filmmakers get frustrated, they'll stop making films.

Except the frustrations, and the filmmakers, are not going away.

In this final chapter, I offer a reality check on what awaits directors during this last leg of their journey. I report on aggravations and challenges. I cite the dismissed and the disgruntled. I recount my own dispiriting experiences. But I also suggest some strategies and solutions for plowing ahead, against all odds, to finding a respectable, satisfying home for your film, one that ensures your artistic vision and your lean team philosophy will remain intact, one that will make you—the filmmaker—the ultimate decision-maker.

Let's pick up where we left off in the last chapter. Your lean team documentary film is locked. You've watched it over and over again on your computer monitor. Time now to get it in front of audiences, which usually means your next step is to start submitting it to film festivals. At first you might find this exciting, daydreaming about the moment your movie plays for an audience of strangers in New York, Austin, Toronto, or even Park City, Utah, at the Sundance Film Festival. However, for the vast majority of filmmakers— experienced, skilled, artistic filmmakers—such daydreams quickly dissolve in the harsh glare of reality.

Don't get me wrong. There really is no reason not to submit your film to all of the most high-profile film festivals. You might have made a film they want to show. But the odds are against you. In fact, if you haven't assembled an experienced team of sales agents and executive producers, and if you haven't raised the money this team requires to navigate the heady waters of the Tribeca, South by Southwest, Toronto, or Sundance festivals, the odds can be downright overwhelming. That's okay. There are literally thousands of other film festivals out there, and some of them may want your movie.

Or not.

The most difficult, most frustrating, and, at times, most depressing part of documentary filmmaking is convincing people to watch your movie. I say "convincing" because that's often what the process feels like: pleading with festival programmers, judges, and directors to just give your movie a chance in front of an audience.

There will always be a group of documentary filmmakers who never experience this grueling process (or haven't for a very long time). These filmmakers are invited to festivals across the globe, they seem to have an easier time securing funding, and they long ago left behind the humbling snub of rejection. Many of these filmmakers are centered in or near New York City, which is, regrettably, the current epicenter of the genre. It's regrettable because most artists can't afford to live there, or even make more than one extended business trip a year to the city. Yet that is where the networking, conferencing, funding, endorsing, publicity-making, praise, respect, and consent all happen.

While great work is made and deservedly applauded by the New York City documentary business-artistic community, a lot of mediocre work is also made and applauded by that same community. That is the problem with this idea of "community" when it comes to art-making. Communities tend to self-censure and self-congratulate; they're unwilling to admit outsiders or criticize insiders. This results in conventional work, or maybe *marginally* adventurous work, that fits neatly into the community's circle of accepted ideas. Even the respected but decidedly out of the mainstream director Lucien Castiang-Taylor (*Sweetgrass, Leviathan*) laments this "narrow repertoire sanctioned by the gatekeepers of documentary practice."[1]

For those who believe they've made a worthy film that should be judged solely on its craft and storytelling, the film festival route can be a demoralizing journey. And like so many other phases of filmmaking that don't involve actually shooting and editing the film, it's a journey that can seem to drag on for years.

I'm not talking only about the rejections that keep you submitting your film to festival after festival in search of the one that will accept it. I'm talking about the feeling you get, especially in the online screening room of the festival universe, that no one is really paying attention to your movie; that you have to wait until you see a festival's schedule posted on its website to realize your film is not on it; that you are flushing money down the drain with every click of your mouse; that by the time your film does get into a festival in Sump Pump, Texas, its topical issues will be yesterday's news. This describes far too many directors' experiences with industry decision-makers and gatekeepers.

But there *is* a different path. Because you are a lean team filmmaker, you are in control of your own destiny. And you are not alone.

Documentary filmmakers are starting to take a long, hard look at both the hurdles and expense of the film festival process, as well as the tacit extortion within the current digital distribution business model. Filmmakers are becoming smarter and more selective. They are looking past the festival circuit directly to DIY distribution outlets, exploring ways to cut out the intermediaries and get viewers to see their work on their own terms. They are willing to adjust their expectations, spend less money, and think of their work as self-expression first and a commodity second, if at all.

The lean team filmmaker is poised to capitalize on these new disruptive trends.

FILM FESTIVALS

In the almost two decades since I made my first documentary, *30 Frames a Second*, the number of global film festivals has increased to a mind-boggling degree. Back in 2000, there simply weren't that many film festivals, and there were very few documentary-only fests. I blindly sent my VHS tape off to the Chicago Underground Film Festival, got accepted, won the Best Documentary Award, and then was invited to another dozen or so film festivals, winning several more awards. One of my proudest achievements was the selection of *30 Frames a Second* by the *Village Voice* as one of the Top 50 Undistributed Films of 2001; such were my modest expectations. Eventually I found a home for the movie with the respected educational distributor Bullfrog Films (and later on with Netflix, although they dropped my movie after ten years to make way for new product).

On his indispensable website stephenfollows.com, the writer, educator, and data analyst Stephen Follows examines film festivals and other independent film industry trends. In 2013, he reported that 75 percent of film festivals had come into existence in just the previous ten years, which pushed the overall total to 9,706 festivals that were active for at least one year in that ten-year period.[2] He estimated that three thousand fests were currently active, a number that has no doubt wavered up and down, mostly up, in the past few years. In a cursory look at festivals dedicated solely to documentaries, I counted more than 150 in operation around the world.

A rejection letter we received from Toronto's Hot Docs Film Festival, one of the largest and most popular doc-only fests, read, "Thank you for allowing us to consider your documentary for Hot Docs 2016. I'm sorry to inform you that it was not selected for the Festival. Given that we received over 2500 submissions, along with films seen at other events, the competition for limited festival slots has never been more intense."

Over 2,500 submissions! And all were competing for around one hundred feature-length and short-documentary slots, which make up about 50 percent or less of the fest's total slots. The others were taken up by films invited to the fest, meaning they didn't have to compete with the great unwashed mass of blind submissions. Do the math. If you submit your film to this fest, you have about a 4 percent chance of its getting accepted. To put it another way, that's a *96 percent chance of its being rejected.*

In 2018, the Sundance Film Festival received more than 13,000 fiction, documentary, and short submissions. They programmed 229 total films. Out of 1,635 documentaries submitted, only 47 were accepted. This is an acceptance rate of 2.9 percent— in other words, a rejection rate of *97.1 percent!*[3]

Think of it like this: if someone invited you to what sounded like a really fun party and told you the invitation would cost a hundred dollars, the payment was nonrefundable, and there was a 97.1 percent chance you'd never be allowed through the door, you'd tell them to take their party and shove it.

The odds aren't much better for smaller film festivals. A volunteer for the San Francisco Documentary Film Festival, known as SF DocFest, told me they received eight hundred submissions in 2016 for about sixty available slots, including shorts. That's a 92 percent chance of getting rejected. Yet hopeful filmmakers from around the world dutifully pay their submission fees anyway, thinking their film will be the one to beat the nearly insurmountable odds and get in. In the rejection email I received from the Margaret Mead Film Festival, festival organizers stated they received eight hundred submissions for around fifty slots, a 94 percent chance of rejection. The festival should be applauded for programming mostly under-the-radar films, but these numbers still point out two inescapable facts of the entire film festival world: thousands of people submit documentaries to festivals, and nearly all face rejection.

The festival landscape is littered with scrappy regional upstarts, two- to four-day festivals bringing films and their directors to small or midsize towns for a weekend of collective viewing, parties, and an array of awards that look nice framed inside the digital laurels filmmakers affix to their online movie posters. I'm not knocking it. I've also eagerly mopped up these little stickers of recognition in order to make our films appear more successful to online buyers (see Figure 6.1).

FIGURE 6.1 Film festival laurels adorn the website for *Zona Intangible* (2017) to make the film look more appealing to potential distributors and viewers. (Screen capture from website.)

Yet there is something out of whack about this gluttonous reliance on smaller and smaller film festivals to impart significance or meaning to films. Even the founder of Sundance, Robert Redford, admitted that "there are probably too many film festivals . . . a festival in every neighborhood . . . I don't know about the overriding value except that we'll get the chance to see more films."[4] When he says "we," he means the viewers in those small to midsize towns. But what about the filmmakers themselves and that elusive "overriding value" Redford refers to?

Film festivals are paradoxically all too expensive *and* all too easy to enter. The online film-entry website Withoutabox is really only a system for keeping track of how much money you are spending. Another popular website, FilmFreeway, advertises less onerous fees for those film festivals that use it, but it's also just a conduit for collecting the entry fees that festivals need to survive. It doesn't increase your chances of getting your film accepted. Jacob Bricca, the director-editor of the feature doc *Finding Tatanka*, spent around $3,000 submitting his film to 117 festivals over an eighteen-month period. He was rejected from all but 12, finally premiering the movie at the Big Sky Film Festival in Missoula, Montana. To his credit (and indomitable persistence), he considered this a success.

In a much discussed article called "The Great Film Festival Swindle" on his Rumpus website,[5] writer and filmmaker Stephen Elliott conducted an (admittedly unscientific) investigation into filmmakers who pay a fee to get their films into festivals and those who do not. He found a huge disparity. Films that receive a submission waiver are generally considered films a festival wants to program. Those requiring payment are generally disregarded. It's not a stretch to conclude that film festivals derive their profits from the submission fees of filmmakers whose work they basically already plan on rejecting. Granted, this is an extremely broad assertion. Elliott is talking about fictional feature films, not docs or shorts, and there are many smaller film festivals that don't fit this pattern. But in my view, he exposes a greater problem with film festivals, one that nearly all filmmakers need to be aware of and perhaps actively engage with to change. That problem is transparency.

Film festivals could go a long way toward mitigating filmmakers' frustration, dejection, and thinning wallets if they were more transparent about their process. Transparency would mean a festival honestly stating on its website that, for example, it receives two thousand blind submissions for only thirty available slots, meaning a 98.5 percent chance of rejection. That knowledge would help filmmakers determine if they want to roll the loaded dice. But transparency would mean less revenue for festivals, which depend mostly on entry fees to pay staff and expenses. The chances of festivals coming clean about their mysterious, behind-the-curtain operations are probably nil.

Another way festivals could be more transparent is by providing feedback, even if that feedback consisted only of the notes screeners took while watching your film. I've always thought the standard festival response ("the high volume of submissions prevents us from providing feedback, blah blah blah") is rather lame. The very least that a festival can do after taking your entry fee is tell you they watched your entire film and then provide a few comments on why it didn't get accepted (e.g., "We had a total of five films about surfing cocker spaniels submitted this year. We could only take one."). This lack of acknowledgment is why film festival snubs hurt. Filmmakers get the same boilerplate rejection email from every film festival, without a single hint as to the reason behind the rejection. I'm not asking here for a critical evaluation of a film's worth, just a few scraps of insight into the decision process. Getting feedback will not take the sting out of rejection, but it will at the very least confirm that your film was watched and fairly evaluated.

The D-Word, a website devoted exclusively to documentary filmmakers sharing their experiences, hopes, dreams, and defeats with other filmmakers, is a good place to engage in conversation and argument about the value or need for film festival feedback. Some feel that it is asking too much of festivals to provide any personal feedback about your movie. Others feel that any feedback is irrelevant. Some say that festivals are only in the film-exhibition business and don't have the critical skills to provide feedback. Others agree but add that they are also in the film-judgment business, which means they should at least provide a filmmaker with a baseline result of that judgment.

The 2016 Oaxaca Film Festival established a novel but dubious solution to this problem. They offered to provide a written critique of our film at a price of, ahem, $24.99, an offer they promoted after we'd paid the entry fee and while we were waiting to see if our film would be rejected or accepted. The email from the festival's director of operations claimed that "nowhere on the International Festival Circuit will you find any major Selection Team willing to do this especially for you at such a low price." I received a dozen or more emails touting this exclusive come-on, claiming that seven hundred filmmakers had already purchased this packaged critique. *Seven hundred filmmakers!* That added up to a tidy *additional* $17,500 the festival took in from filmmakers who probably had a 90 percent chance or more of being rejected. (The festival didn't stop there; a week after the submission deadline passed, they sent out fundraising emails asking filmmakers to donate $10 in a kind of film festival pledge drive.)

This reeks of a money grab. Festival screeners already keep some kind of tally or point system for each film they watch. Why is it too much to ask that they pass those metrics along to you at no extra charge? Instead, a festival such as Oaxaca exploits filmmakers who are starved for feedback about their movies.

Another regrettable little secret of the film festival world is that many films are never viewed past the first ten to twenty minutes. Volunteers for two small but well-organized regional festivals I attended confirmed this, telling me that because they are inundated with submissions, films that don't fit their programming theme or don't engage the particular whims of the volunteer watching them are dismissed within fifteen minutes.

It's fairly easy now to find out if and when film festivals (and funding organizations) are watching your movie, thanks to the analytic statistics now available on sites such as Vimeo, which most filmmakers use as an online submission portal to fests. The numbers quite often reveal that very few festivals watch your entire film; in fact, many watch only 20 percent of it.

This opens a whole can of worms for the anxiety-ridden filmmaker. Does this mean your movie falls apart at the fifteen- or twenty-minute mark, and no one can bear watching any more of it? Will you go back in and try to "fix" what's wrong, even though nothing may be wrong, other than that a very exhausted volunteer screener had a digital stack of other films to get through? How do you know that festival screeners aren't simply letting your movie run on their laptop while they do other tasks, meaning it may look like someone watched the whole movie, but you can't really be sure?

Filmmaker Chris Suchorsky, writing on the website No Film School, admits that his first blind submission film festival experience left him so dispirited that he didn't finish another film for ten years.[6] With his next film, he decided to scrutinize the data on who was watching and for how long, and he called out one high-profile documentary festival (which he didn't identify) for sending him a rejection email in which they claimed to have "thoroughly and thoughtfully" considered his film, even though they'd watched only the first twenty minutes of the ninety-seven-minute movie. He wrote them a letter and received a refund, but not an apology.

I can't blame festival programmers for this practice; I only wish they were upfront and on-the-record about it. Wouldn't it be refreshing to see the following statement on a festival's website: "If your film clearly does not meet our standards for production value or content in its first fifteen minutes, we reserve the right to not watch the film in its entirety and refund your entry fee." You can read comments from the festival perspective by digging further into Stephen Follows's website, where programmers air their comments on what annoys them the most about the films they receive and the directors they deal with.[7]

Festival executives also complain about the flood of submissions, yet they aren't doing anything to mitigate this problem. Could they shorten their submission window from, say, six months to one month? Could they cap the number of submissions at five hundred or a thousand rather than accept all comers? Could they state what types of films they aren't interested in seeing? The True/False Film Festival does just that (as discussed later), but they are the exception.

In addition to the cost of entering film festivals, there's the expense of actually attending them. Some festivals pay for lodging but not airfare, and very few pay you a screening fee. Will you be prepared to shell out the cash for airfare, rental car, hotel room, and restaurant meals simply for the thrill of seeing your film once on a theater screen in a city a thousand miles away? My wife and I did.

We flew from Seattle to Kansas City to attend the Kansas International Film Festival for a screening of *The Church on Dauphine Street*, renting a car so we could drive to our cookie-cutter room in a suburban Holiday Inn, and then went on to a shopping mall where every business was shuttered except the movie theater, only to present our film to about forty people who asked a half-dozen questions before it was time for the next film. When the movie then got invited to the Tampa Independents Film Festival, we decided to stay home, only to find out later we won the Best Documentary Award. We wished we could have afforded to go.

A colleague of mine was invited to a Southern California festival where, she was told, her hotel room and that of her co-director would be paid for. They arrived only to find out a major funder of the fest had backed out at the last minute, meaning they were now on the hook for the hotel bill. To add insult to injury, their movie screened just once in a Monday morning time slot where the only people in attendance were the filmmakers and two of their relatives.

In all fairness, there are many festivals that go out of their way to offer filmmakers a pleasant experience, and we have several happy memories of small-town fests that were welcoming and truly appreciative of the work we'd done. The audiences at those modest festivals were engaged, thoughtful, and intelligent. But the question still remains: Is the ego-salving appeal and audience engagement of a few screenings in regional film fests worth the cost, the time, and the several rejections you endured to get there?

"I think it's a very broken system that no one has taken the time to critique or reform," one longtime member of the D-Word community told me. "What's worse is that those who run film festivals (or who have run them previously) don't want to hear anything from filmmakers about why the whole process is incredibly opaque, often unfair, and a monumental waste of money and resources."

You can read more about these frustrations by Googling "film festival rejections." The commiseration helps heal your bruised self-esteem, but it doesn't necessarily cure you of the fevered dream of a film festival premiere. In that case, it is time to take a step back and consider a different approach, an approach that aligns with the LTDF credo of artistic satisfaction, personal reward, and cost-saving strategies.

Before you start throwing good money after bad, thoroughly research every festival you plan to enter. Start with documentary film festivals only, and then widen out to include all types of fests. Review their archives to see what types of films they program and how many they accept. Keep track of the festivals that have, in the past, screened the same ten to twelve films as other fests, films that no doubt premiered at one of the major fests (Hot Docs, Full Frame, CPH:Dox, Sheffield, IDFA) and are making the rounds of the second-tier festivals, taking up valuable screening slots. Remember that festivals want to lure paying audiences, so booking a film with prepackaged buzz is considered the best way to do this. But the more of these films you see in a festival's previous lineup, the lower your chances of getting in.

One of the best-curated documentary film festivals in the country is the True/False Film Festival in Columbia, Missouri, which consistently programs a diverse schedule of films from Sundance and international fests. These films range from straightforward entertainment to more experimental, formally challenging works. You can attend the festival—which is impeccably organized and presented—and dream of it as the perfect place to premiere your movie. But take a closer look. The True/False schedule is made up almost entirely of films from those other festivals, and its 2018 website very clearly states what kinds of films its programmers are interested in screening. True/False "values formal inventiveness and craftsmanship; it gives no extra points to 'important' messages or stories. True/False does not screen didactic work nor does it play documentaries best suited for the small screen."[8] The fest can be applauded for steering clear of preachy docs, but one could quibble with the last restriction. Do they mean to say they prefer cinematic nonfiction over works of broadcast journalism, or are they making smug pronouncements on what movies they consider too small for their prestige festival? Taken literally, most docs end up being watched on small screens anyway.

If your doc fits certain themes—social justice, the environment, sports, spirituality, LGBTQ issues—insert those terms in the FilmFreeway and Withoutabox online search engines to find fests that concentrate on these issues. Use your regular browser as well, since many fests don't subscribe to either FilmFreeway or Withoutabox (True/False, in fact, has discontinued Withoutabox and instead uses its own system). You may discover festivals that cater to films with exactly your subject matter.

We did just that with our film *Zona Intangible*. We recognized it was a small and rather eccentric movie, with specific appeal in a few key areas, so we changed our festival strategy from focusing on the major documentary festivals to seeking out ones with themes such as global health, immigration, religion, human rights, and Latino subject matter; we contacted festivals that had accepted our other films; and we connected with festival representatives or board members with whom we had previous relationships. I even emailed the festival directors to tell them about our film. These approaches paid off, albeit in a small-scale way. We were accepted into a few minor but well-run fests (including three specializing in Latino-themed content), and we were even invited to an attractive little festival in Paris called the Ethnografilm Festival, partly because I took the time to connect with the festival director.

Even with a more direct and refined strategy, you still need to pay attention to how many feature-length docs smaller fests actually program. If they screen only five or six each year, why do you think your film would be picked? Scrutinize the entry fees. If a festival is imposing a fee of $50 or more, even for early-bird submissions (when the fee should be much lower), it is probably a festival more interested in taking your money than screening your film. Beware of scams. Some festivals that list a call for submissions on Withoutabox and FilmFreeway don't even exist.

Try sending emails to small or midsize festivals before you submit your film. Tell them a little about it and admit you're skittish about paying the fee, since you're not sure if your film would be a good fit. You may get a waiver or discount on the fee, or they may tell you your film is indeed not right for them. A friend of ours thought *Zona Intangible* might work for festivals celebrating urban design, but I was skeptical. Rather than pay the $100 entry fee to these very specialized fests, I contacted the directors, mentioned my doubts, and asked them to waive the fee. They did, and our film was not accepted, but it didn't cost us anything. This email approach will probably not work for the big festivals. But it's worth a try for subject-specific or regional festivals.

If you know someone personally connected with a festival, go ahead and email them to see if you can get on an inside track. Festival programmers will tell you they don't play favorites (a claim always contradicted by evidence of the same filmmakers getting accepted to the same fests again and again), but it doesn't necessarily hurt your chances to get on a festival's radar with a more personal appeal.

Some programmers advise you to submit your film early to a fest, before they are overwhelmed with submissions. But there is no evidence this strategy pays off, other than by saving you the higher entry fees of a later submission. With the ability to check your film's viewing stats on your Vimeo page, you can always see a suspicious flurry of views in the week before the rejection email arrives, despite the fact that your film has been sitting on that page unwatched for the past three months. If programmers are waiting until the last minute to view your film, they're waiting until the last minute to view everyone else's film, too. How selective can they be if they're rushing to get through the final laundry list of submissions?

We all want to see our film play to an audience, and film festivals provide this opportunity as a first stop on your movie's journey. But before you stumble blindly down this path, manage your expectations from the outset. Ask yourself what, in the end, you will be satisfied with. Do not let film festivals define the success or failure of your film.

DISTRIBUTION

If your film is accepted by the Sundance Film Festival, congratulations. You have a four out of five chance of getting a distribution deal, according to statistics released by the fest.[9] These statistics don't tell you what *kind* of distribution deal, only that a company will scoop up your film and will do some—not all—of the grunt work involved in getting it out to the public through, most likely, streaming venues such as Amazon, iTunes, and cable TV on-demand services. But nearly every deal with a distributor involves a substantial loss of control on the part of the filmmaker. Most contracts guarantee less than 30 percent of net profits to the director, a percentage that kicks in only after the distributor has recouped all the upfront costs, which include the digital delivery fees to the above-mentioned platforms and marketing expenses. Your film has to make a lot of money before you see much of a return.

Theatrical releases for documentaries are rare, and unless you are Michael Moore, a release means a one-week or three-day run in an art-house theater in a few cities, where the film will likely play to small audiences. Playing for a few days in a handful of major cities is better than nothing, and you should be proud if your film makes even a small, positive contribution to the endangered future of the art-house theater. But the money will not come flowing in.

Box Office Mojo created a list ranking the one thousand most financially successful theatrically released documentaries since 1982.[10] From that list I picked one film, *Big Men*, directed by Rachel Boynton, to see how it did. I chose it because I briefly spoke to Boynton at the True/False Film Festival, where she told the audience her film had a "nearly one-million-dollar budget."

Big Men, which is about an American oil company exploiting resources in Ghana, enjoyed a healthy festival run before its theatrical release. It played in three theaters for a total of ninety-eight days and earned $56,286.[11] After that, the film moved to Netflix, where it was viewed thousands of times (although the viewing statistics have now been removed). Netflix pays an exclusive fee for streaming rights, not a pay-per-view percentage. Whether your movie receives five thousand or fifty thousand views, that initial fee is all you get. And if you have a traditional industry distributor for your film, you get only a percentage of that upfront fee.

The budget and financial returns for *Big Men* were the subject of an article for *IndieWire*, which reported that "as ambitious and well-crafted as the film may be, *Big Men* has been cut down to size by a shifting marketplace."[12] That marketplace predetermines which kinds of films it wants to throw its weight behind, which apparently doesn't include films set in Africa. Boynton was told by an industry insider that "people don't care about Africa." The movie was partially funded by Impact Partners, whose cofounder, Dan Cogan, said that "it's always been a challenge to make documentaries at that budget level."

We should applaud the success a documentary like *Big Men* enjoyed in bagging the trifecta of the documentary filmmaker's dream: generous funding, film festival recognition, and a theatrical run. But in a climate increasingly geared toward financial return, where there is less money to spread around and more pressure to produce a payoff, it should concern all filmmakers that a film costing as much to make as *Big Men* (an intrepid movie, shot in a lean team style, that hardly *looked* that expensive) returned such small sums to its investors. If someone gave me a million dollars to make one movie, I would ask if I could use that dough to make ten movies instead.

We first dipped our toes in the online streaming market in 2010 through a company called FilmBuff (now rebranded as Gunpowder and Sky Distribution). They licensed three of our documentaries for online streaming platforms, including my first doc, *30 Frames a Second,* to Netflix (it was already on Netflix as a DVD rental, as part of a deal with a previous distributor, Passion River Films). Even though my movie was already ten years old, it quickly gathered thirty thousand online Netflix views. I was pleased to see that FilmBuff was indeed holding up its end of our lopsided bargain, mailing us quarterly checks, each amounting to $1,000 or $2,000. But over the course of the more than eight years that all of our films have been distributed by the company, we've made less than $20,000.

The purpose of my digression into this unseemly terrain of profit and loss is to once again pull us back to the basic reality of a documentary's earning potential in the so-called marketplace. You made your lean team doc not because you dreamed of riches and lengthy runs in the nation's multiplexes. You wanted to make a film to express an idea or tell a story. You also wanted to share that creative act with an audience, which is the last artistic step in the process. High-profile and deep-pocketed investor-distributors may never cross your path, but this leaves you with the option that many filmmakers find themselves considering: do-it-yourself distribution.

DIY distribution is elbowing its way into the traditional pathways of viewership. Now anyone can get their film on popular online platforms if they are willing to pay the upfront costs to an ever-growing number of distribution hubs. These hubs have names like Distribber, Distrify, and the Film Collaborative, and there are dozens of other sites, all with varying distribution options, filmmaker percentages, audience reach, special incentives, etc.

The choices are mind-boggling. You will need to pay these sites anywhere from $1,200 to $2,000 to encode and deliver your film to iTunes, Amazon, etc., and then you will have to do nearly all of the legwork to let audiences know it's there. This means the future of your film is in your hands, and you reap most of the profits from your hard work (a range of 70 to 90 percent). Keep in mind, though, that the royalties will be meager and slow to come, especially if viewers have to pay as little as 99 cents to watch your movie on Amazon.

A truer DIY option is to set up a website and distribute the film via your own online portal. Filmmaker Sean Dunne has completely rejected the usual avenues of industry exposure, releasing all of his long and short documentaries, such as *Oxyana* and *Cam Girlz*, for free via Vimeo links on his website.[13] He isn't enjoying the supposed benefits of worldwide exposure offered on Amazon or Hulu, but he is in complete control of his own work. Another option somewhere in between pseudo-DIY and true DIY is offered by Vimeo On Demand, where you control nearly all aspects of how your film is packaged and sold (see Figure 6.2).

Vimeo On Demand has taken off in the past few years, as it offers a simple and elegant user interface for uploading your film, trailer, poster, and thumbnail image, along with a

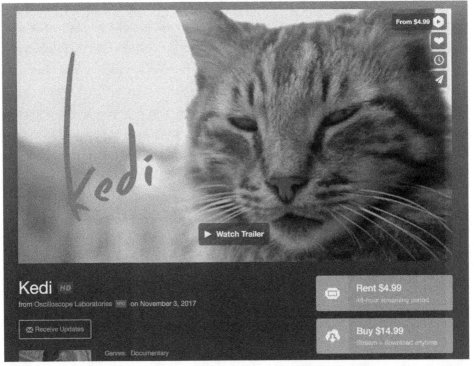

FIGURE 6.2 Distributors and filmmakers are using Vimeo On Demand to sell their films directly to viewers and keeping most of the profits. (Screen capture from website.)

quick way to set your own pricing. *Unrest*, a festival winner by Jennifer Brea, was available on Vimeo before it made its way to the PBS series *POV*. The festival and critical favorite *Kedi* can also be found on Vimeo, as can many films that are shut out of festivals and traditional distribution outlets. More than thirty thousand fans of the late renegade Austin musician Blaze Foley have experienced the cheesy homemade charm of Kevin Triplett's homage *Duct Tape Messiah*, which the director offers for free on Vimeo.

I spent a weekend setting up individual pages for eight of our films and found the whole process rewarding and empowering (even with the knowledge that the marketing of our films would be totally our responsibility). Vimeo promises 90 percent revenues to the filmmaker, which is enticing, but a closer read of the buried fine print reveals they return that 90 percent only after their 4 to 17 percent recoupment of transaction fees, a vague term referring to how much it costs Vimeo to get the money from your credit card company. Still, this is a much better deal than you'd get through almost any other outlet.

It's revealing to read the mission statements of these new distribution models. Many of their founders have been screwed by traditional methods and are fighting back with "filmmaker first" directives. Here is what Orly Ravid, founder and co-executive of the Film Collaborative, states on her website: "With seventeen years of acquisitions, distribution and sales experience, I conceived of *The Film Collaborative* because I was sick of the layers of middlemen standing in between filmmakers and the revenues they deserved but were often not receiving. I was further bothered by the wasted money and inefficiency, to say nothing of greed and cheating. And frankly, the old model of giving up rights never made any sense to me."[14]

There is yet another distribution angle that requires almost no upfront fees and guarantees your film both access to specific audiences *and* financial return: the educational market. Bullfrog Films and Women Make Movies are two veteran distributors; others include Collective Eye, Cinema Libre, Good Docs, Alexander Street Press, and many additional outfits in a vast market. These companies will include your film in their catalogs and make it accessible to universities, libraries, and nonprofits around the country. But they won't take just any film. They sometimes shy away from first-person films or experimental works, and they tend to focus on the issues presented in the films rather than their aesthetic components. However, our first-person doc *Zona Intangible* was acquired by Alexander Street (as described later), so it's always worth a try to directly contact these companies.

Those in charge of acquiring titles for their schools know how to search the distributor sites for topic-specific movies, and they'll either buy them (at a cost in the $300 range) or rent them for specific screenings (at around $100 to $250 per screening). Your cut is still in the area of 25 to 40 percent, but the distributor is renting and selling your film at a high price point. Two of our films have made more than $30,000 combined in the educational market, a respectable profit considering they sported lean team production budgets of less than $10,000 each.

No, we aren't getting rich, but we have the truly satisfying knowledge that our films are in the curriculum of universities across the country. If you add up our royalties from our educational and streaming distributors, we have made more than $50,000 in the eighteen years our films have been in the marketplace. That is a pittance when spread out over nearly two decades, which is why we've never quit our day job making *paid* films for nonprofits. (I still receive quarterly checks from Bullfrog Films for *30 Frames a Second*; yesterday New York University bought a DVD of the movie for $50. My cut was $12.50.)

How do you get your film picked up by an educational distributor? Either by meeting these distributors at festivals, networking events, or marketplaces like the Independent Filmmaker Project and the Hot Docs Conference or by researching them online and pitching your film to their acquisitions staff. This is exactly what we did with *Zona Intangible.*

Since we were tired of spending even more of our money on film festival entry fees and we had avoided markets altogether, we made direct email pitches to five different distributors. Four turned us down, but Alexander Street Press acquired the film after I noticed they had introduced a new catalog of films about border and migration issues and had a whole section of ethnographic docs. Since our film dealt with issues of migration, and we had recently been invited to the Paris Ethnografilm Festival, our timing was good. They picked up our film despite the fact that we'd screened at only seven festivals, none of which were high-profile or prestigious. We had faith in the quality of our film, and so did they.

Be aware that the educational market is experiencing the same budget woes as much of the doc industry. John Hoskyns-Abrahall, founder of Bullfrog Films, told me that "the market is weak for various reasons. First, money is not flowing into education. Second, technology is changing, and DVD budgets were down 30 percent in 2016, according to some. We have certainly felt the pinch."

Global streaming platforms like Kanopy and Hoopla are helping these distributors make up for the loss in traditional sales, and Alexander Street sells films in large collections, but it's still tough to make a buck. As Hoskyns-Abrahall told me, "Senior and knowledgeable video librarians are retiring or being let go because of their relatively high salaries. Often, they're replaced by younger IT people who have no knowledge or interest in the field. Their concern is to buy enough films in every subject area to cover their instructors' needs. But of course, the price being paid per title is very low, by comparison with DVD anyway" (see Figure 6.3).

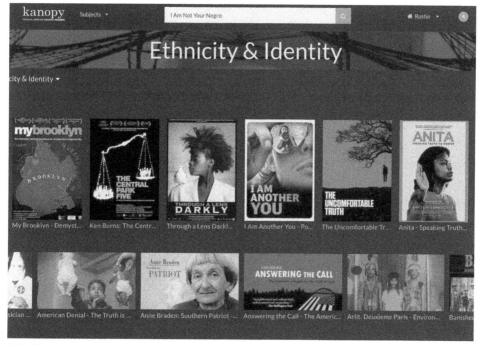

FIGURE 6.3 Educational streaming services like Kanopy and Hoopla are partnering with libraries to offer free streaming of thousands of films. (Screen capture from website.)

I have high praise for these educational distributors. They tend to be honest, reachable by email, and passionately committed to finding homes for films that may otherwise disappear, films that can inspire and educate students around the globe. They actually treat filmmakers with the respect and transparency they deserve.

BROADCAST

A traditional television broadcast remains the only way to reach the largest possible audience in one fell swoop. A single screening of your film on your city's local PBS affiliate can mean an audience of thousands; a run on the PBS series *POV* can reach hundreds of thousands more. If your film's subject matter is about nature, food, science, women's issues, history, or sports, you may be able to place it on cable channels such as Discovery, the Food Network, Science, Bravo, ESPN, and dozens of others. But be aware that these major channels have strict guidelines about length, presentation, and political bias. Your movie may be edited, packaged, and promoted in ways you don't agree with. And the money they pay may not be enough to outweigh the compromises. Even the great exposure from a Netflix deal may come with too many conditions on your film.

Venues such as *POV, Independent Lens, Wide Angle, World Channel,* and various PBS offshoots such as Latino Public Broadcasting and Native American Public Telecommunications are worth contacting, but if you succeed in getting picked up by any of these programs, read the fine print on their licensing contracts, which can sometimes limit digital screening rights for years to come and restrict other opportunities to show your film. The funding source Independent Television Service (ITVS) has a long relationship with PBS. If you get ITVS money (which, again, can take years), your film is almost guaranteed a broadcast window on one of their programs.

Another way to get your documentary on public television stations is by going through a submission process with American Public Television (APT). APT Exchange, one of APT's three programming divisions, supplies programming to public TV stations, and virtually all US public television licensees subscribe to the APT Exchange services. This allows regional PBS affiliates access to the APT inventory.

The service most likely to appeal to documentary filmmakers is APT Syndication, which will evaluate your film to see if it fits their programming needs. They don't charge outright to consider your film, but they also don't pay an acquisition fee, and you won't receive any royalties after the film is aired. In fact, it is difficult to know when and where it does air. APT offers what they call a "carriage service" to track which stations screen your film, but they charge $200 to $3,000 for it, according to an email I received from APTonline.org. You'll need to provide errors and omissions insurance (E&O), which protects the broadcaster from liability in case anyone connected with the film sues you. And you'll have to pay for closed captioning of your film, which can run in the hundreds of dollars.

As you can see, the costs of contracting with APT may not be worth all of the unknowns in the PBS system, a system that is seriously underfunded and continually asking for money, hence the endless banalities you'll find in their pledge drive programming schedule of *Antiques Road Show, Masterpiece Theater,* and *Rick Steves' Europe.*

An educational distributor will sometimes have luck finding foreign broadcasters for your film. Women Make Movies distributed *Quick Brown Fox* to Finland's and Israel's public TV networks; we ourselves sold *The Church on Dauphine Street* to RTE, Ireland's version of PBS. We were respectably paid for these international broadcasts.

Your best option, if you live in a city large enough to have its own regional PBS station, is to contact that station directly, tell them about your film, and see if they are interested in supporting a local filmmaker by screening your work. You'll receive next to nothing for offering up your creative work, but you'll at least have an audience. Four of our films have aired on KCTS-TV, the PBS station in our home city of Seattle, but the station has since discontinued airing its series of local, independently produced documentaries.

SPECIAL SCREENINGS

This far-ranging category can yield experiences both satisfying and exhausting. By booking your own screenings with groups or institutions interested in your movie's subject matter, you'll enjoy the benefit of one-to-one connections with audiences who are there only for you. Some people at these screenings might connect you to colleagues who may also want to book your film. You could enjoy a run of community screenings that can rival the film festival experience. We've often found art museums and nonprofit film societies to be welcoming and stimulating venues for screenings, since the audience tends to be more engaged in your film than they would be at a festival, where there are so many other films competing for their attention.

The team behind the climate documentary *This Changes Everything*, based on the book by Naomi Klein, decided to skip most film festivals, opting for a grassroots approach to quickly get their film in front of community audiences and online streaming outlets. True, they had a relatively healthy budget and the advantage of name recognition to fuel their publicity, but they demonstrated how to get your film seen by taking it straight to the people.

This can be a grueling approach. You'll need to weigh whether it's worth the time and expense, and whether you have the stamina to spend months and months in the trenches of community screenings. This strategy can involve renting a community gathering space or theater and then connecting to local film societies or nonprofit organizations that may share your film's message. You'll need to do much of your own publicity: contacting the media for interviews and taking out ads in local publications, shipping posters and other materials to the venue organizers, and showing up at the screenings for audience Q&A.

These decisions depend on your personal goals as a filmmaker. If you are eager to move on to making your next movie, a better route might be to cough up the money for DIY online distribution, flack your film on social media as time allows, and get back to making movies (or, in true lean team fashion, release your movie for free on your own website).

To get a firsthand sense of the long-term commitment involved in self-distribution, read an article on *IndieWire* titled "Here's How These Filmmakers Self-Distributed Their Documentary . . . And Actually Made Money."[15] You'll soon realize that after your film is finished, you must exchange your artist hat for your marketing hat. It's not necessarily a one-size-fits-all arrangement.

A particularly inspiring distribution success story revolves around the luminous *Kedi*, a first film by Ceyda Torun and Charlie Wuppermann.[16] A hit at film festivals but rejected by nearly all distribution gatekeepers, the film was finally picked up by the company

Oscilloscope. By working with the filmmakers on an ambitious strategy, Oscilloscope helped the movie take in nearly $3 million in theatrical and digital venues.

The Sundance Institute is attempting to help filmmakers secure distribution through a unique program called the Creative Distribution Fellowship. Its goal is to empower filmmakers who want to sidestep traditional distribution by giving them access to money, mentorships, and prenegotiated distribution deals. It's competitive, of course, but at least the institute has its eyes open regarding the wide-open digital distribution landscape.

A BRIEF WORD ABOUT ETHICS

"Ethics" refers to the moral principles that govern a person's behavior or an activity. It's an especially important concept during these difficult times, when the ethical behavior of some of our elected leaders is particularly challenged. It has always been a key consideration in the practice of documentary filmmaking. I've chosen not to include a chapter on ethics in this book simply because there are so many other fine books that cover this territory comprehensively: Barry Hampe's *Making Documentary Films and Videos*, Bill Nichols's *Introduction to Documentary*, and Alan Rosenthal and John Corner's anthology *New Challenges for Documentary* all discuss this topic at length. And the filmmakers interviewed in Liz Stubbs's *Documentary Filmmakers Speak* confront ethical considerations whenever they go into the field. It may surprise you that many of them— Albert Maysles, Susan Froemke, Nick Broomfield, Joe Berlinger—have given money to their subjects, either as honorariums or by paying for food or transportation. Usually this money is handed out with the understanding that the subject can still bow out of the film at any time. Much of Nina Davenport's *Operation Filmmaker* deals with the delicate question of how much financial help filmmakers should give their subjects in order to keep filming.

I learned the basic ethical principles of documentary filmmaking in my broadcast journalism courses in college. My wife learned them on the job writing for City News Bureau of Chicago and then producing for a CBS News affiliate in Seattle. We both approach all of our films from the same ethical standpoint, which can be boiled down to one simple practice: honesty. We never mislead our subjects when we're gathering our footage, and we strive never to misrepresent them in the finished film. This doesn't mean some of our subjects haven't been annoyed with the results. But we've never manipulated footage to change the meaning of something; we've never staged recreations without it being obvious; we've never made people look bad out of spite or revenge; we've never lied or fudged or buried the truth when it was inconvenient.

However, not everything we do is strictly truthful, simply because the act of pointing a camera at someone instantly alters the truth of the moment. The subject is now responding to your presence, even acting for you, even if neither you nor your subject are aware of it. Your involvement in subjects' lives can reverberate far beyond the few moments or days you spend with them. "With the best intentions in the world," ethics scholar Calvin Pryluck writes in *New Challenges for Documentary*, "filmmakers can only guess how the scenes they use will affect the lives of the people they have photographed; even a seemingly innocuous image may have meaning for the people involved that is obscure to the filmmaker."[17]

The making of one of the earliest known documentaries, Robert Flaherty's *Nanook of the North* (1922) involved ethically dubious techniques, such as faked Eskimo hunting sequences and the use of a set-designed igloo. In Luis Buñuel's *Land Without Bread* (1933), the director filmed two animals he asked to be slaughtered for key scenes. And the storytelling in the groundbreaking nonfiction series *An American Family* was influenced as much by the presence and promises of the filmmaking crew as it was by the behavior and relationships of the family members portrayed.

The contemporary film landscape includes many films in which the choices made by directors proved to be ethically controversial: Michael Moore's fast and loose reordering of chronology in *Roger & Me* (1989); the questionable motivations of Henry Joost and Ariel Schulman's *Catfish* (2010); the faked home-movie footage in Sarah Polley's *Stories We Tell* (2012); a staged scene of "rat fishing" in Theo Anthony's *Rat Film* (2017); and the brazen recreation of genocidal murders by the actual killers in Joshua Oppenheimer's highly praised *The Act of Killing* (2012), a film that Nick Fraser, formerly the editor of BBC's *Storyville* documentary series, called a "high-minded snuff film."[18] Everyone has a breaking point when it comes to stretching ethical boundaries.

I wished Polley's intriguing film had revealed, right away, her subterfuge regarding the home-movie material. I felt duped when I found out it wasn't real. I also had a problem with Anthony's employment of an actor to play one of the guys fishing for rats, using a hook, line, and peanut butter for bait, in a scene that played as if this were something these two did all the time. It was a fabrication but was never identified as such in the film (he reveals the fiction in an interview for RogerEbert.com).[19] I also shared some of Fraser's feelings about *The Act of Killing*. The film was both fascinating and appalling, inviting us to spend two hours in the company of charismatic killers, while expecting us to also recoil at their blasé reenactments of torture and homicide.

Deception can occur in both the making and the presentation of documentary films. The challenge for filmmakers is to respond to their subjects, and their audience, with decency and honesty. Even matters such as getting written releases from your subjects or asking people not to stare at the camera can be ethically tricky. We were advised by our interpreters in Peru not to ask people in squatter communities to sign releases, since they were suspicious of written contracts. Yet in the United States, releases signed by your key participants are a legal must (this isn't true for incidental bystanders; you don't have to worry about getting releases for people who show up on the periphery of your film).

If people stop what they're doing and stare at the camera, do you interfere and ask them not to, especially if you were trying to film them candidly? If this happens when I'm shooting, I keep rolling while I look away from the viewfinder and pretend to read a text on my phone. When I peek again, the subject has gone back to what they were doing. Then again, sometimes people stare at my camera, and it turns out to be exactly what I want them to do (see Figure 6.4).

Honesty, respect, decency: it shouldn't be too hard to follow these principles in filmmaking. A documentary filmmaker needs to be especially aware that the camera, as Susan Sontag wrote in *On Photography*, "is a kind of passport that annihilates moral boundaries and social inhibitions, freeing the photographer from any responsibility toward the people photographed."[20] For that reason, we must try to view our presence and our resulting product through eyes other than our own.

As Pryluck eloquently puts it, "We are all outsiders in the lives of others . . . In the end, since the dignity of others is best protected by a well-informed conscience, sober consideration of our ethical obligations may serve to impress all of us—beginner and old pro—with the power we carry around when we pick up a camera."[21]

FIGURE 6.4 A woman in Manchay, Peru, stares at the camera (and the filmmaker) in *Zona Intangible* (2017), by Ann Hedreen and Rustin Thompson. (Still capture from digital file.)

CONCLUSION

The decision to make a documentary starts with a cause, a concept, a rumination, a reflection, a curiosity, or a passion. It can be an exciting, expensive, and sometimes exhausting journey of endurance, or it can be a rewarding, temperate, enjoyable journey of artistic fulfillment, one that doesn't deplete your bank account, break your spirit, or blow up the other things in life you enjoy. The latter is the kind of journey I'm encouraging you to make: your documentary doesn't have to change the world, change the conversation, or even change your life (although it's okay if it does any of those things); rather, it should be a documentary into which you've poured your talents as an artist, one in which you've taken creative risks and cultivated a personal vision—one you can look back on after it's finished and say, "I made that. I'm proud of it. It's mine."

In the introduction to this book, I wrote about keeping your eyes wide open when working with the documentary industry, an industry that exists not only to help bring vital films to audiences worldwide but also to make money. Like any other industry, it's not particularly prone to taking risks. It would much rather work with established artists than newcomers, and if it does work with newbies, it will scrutinize their films for their salable or socially impactful elements first and worry about their artistic approach second. It's an industry that can sometimes be hampered by that high-mindedness Nick Fraser referred to in "The Act of Killing." In his view, "documentaries are the art of the journeyman. They can be undone by too much ambition."[22]

Industry gatekeepers are sometimes guilty of aiding and abetting that ambition, making far too much of filmmakers' prosaic and trendy do-gooderism, elevating their documentaries to an exalted level that is, when all is said and done, self-serving and rather absurd. These are, after all, only movies. That's how we (and our audiences) should think of them. Whenever I hear filmmakers or their patrons taking themselves too seriously, or tuning into the echo chamber of praise for the same half-dozen docs every year, or laying down arbitrary rules, I get suspicious.

As in any other industry, the people pulling the business strings of documentary filmmaking depend upon willing filmmakers to supply them with product and to justify their existence. Those in charge, from funding organizations to film festivals, earn their living (or at least part of it) by deciding who advances and who gets ignored. As a lean team documentary filmmaker, you can either engage with these gatekeepers or call your own shots, from first idea to final film.

In this book, I've tried to lay out a few guiding principles.

If you work on the industry side of things, strive for parity and transparency. Instead of giving $1 million to one filmmaker, give $50,000 each to twenty filmmakers. Instead of rejecting 96 percent of movies submitted to your festival, limit the number of admissions or shorten the admission window. Offer more slots to unknown filmmakers. Be honest with directors, give them some feedback, and refund their money if their movie is clearly not even in consideration for your festival.

As a filmmaker, keep your gear simple; eliminate barriers; work by yourself (or, at the most, with one other person); give yourself the gift of learning how to edit; research funding, film festivals, and distribution options with a realistic goal in mind; manage your expectations and keep your budget small.

If your movie becomes a smash hit, it happened because you *stuck* to your lean team principles, not because you abandoned them. If your film yields a richly satisfying personal experience, with modest rewards and great memories, there's nothing wrong with that. You didn't compromise your vision, and you're not broke, dejected, or defeated, so you can now think about making another movie. You can become a constant filmmaker.

Go right ahead and do it. No one is stopping you. And remember to *get close.*

NOTES

INTRODUCTION

1. Adam Leipzig, "Park City Climate: Sundance Infographic 2017," *Cultural Weekly* (January 23, 2017), https://www.culturalweekly.com/sundance-infographic-2017/.
2. Peter Hamilton Consultants, "Inside PBS's POV Strand," DocumentaryBusiness.com (May 5, 2013), https://www.documentarytelevision.com/commissioning-process/inside-pbss-flagship-pov-strand-12-how-many-projects-are-funded-what-do-they-pay-for-which-rights/.
3. John Anderson, "Documentary Filmmakers Find That an Agenda Helps with Financing," *New York Times* (July 8, 2016), https://www.nytimes.com/2016/07/10/movies/documentary-filmmakers-find-that-an-agenda-helps-with-financing.html?_r=0.
4. Independent Feature Project, http://www.ifp.org/.
5. John Anderson, " 'Respect the Feathers': Who Tells Standing Rock's Story?" *New York Times* (December 16, 2016), https://www.nytimes.com/2016/12/16/movies/standing-rock-sioux-tribe-filmmakers.html?_r=0.

CHAPTER 1

1. Jean-Luc Godard, "Photography is truth. The cinema is truth twenty-four times per second," from *Le Petit Soldat* (1960).
2. Center for Media and Social Impact, "Fair Use, Free Speech & Intellectual Property," http://cmsimpact.org/program/fair-use/.
3. Wu Wenguang, "Individual Filmmaking," in *The Documentary Film Reader: History, Theory, Criticism*, ed. Jonathan Kahana (Oxford: Oxford University Press, 2016), 959.

CHAPTER 2

1. Samantha Power, "Ambassador Samantha Power's 2016 Class Day Address," *Yale News* (May 22, 2016), https://news.yale.edu/2016/05/22/ambassador-samantha-powers-2016-class-day-address.
2. Robert Capa, Biography page, Magnum Photos, http://pro.magnumphotos.com/C.aspx?VP3=CMS3&VF=MAGO31_9_VForm&ERID=24KL535353.
3. Caravaggio, *The Taking of Christ*, National Gallery of Ireland, https://www.nationalgallery.ie/sites/default/files/2017-04/w1500-Caravaggio-Taking-Christ.jpg.
4. Joan Churchill, "Inside Out: Joan Churchill," *Documentary* magazine (August 24, 2017), https://www.documentary.org/feature/inside-out-joan-churchill.
5. B&H Photo-Video-Pro Audio, https://www.bhphotovideo.com/c/product/856444-REG/Opteka_OPTCXS300_CXS_300_Dual_Grip_Video.html.
6. James Estrin, "Mary Ellen Mark, Photographer and Force of Nature," *New York Times* (May 26, 2015), https://lens.blogs.nytimes.com/2015/05/26/mary-ellen-mark-photographer-and-force-of-nature/.
7. David MacDougall, "Beyond Observational Cinema," in *The Documentary Film Reader: History, Theory, Criticism*, ed. Jonathan Kahana (Oxford: Oxford University Press, 2016), 566.

8. Liz Stubbs, "Nick Broomfield: Modern Adventurer," in *Documentary Filmmakers Speak* (New York: Allworth Press, 2002), 133.

9. Scott Macdonald, Interview with Michael Glawogger, in *Avant-Doc: Intersections of Documentary and Avant-Garde Cinema* (Oxford: Oxford University Press, 2015), 259.

10. Bill Nichols, "Introduction: How Can We Define Documentary Film?," in *Introduction to Documentary*, 2nd ed. (Bloomington: Indiana University Press, 2010), 30–33.

11. Bill Nichols, "How Can We Differentiate among Documentaries?," in *Introduction to Documentary*, 161–162.

12. David Edelstein, "How Documentary Became the Most Exciting Kind of Filmmaking," Vulture (April 14, 2013), http://www.vulture.com/2013/04/edelstein-documentary-is-better-than-filmmaking.html.

13. Chris Boeckmann, "Projecting Outside the Echo Chamber," *Filmmaker* magazine (April 13, 2017), http://filmmakermagazine.com/102137-projecting-outside-the-echo-chamber/#.WjP_CFQ-fx5.

14. Impact Partners website, About Us page, https://www.impactpartnersfilm.com/about-us.

15. Paula Bernstein, "Make a Movie, Change the World: What It's Like to Work with Impact Partners," *IndieWire* (January 22, 2015), http://www.indiewire.com/2015/01/make-a-movie-change-the-world-what-its-like-to-work-with-impact-partners-66022/.

16. Daniel Walber, "Notes from Art of the Real: What Critics Can Learn from Great Programming," Nonfics: Real Stories, Real Insight (April 22, 2017), https://nonfics.com/art-of-the-real-2017-d15cd00d2e37.

17. Interview with Kim Longinotto by Martin Svoboda for the D-Word (March 20, 2018), The D-Word, https://www.d-word.com/topics/62-Documentary-Festivals?post=359149.

18. Macdonald, Interview with Michael Glawogger, 249.

19. Barry Hampe, "The Documentary Idea," in *Making Documentary Films and Videos* (New York: Holt Paperbacks, 2007), 50.

20. Scott Macdonald, Interview with Nina Davenport, in *Avant-Doc*, 182–183.

21. Filmmaker interview, Jesse Moss, "The Overnighters," *POV*, PBS, http://www.pbs.org/pov/theovernighters/interview/.

22. Werner Herzog Teaches Filmmaking, "Lesson 5: Financing First Films," Masterclass, https://www.masterclass.com/classes/werner-herzog-teaches-filmmaking.

23. Barry Hampe, "What Is *Not* a Documentary?" in *Making Documentary Films and Videos*, 27.

24. Muriel MacDonald, "Don't Drive Here," *The City Fix* (blog) (September 5, 2013), http://thecityfix.com/blog/dont-drive-heretelevision-takes-on-road-safety-peru-muriel-macdonald/.

25. Renee Tajima-Peña, "#DocsSoWhite: A Personal Reflection," *Documentary* magazine (August 30, 2016), https://www.documentary.org/feature/docssowhite-personal-reflection.

26. John Anderson, "Documentary Filmmakers Find That an Agenda Helps with Financing," *New York Times* (July 8, 2016), https://www.nytimes.com/2016/07/10/movies/documentary-filmmakers-find-that-an-agenda-helps-with-financing.html?_r=0.

27. Anthony Kaufman, "Reality Checks: This Year's Sundance Showed How the Documentary Film World Is Changing," *IndieWire* (January 29, 2016), http://www.indiewire.com/2016/01/reality-checks-this-years-sundance-showed-how-the-documentary-film-world-is-changing-30443/.

28. Marjorie Baumgarten, "Look & See: A Portrait of Wendell Berry," *Austin Chronicle* (September 1, 2017), https://www.austinchronicle.com/calendar/film/2017-09-01/look-and-see-a-portrait-of-wendell-berry/.

29. Nell Minow, "Look & See: A Portrait of Wendell Berry," RogerEbert.com (June 30, 2017), https://www.rogerebert.com/reviews/look-and-see-a-portrait-of-wendell-berry-2017.

30. John Hewitt and Gustavo Vazquez, "Paying for It: Fundraising," in *Documentary Filmmaking: A Contemporary Field Guide*, 2nd ed. (Oxford: Oxford University Press, 2014), 62.

31. Ibid., 68.

32. Additional Teaching Resources webpage, Edit Media, http://www.editmedia.org/resources/.

33. Oakley Anderson-Moore, "Where the Money Is: The Grants Behind This Year's Sundance Documentaries," No Film School (January 28, 2014), https://nofilmschool.com/2014/01/the-grants-behind-this-years-sundance-documentaries.

34. Funding submission FAQ, #29: What percentage of applications are actually funded? Sundance Institute, http://applications4.sundance.org/res/p/faq/#29.

35. "Challenges for Freelance Documentary Filmmakers in Today's Market," Whicker's World Foundation (February 2016), https://whickersworldfoundation.com/2016/02/challenges-for-freelance-documentary-filmmakers-in-todays-market/.

36. Ibid.

37. "'Cost of Docs' 100 Survey: Trends and Challenges Facing Documentarians in Today's Market," European Documentary Network (September 28, 2017), http://edn.network/news/news-story/article/cost-of-docs-100-survey-trends-and-challenges-facing-documentarians-in-todays-market/?tx_ttnews%5BbackPid%5D=111&cHash=af111081414842c39781ec199c7e25f.

38. "State of the Field: A Report from the Documentary Sustainability Summit," National Endowment for the Arts and International Documentary Association (August 2017), https://www.documentary.org/sites/default/files/images/articles/Stateofth eField_mediaartssummit2017.pdf.

39. Anthony Kaufman, "The Top 8 Pitches at the Hot Docs Forum: What Worked and What Didn't," *IndieWire* (May 1, 2015), http://www.indiewire.com/2015/05/the-top-8-pitches-at-the-hot-docs-forum-what-worked-and-what-didnt-62464/.

40. John Anderson, "At Hot Docs, Filmmakers Make Pitches and Face Brutal Feedback," *Current* (May 7, 2015), https://current.org/2015/05/at-hot-docs-filmmakers-make-pitches-and-face-brutal-feedback/

41. Manori Ravindran, "The Risks and Rewards of International Pitch Forums," *Documentary* magazine (January 17, 2017), https://www.documentary.org/feature/risks-and-rewards-international-pitch-forums.

42. The Documentary Core Application Project, International Documentary Association, https://www.documentary.org/funding/documentary-core-application-project.

43. Lance Kramer, "The Messy Truth Behind a Day Job as a Documentarian," *Documentary* magazine (April 26, 2017), https://www.documentary.org/feature/messy-truth-behind-day-job-documentarian.

CHAPTER 3

1. Lauren Wissot, "Shooting under Fire: Running and Gunning with the Renaud Brothers," *Filmmaker* magazine (December 17, 2013), http://filmmakermagazine.com/82852-shooting-under-fire-running-and-gunning-with-the-renaud-brothers/#.WjU-gFQ-fx4.

2. Stanley Leary, "If Your Pictures Aren't Good Enough, You're Not Close Enough," Black Star Rising (January 7, 2009), http://rising.blackstar.com/if-your-pictures-arent-good-enough-youre-not-close-enough.html.

CHAPTER 4

1. Biography page, Fondation Henri Cartier-Bresson, http://www.henricartierbresson.org/en/hcb/.

2. Werner Herzog Teaches Filmmaking, "Lesson 10: Camera Shooting Strategy," Masterclass, https://www.masterclass.com/classes/werner-herzog-teaches-filmmaking.

3. Interview with Kim Longinotto by Martin Svoboda for the D-Word (March 20, 2018), https://www.d-word.com/topics/62-Documentary-Festivals?post=359149.

4. Scott Macdonald, Interview with Michael Glawogger, *Avant-Doc: Intersections of Documentary and Avant-Garde Cinema* (Oxford: Oxford University Press, 2015), 254.

5. Betsy A. McLane, "Video Arrives," in *A New History of Documentary Film*, 2nd ed. (London: Continuum, 2012), 273.

6. Catie L'Heureux, "Mississippi's Last Abortion Clinic, Captured," The Cut, https://www.thecut.com/2016/06/jackson-documentary-last-abortion-clinic-mississippi.html.

7. "Errol Morris Interviews Errol Morris," *FLM Magazine* (Winter 2004), reprinted at http://www.errolmorris.com/content/eyecontact/interrotron.html.

8. Werner Herzog Teaches Filmmaking, "Lesson 10: Camera Shooting Strategy."

9. Henry Jaglom, *The Movie Business Book*, 4th ed., ed. Jason E. Squire (Milton Park: Taylor & Francis, 2016), 54.

10. "The Edit 10: Best Practices for Inclusive Teaching in Media," Edit Media, http://www.editmedia.org/best-practices/.

11. Dan Fox, *Pretentiousness: Why It Matters* (Minneapolis: Coffee House Press, 2016), 116.

CHAPTER 5

1. Robert Drew, "An Independent with the Networks," in *New Challenges for Documentary*, 2nd ed., ed. Alan Rosenthal and John Corner (Manchester: Manchester University Press, 2005), 286.

2. Boris Kachka, "How Alex Gibney Is Reinventing Documentary Filmmaking," Vulture (June 29, 2016), http://www.vulture.com/2016/06/alex-gibney-is-reinventing-documentary-filmmaking.html.

3. Jacob Bricca, "Introduction: The Construction of Meaning in Documentaries," in *Documentary Editing: Principles and Practice* (Waltham, MA: Focal Press, 2017), xii.

4. Liz Stubbs, "Ken Burns: Emotional Archaeologist," in *Documentary Filmmakers Speak* (New York: Allworth Press, 2002), 82.

5. Ibid.

6. Jamie Lang, "My French Film Festival: Spotlighting Swiss Doc 'Before Summer Ends' and Director Maryam Goormaghtigh," *Variety* (January 18, 2018), http://variety.com/2018/film/festivals/spotlighting-swiss-doc-before-summer-ends- 1202669281/.

7. Walter Murch, *In the Blink of an Eye: A Perspective on Film Editing*, 2nd ed. (Hollywood: Silman-James Press, 2001), 18.

8. Dave Walker, "*The Church on Dauphine Street* Celebrates the Spirit of Volunteers," *New Orleans Time-Picayune* (October 19, 2007).

9. Stubbs, "Ken Burns: Emotional Archaeologist," chap. 5.

10. John Corner, "Sounds Real: Music and Documentary," in *New Challenges for Documentary*, 2nd ed., ed. Alan Rosenthal and John Corner (Manchester: Manchester University Press, 2005), 246.

11. Josh Hanig, "The Politics of Documentary: A Symposium," in Rosenthal and Corner, *New Challenges for Documentary*, 154.

12. Kate Taylor, "Why the Narrating Voice of God Has Disappeared at Hot Docs," *Globe and Mail* (April 24, 2015), https://www.theglobeandmail.com/arts/film/kate-taylor-why-the-narrating-voice-of-god-has-disappeared-at-hot-docs/article24106026/.

13. Fernanda Rossi, "Doc Doctor's Story Strategies: Is Narration a Storytelling Red Flag?," *Independent* (November 23, 2009), http://independentmagazine.org/2009/11/narration/.

14. Scott Macdonald, Interview with Ross McElwee, in *Avant-Doc: Intersections of Documentary and Avant-Garde Cinema* (Oxford: Oxford University Press, 2015), 147.

15. Richard Brody, "'Cameraperson' and the Conventions of Documentary Filmmaking," *New Yorker* (September 9, 2016), https://www.newyorker.com/culture/richard-brody/cameraperson-and-the-conventions-of-documentary-filmmaking.

16. Ibid.

17. Rustin Thompson, "Too Much? A Movie Gives Us an Inside View of Poverty," *Crosscut* (August 14, 2014), http://crosscut.com/2014/08/poverty-what-movie-can-tell-us-rich-hill/.

18. Clayton Dillard, "Rich Hill," *Slant* (July 29, 2014), https://www.slantmagazine.com/film/review/rich-hill.

19. Luke Moody, "The Silent Return of the Voice of God in Documentary," *11Polaroids: Journal of Film, Sound & Art* (n.d.), https://11polaroids.com/2016/07/21/silent-return-of-voice-of-god-in-documentary/.

20. Godfrey Cheshire, Review of "Machines," RogerEbert.com (August 9, 2017), https://www.rogerebert.com/reviews/machines-2017.

21. Tom Isler, "Making the Cut," *Documentary* magazine (February 28, 2008), https://www.documentary.org/feature/making-cut.

22. Ibid.

CHAPTER 6

1. Scott Macdonald, "Sensory Ethnography," in *Avant-Doc: Intersections of Documentary and Avant-Garde Cinema* (Oxford: Oxford University Press, 2015), 403.

2. Stephen Follows, "The Seismic Shift in the World of Film Festivals," Stephen Follows: Film Data and Education (April 3, 2016), https://stephenfollows.com/the-revolution-in-film-festivals/.

3. Adam Leipzig, "Sundance Infographic 2018: As Climate Changes, Indies Retrench," *Cultural Weekly* (January 17, 2018), https://www.culturalweekly.com/sundance-infographic-2018-climate-changes-indies-retrench/.

4. Eric Kohn, "Sundance 2013: Robert Redford Says There Are Too Many Film Festivals," *IndieWire* (January 17, 2013), http://www.indiewire.com/2013/01/sundance-2013-robert-redford-says-there-are-too-many-film-festivals-241604/.

5. Stephen Elliott, "The Great Film Festival Swindle," Rumpus (May 31, 2016), http://therumpus.net/2016/05/the-great-film-festival-swindle/.

6. Chris Suchorsky, "How to Make Sure Film Festivals Actually Watch Your Movie—And Hold Them Accountable," No Film School (May 9, 2017), https://nofilmschool.com/2017/05/film-festivals-submissions-actually-watch-your-movie.

7. Stephen Follows, "What Film Festival Directors Really Think," Stephen Follows: Film Data and Education (September 1, 2013), https://stephenfollows.com/what-film-festival-directors-really-think/.

8. True/False Film Festival, Call for entries webpage (2018), https://truefalse.org/submit/features-and-shorts.

9. Adam Leipzig, "Park City Climate: Sundance Infographic 2017," *Adam Leipzig* (blog) (January 19, 2017), https://www.adamleipzig.com/blog/park-city-climate-sundance-infographic-2017-million-piracy-losses-distribution-changes-and-slamdance-stats/.

10. Genre: Documentaries, Box Office Mojo.com, http://www.boxofficemojo.com/genres/chart/?id=documentary.htm.

11. "Big Men," Box Office Mojo, http://www.boxofficemojo.com/movies/?id=bigmen.htm.

12. Anthony Kaufman, "This Documentary Executive Produced by Brad Pitt is Struggling at the Box Office. Here's Why," *IndieWire* (March 18, 2014), http://www.indiewire.com/2014/03/this-documentary-executive-produced-by-brad-pitt-is-struggling-at-the-box-office-heres-why-28902/.

13. Sean Dunne, http://www.veryape.tv/.

14. Orly Ravid, "About" website page, The Film Collaborative, http://www.thefilmcollaborative.org/about/.

15. Alex Steyermark, "Here's How These Filmmakers Self-Distributed Their Documentary . . . And Actually Made Money," *IndieWire* (June 12, 2015), http://www.indiewire.com/2015/06/heres-how-these-filmmakers-self-distributed-their-documentary-and-actually-made-money-61050/.

16. Peter Broderick, "The One-of-a-Kind Model: Kedi," *Distribution Bulletin #2* (May 9, 2017), http://www.peterbroderick.com/distributionbulletins/files/82af2fffd270e588750660938b2e1f18-37.html.

17. Calvin Pryluck, "Ultimately We Are All Outsiders: The Ethics of Documentary Filming," in *New Challenges for Documentary*, 2nd ed., ed. Alan Rosenthal and John Corner (Manchester: Manchester University Press, 2005), 197.

18. Nick Fraser, "The Act of Killing: Don't Give an Oscar to This Snuff Movie," *Guardian* (February 22, 2014), https://www.theguardian.com/commentisfree/2014/feb/23/act-of-killing-dont-give-oscar-snuff-movie-indonesia.

19. Matt Fagerholm, "Hot Docs 2017 Interview: Theo Anthony on 'Rat Film,'" RogerEbert.com (April 28, 2017), https://www.rogerebert.com/interviews/hot-docs-2017-interview-theo-anthony-on-rat-film.

20. Susan Sontag, "America, Seen Through Photographs Darkly," in *On Photography* (London: Picador, 1977), 41.

21. Pryluck, "Ultimately We Are All Outsiders," 207.

22. Fraser, "The Act of Killing."

GLOSSARY

16:9 ratio: The width (16 units) and the height (9 units) of the image size commonly used for documentary-style shooting in cameras and for the displays of computer monitors and TV screens. This ratio yields a more cinematic image than the old standard ratio of 4:3. Most cameras and TV screens can be switched to 4:3 if desired.

1920 × 1080: The standard resolution, in pixels (1,920 wide by 1,080 high), of cameras that shoot high-definition video in the 16:9 ratio.

35mm sensor: An image sensor in high-definition video cameras that is the same size as a frame of traditional 35mm film. Sometimes called "full frame," the sensor and its resulting image come close to replicating the look of film.

4K format: A resolution of 4,000 horizontal pixels, now available as a shooting format on many cameras and even camera phones, which can then be screened on 4K display monitors.

Adobe After Effects: Postproduction editing software used to create special visual effects and motion graphics.

Aperture and iris: The aperture is the opening or hole in a lens through which light enters. The iris controls the size of the opening.

Automatic gain control (AGC): A term that refers to both audio and image. Setting your camera to AGC allows it to artificially enhance an image in low light or automatically adjust audio levels when you are shooting in the field.

Beta SP tape: A new type of Betacam tape—the SP stands for "Superior Performance"— introduced in 1986 so Sony could make more money in conjunction with their Beta SP cameras. It was the news industry standard well into the early 2000s.

Bokeh: From the Japanese word for "blur," this term refers to the blur produced by out-of-focus parts of an image. I have never used this word before and you will probably never hear it used either, but I just thought you should know what it is.

B-roll: The footage or visual evidence used to support the primary footage, which is usually made up of interviews or sound from interviews.

Camera slider: A flat metal rail upon which you can attach your camera and push it to achieve a smooth dolly or tracking effect, the camera gliding from one end to the other. Camera sliders come in several lengths, weights, and price points and can be affixed to a tripod or used independently.

CCD and CMOS sensors: The sensors in video cameras that convert light into images. CCD (charge-coupled device) sensors, while considered more stable and of higher quality, have been slowly replaced by CMOS (complementary metal oxide semiconductor) sensors, which are much less expensive to manufacture, have a much longer battery life, and are improving in quality. Don't worry, no one will ever ask you what CMOS means, but the use of these sensors has led to a reduction in the price of video cameras across the board.

Chyron (or super): A caption or text on-screen, usually used to identify people on-screen. The term was commonly used in newsrooms from the Cro-Magnon era.

Cinema vérité: French for "cinema of truth," it's also been called observational cinema, and it's also been called bullshit, since any injection of a camera and the person wielding it into a situation often results in "truthiness" instead of unvarnished truth. Consider the term worthy of discussion, but as a definitive label of a style of filmmaking it has become rather meaningless.

Color grading: The postproduction process of enhancing or improving the color of a video image.

Color temperature: This term refers to the color of the light illuminating the image, as well as the camera settings that can be manipulated to reflect that color accurately. Higher color temperatures (5,600 K, or kelvins, is the midpoint) are considered cool, or blue; lower color temperatures (a midpoint of 3,200 K) are warm, or orange.

Cutting on action: Editing the in-points and out-points of individual shots while action, rather than stasis, is taking place. Also, a specific edit that matches the action of one shot to the next (e.g., a wide shot of a basketball player releasing a jump shot cuts to a close-up of the ball just entering the net).

dB (decibel level in audio recording): A measure of how loud a sound is.

dB (signal-to-noise ratio in video cameras): Denotes the sensitivity of a camera's imaging system, or gain (see below). Usually dB is set at zero but can be increased in increments to electronically enhance the ability of a camera to shoot in low light.

DCP (Digital Cinema Package): A digital file containing the highest possible resolution of a finished film. DCPs are transferred to hard drives and used for top-tier film festival and theatrical screenings. At an encoding cost of about $40 per minute, cash-strapped filmmakers need $3,000 to $4,000 to make a DCP of their movie.

Depth of field: The distance between the nearest and farthest objects in a scene or image that appear in focus. A deep focus means most of the image is in focus; a shallow focus means only one area is in focus while the rest is blurred.

Diegetic music: Music whose source is visible on the screen, or can be assumed to be coming from somewhere off-screen, rather than added in postproduction.

DIY: Do-it-yourself.

Drag: Controlled by a lever on a tripod, drag adjusts the friction to ensure smooth, jerk-free panning and tilting. Can also refer to your current boss.

DSLR: A digital single-lens reflex camera with the ability to shoot high-quality, high-definition video.

E&O (errors and omissions) insurance: A scary term for liability insurance intended to protect a distributor or broadcaster against any copyright lawsuits brought against you. It means you'll get sued but they won't.

Fair use: Copyrighted material (not including music) used for purposes of comment, criticism, parody, or education that is unaltered and appears briefly, without the need for permission from the copyright owner. A film clip or TV news excerpt is okay if used sparingly and in the correct context. Fair use standards are not uniform or written in stone.

Fluid head: A tripod head to which a camera is attached and can then be panned and tilted smoothly and adjusted to various levels of friction. Also, quite possibly the name of an underground speed-metal band from the 1980s.

Focus group: A preselected group of people who are interviewed about their reactions to a film or other product.

Foley: Sounds recorded in a studio that mimic sounds heard in real environments. These are available to filmmakers in online production effects libraries.

fps (frames per second): A measure of how many video frames are contained within one second of video. 24fps is the current video standard; 30fps and 60fps are also used in some cases.

f-stop: A camera setting corresponding to a particular number (e.g., 2.4, 2.8, 3.2), which indicates the size of the aperture. The higher the number the smaller the aperture.

Gaffer tape: A heavy cotton cloth tape, usually a few inches wide and sold in rolls, with many different uses in video and film shoots.

Gain: In video cameras, gain (measured in decibels, see dB above) boosts the camera's sensitivity to light (e.g., 6 dB, 9 dB, 18 dB, 24 dB), allowing you to shoot in dark situations.

H.264 video: A commonly used format for the compression of high-resolution video content into a high-quality but compact digital file that can be easily shared on the internet.

Half-inch videotape: Half-inch-size videotape cassettes (Betacam) that were introduced in 1982 and used in recorders that were the first to be built into cameras rather being part of a separate tape deck.

HDV format: A short-lived but popular tape format designed for high-definition video recorded on the last of the tape-based camcorders. It was soon replaced by memory cards for high-definition cameras.

Hot shoe: A postage-stamp-sized metal plate on the top section of a video camera or camera handle; lights and wireless transmitters can be screwed onto the plates. In still photography, the hot shoe provides an electrical connection for synchronizing a flash accessory. Can also refer to a sneaker that has been set on fire.

Intertitles: On-screen text usually used to help move the narrative of a film forward, or to comment on or explain something to the viewer, or to plug holes in a story the director should have shot footage for.

Jump cut: The abrupt cutting from one shot to another without concern for spatial or sequential logic. Some say the jump cut was first used by Jean-Luc Godard in his 1960 film *Breathless*, but in that same year Robert Drew used jump cuts in his documentary *Primary*.

Key light: The main source of light in a shot. It can be a light you set up yourself, a lamp that already exists in a room, daylight coming through a window, or the sun.

Lavalier microphone: I've always wondered where this name came from, so I looked it up. Originally named for a pendant worn by the French Duchesse de La Vallière in the late 1600s, it refers to a small microphone that can be clipped to clothing or placed anywhere in a scene.

LED: You will never say, "I need a light-emitting diode for this shot," but that's what LED means. It's a light source that never gets hot, can run off batteries or AC power, is small and lightweight, and has adjustable color temperature dials.

Loupe: A tubelike attachment for a camera's fold-out viewfinder screen that blocks out surrounding light and can also help magnify the image for better clarity.

Macro (in camera or lenses): A macro lens or adaptor is capable of producing sharp, extreme close-ups.

Memory card: The now-common device for storing all of the video and audio you capture in the field. It slides into a slot on the side of most cameras.

MiniDV: The first digital video tape designed for the earliest prosumer (professional-consumer) cameras such as the Sony PD-150.

Neutral-density (ND) filter: Reduces the amount of light entering the lens, correcting for overexposure without altering the color or intensity.

Nonlinear editing (NLE): A revolutionary kind of software that allows for easy manipulation of the placement of video and audio content during the editing process. Final Cut Pro, AVID, Premiere, and DaVinci Resolve are all types of NLE systems.

Nouvelle Vague: The New Wave of 1950s and '60s French filmmakers who brazenly rejected conventional feature filmmaking style by applying the portable techniques of documentaries and inventive uses of image and sound to create radical social and political works.

Plug-ins: Additional software that some nonlinear editing systems may require to handle motion graphics, format conversions, color enhancement, etc.

Prime lens: A lens of fixed focal length that cannot be zoomed in or out.

Rack focus: The once-ubiquitous technique of changing the focus during a shot, usually when the lens was zoomed into one object and then *racked* (turning the focusing ring on the lens barrel) to another object closer or farther away. It still produces a cool look, although a bit showy, and it's harder to do with camcorder lenses that can be turned continuously rather than in a defined range.

Room tone: The ever-present white noise (e.g., air conditioner, heater, buzzing lights) emitted by certain rooms. Either room tone is recorded in the field or digital versions can be found in production sound effects libraries.

Servo lens: Refers to a lens with an internal motor used for zooming and focusing.

SFX: Short for sound effects.

Shooting ratio: The ratio of hours of raw video shot to one hour of edited video in the final film.

Shotgun microphone: Excuse the violent imagery, but a shotgun mic is one that can be detached from the camera, held in the hand or placed on a boom pole, and can be pointed at a sound source from a discreet distance to record high-quality audio.

Shutter speed: The length of time, in a wide range, that a camera's digital sensor is exposed to light to capture an image.

Thread size (in lenses): The little grooves, or threads, around the inside of a lens, and measured as the diameter of the lens, that allow you to screw on a filters or adaptors.

Three-act structure: A narrative model used in scriptwriting that breaks the running time of a story into three parts or acts: the setup, confrontation, and resolution.

Three-quarter-inch videotape: Sometimes called U-matic, which refers to a subset of early hominids who used the format to record home movies of their children running from giant snakes. In 1971, it became the first portable version of videotape enclosed in a cassette (with a total running time of twenty minutes), making it easier to insert directly into recorders that were then attached via a cable to broadcast cameras.

Time code: The electronically generated time stamp—in hours, minutes, seconds, and frames—on recorded video. The numerals do not appear on the recorded media.

Timeline: The horizontal graph containing the video and audio tracks in nonlinear editing systems.

Tripod spreader: The three rubber or metal arms connecting to the three legs of a tripod, which can be expanded or contracted and help prevent the tripod from collapsing.

TRT: The total running time of a length of video.

Tungsten: The quality of light produced by a common household bulb or professional lighting system, which produces a warm or orange hue.

Upcut: A piece of audio that is clipped or interrupted when inserted into a timeline, resulting in a jarring, distracting sound.

Vignetting: The darkening of the corners or outer borders of an image; can sometimes occur with the use of wide-angle adaptor lenses.

White balance: To "white balance" is the process of obtaining realistic color in a scene by selecting a setting on your camera and then pressing a button. This is the thing I kept screwing up on my very first professional job. Hard to believe they didn't fire me on the spot.

XLR: A three-pin electrical connector used on nearly all professional microphones and audio cables. Also, quite possibly the name of an underground post-punk band from the 1990s.

LIST OF FILMS

This list is confined to those films considered classic or must-see documentaries, films that were made in a lean team style, and other films discussed more in depth within the book.

Ai WeiWei: Never Sorry (Alison Klayman, 2012)
Always for Pleasure (Les Blank, boxed set, 2014)
Approaching the Elephant (Amanda Wilder, 2014)
Barzan (Bradley Hutchinson and Alex Stonehill, 2013)
Before Summer Ends (Maryam Goormaghtigh, 2018)
Behemoth (Zhao Liang, 2015)
Below Sea Level (Gianfranco Rosi, 2008)
Biggie and Tupac (Nick Broomfield, 2002)
Big Men (Rachel Boynton, 2013)
Bob Dylan: Dont Look Back (D. A. Pennebaker, 1967)
Boone (Christopher LaMarca, 2016)
Boxing Gym (Frederick Wiseman, 2010)
Cameraperson (Kirsten Johnson, 2016)
Capturing Reality (Pepita Ferrari, 2008)
Cartel Land (Matthew Heineman, 2015)
Casting JonBenet (Kitty Green, 2017)
Children of the Kalahari (Velina Ninkova, 2015)
Chronicle of a Summer (Edgar Morin and Jean Rouch, 1961)
Circo (Aaron Shock, 2010)
Citizenfour (Laura Poitras, 2014)
City of Ghosts (Matthew Heineman, 2017)
City of Trees (Brandon Kramer and Lance Kramer, 2015)
Dawson City: Frozen Time (Bill Morrison, 2016)
Dope Sick Love (Felice Conti, Brent Renaud, and Craig Renaud, 2005)
Eldorado XXI (Salomé Lamas, 2016)
El Mar La Mar (J. P. Sniadecki and Joshua Bonnetta, 2018)
Encounters at the End of the World (Werner Herzog, 2007)
Field Niggas (Khalik Allah, 2015)
Foreign Parts (J. P. Sniadecki and Véréna Paravel, 2010)
Forest of Bliss (Robert Gardner, 1986)
Fuck Cinema (Wu Wenguang, 2004)
Grey Gardens (Albert Maysles and David Maysles, 1975)
Grizzly Man (Werner Herzog, 2005)

Guerrilla: The Taking of Patty Hearst (Robert Stone, 2004)

Harlan County, U.S.A. (Barbara Kopple, 1976)

Hell on Earth: The Fall of Syria and the Rise of Isis (Sebastian Junger and Nick Quested, 2017)

Hello Photo (Nina Davenport, 1995)

Homo Sapiens (Nikolaus Geyrhalter, 2016)

I Am Not Your Negro (Raoul Peck, 2016)

Into Great Silence (Philip Gröning, 2005)

Into the Abyss (Werner Herzog, 2011)

Iraq in Fragments (James Longley, 2006)

I Travel Because I Have To, I Come Back Because I Love You (Marcelo Gomes and Karim Aïnouz 2009)

Jim: The James Foley Story (Brian Oakes, 2016)

Joyce at 34 (Joyce Chopra, 1972)

Kedi (Ceyda Torun and Charlie Wuppermann, 2016)

Kurt & Courtney (Nick Broomfield, 1998)

Leviathan (Lucien Castaing-Taylor and Véréna Paravel, 2012)

Machines (Rahul Jain, 2016)

Manakamana (Stephanie Spray and Pacho Velez, 2013)

Manufactured Landscapes (Jennifer Baichwal, 2006)

Man with a Movie Camera (Dziga Vertov, 1929)

Marmato (Mark Grieco, 2014)

Medium Cool (Haskell Wexler, 1969)

Memories of a Penitent Heart (Cecilia Aldarondo, 2016)

Nostalgia for the Light (Patricio Guzmán, 2010)

Oil & Water (Laurel Spellman Smith and Francine Strickwerda, 2014)

Operation Filmmaker (Nina Davenport, 2007)

Our Daily Bread (Nikolaus Geyrhalter, 2005)

Photographic Memory (Ross McElwee, 2011)

Pina (Wim Wenders, 2011)

Primary (Robert Drew, 1960)

Quick Brown Fox: An Alzheimer's Story (Ann Hedreen and Rustin Thompson, 2006)

Rat Film (Theo Anthony, 2016)

Rich Hill (Andrew Droz Palermo and Tracy Droz Tragos, 2014)

Roger & Me (Michael Moore, 1989)

Room 237 (Rodney Ascher, 2012)

Sacro GRA (Gianfranco Rosi, 2013)

Salesman (Albert Maysles, David Maysles, and Charlotte Zwerin, 1969)

Sans Soleil (Chris Marker, 1983)

Shape of the Moon (Leonard Retel Helmrich, 2004)

Sherman's March (Ross McElwee, 1985)

Shoah (Claude Lanzmann, 1985)

Stories We Tell (Sarah Polley, 2012)

Streetwise (Martin Bell and Mary Ellen Mark, 1984)

Strong Island (Yance Ford, 2017)

Suitcase of Love and Shame (Jane Gillooly, 2013)

Sweetgrass (Lucien Castaing-Taylor and Ilisa Barbash, 2009)

The Act of Killing (Joshua Oppenheimer, 2012)

The Beaches of Agnès (Agnès Varda, 2008)

The Challenge (Yuri Ancarani, 2016)

The Church on Dauphine Street (Ann Hedreen and Rustin Thompson, 2008)

The Corporation (Mark Achbar and Jennifer Abbott, 2003)

The Fog of War (Errol Morris, 2003)

The Gleaners and I (Agnès Varda, 2000)

The Human Flow (Ai Weiwei, 2017)

The Iron Ministry (J. P. Sniadecki, 2014)

The Joy of Life (Jenni Olson, 2005)

The Look of Silence (Joshua Oppenheimer, 2014)

The Overnighters (Jesse Moss, 2014)

The Pearl Button (Patricio Guzmán, 2015)

The Royal Road (Jenni Olson, 2015)

The Sea Stares At Us From Afar (Manual Muñoz Rivas, 2017)

The Sky Trembles and the Earth Is Afraid and the Two Eyes Are Not Brothers (Ben Rivers, 2015)

The Thin Blue Line (Errol Morris, 1988)

The War Room (D. A. Pennebaker and Chris Hegedus, 1993)

The White Helmets (Orlando von Einsiedel, 2016)

The Wolfpack (Crystal Moselle, 2015)

30 Frames a Second: The WTO in Seattle (Rustin Thompson, 2000)

This Changes Everything (Avi Lewis, 2015)

Three Sisters (Wang Bing, 2012)

Tower (Keith Maitland, 2016)

20 Feet from Stardom (Morgan Neville, 2013)

Uncertain (Ewan McNicol and Anna Sandilands, 2015)

Unrest (Jennifer Brea, 2017)

Untitled (Michael Glawogger and Monika Willi, 2018)

Vincent: The Life and Death of Vincent Van Gogh (Paul Cox, 1987)

Watchers of the Sky (Edet Belzberg, 2014)

We Come as Friends (Hubert Sauper, 2014)

What Now? Remind Me (Joaquim Pinto, 2013)

Whores' Glory (Michael Glawogger, 2011)

Whose Streets? (Sabaah Folayan and Damon Davis, 2017)

Workingman's Death (Michael Glawogger, 2005)

Zona Intangible (Ann Hedreen and Rustin Thompson, 2017)

BIBLIOGRAPHY

Anderson, John. "At Hot Docs, Filmmakers Make Pitches and Face Brutal Feedback." *Current* (May 7, 2015). https://current.org/2015/05/at-hot-docs-filmmakers-make-pitches-and-face-brutal-feedback/.

———. "Documentary Filmmakers Find That an Agenda Helps With Financing." *New York Times* (July 8, 2016). https://www.nytimes.com/2016/07/10/movies/documentary-filmmakers-find-that-an-agenda-helps-with-financing.html?_r=0.

———. "'Respect the Feathers': Who Tells Standing Rock's Story?" *New York Times* (December 16, 2016). https://www.nytimes.com/2016/12/16/movies/standing-rock-sioux-tribe-filmmakers.html?_r=0.

Anderson-Moore, Oakley. "Where the Money Is: The Grants Behind This Year's Sundance Documentaries." No Film School (January 28, 2014). https://nofilmschool.com/2014/01/the-grants-behind-this-years-sundance-documentaries.

Artis, Anthony Q. *The Shut Up and Shoot Documentary Guide*. New York City, NY: Routledge, 2014.

B&H Photo-Video-Pro Audio. https://www.bhphotovideo.com/c/product/856444-REG/Opteka_OPTCXS300_CXS_300_Dual_Grip_Video.html.

Baumgarten, Marjorie. "Look & See: A Portrait of Wendell Berry." *Austin Chronicle* (September 1, 2017). https://www.austinchronicle.com/calendar/film/2017-09-01/look-and-see-a-portrait-of-wendell-berry/.

Bernard, Sheila Curran. *Documentary Storytelling: Creative Nonfiction on Screen*. New York City, NY: Routledge, 2015.

Boeckmann, Chris. "Projecting Outside the Echo Chamber." *Filmmaker* magazine (April 13, 2017). http://filmmakermagazine.com/102137-projecting-outside-the-echo-chamber/#.WjP_CFQ-fx5.

Box Office Mojo. "Big Men." http://www.boxofficemojo.com/movies/?id=bigmen.htm.

———. Genre: Documentaries. http://www.boxofficemojo.com/genres/chart/?id=documentary.htm.

Bricca, Jacob. *Documentary Editing: Principles and Practice*. Waltham, MA: Focal Press, 2017, xii.

Broderick, Peter. "The One-of-a-Kind Model: Kedi." *Distribution Bulletin #2* (May 9, 2017). http://www.peterbroderick.com/distributionbulletins/files/82af2fffd270e588750660938b2e1f18-37.html.

Brody, Richard. "'Cameraperson' and the Conventions of Documentary Filmmaking." *New Yorker* (September 9, 2016). https://www.newyorker.com/culture/richard-brody/cameraperson-and-the-conventions-of-documentary-filmmaking.

Capa, Robert. Biography page, Magnum Photos. http://pro.magnumphotos.com/C.aspx?VP3=CMS3&VF=MAGO31_9_VForm&ERID=24KL535353.

Center for Media and Social Impact. "Fair Use, Free Speech & Intellectual Property." http://cmsimpact.org/program/fair-use/.

Cheshire, Godfrey. Review of "Machines." RogerEbert.com (August 9, 2017). https://www.rogerebert.com/reviews/machines-2017.

Churchill, Joan. "Inside Out: Joan Churchill." *Documentary* magazine (August 24, 2017). https://www.documentary.org/feature/inside-out-joan-churchill.

Corner, John. "Sounds Real: Music and Documentary." In *New Challenges for Documentary*, edited by Alan Rosenthal and John Corner. Manchester: Manchester University Press, 2005, 246.

Dillard, Clayton. "Rich Hill." *Slant* (July 29, 2014). https://www.slantmagazine.com/film/review/rich-hill.

Drew, Robert. "An Independent with the Networks." In *New Challenges for Documentary*, edited by Alan Rosenthal and John Corner. Manchester: Manchester University Press, 2005, 286.

Edelstein, David. "How Documentary Became the Most Exciting Kind of Filmmaking." Vulture (April 14, 2013). http://www.vulture.com/2013/04/edelstein-documentary-is-better-than-filmmaking.html.

Edit Media. Additional Teaching Resources Webpage. "The Edit 10: Best Practices for Inclusive Teaching in Media." http://www.editmedia.org/best-practices/.

Elliott, Stephen. "The Great Film Festival Swindle." Rumpus (May 31, 2016). http://therumpus.net/2016/05/the-great-film-festival-swindle/.

Else, Jon. "The Politics of Documentary, A Symposium." In *New Challenges for Documentary*, edited by Alan Rosenthal and John Corner. Manchester: Manchester University Press, 2005, 246.

Estrin, James. "Mary Ellen Mark, Photographer and Force of Nature." *New York Times* (May 26, 2015). https://lens.blogs.nytimes.com/2015/05/26/mary-ellen-mark-photographer-and-force-of-nature/.

European Documentary Network. " 'Cost of Docs' 100 Survey: Trends and Challenges Facing Documentarians in Today's Market" (September 28, 2017). http://edn.network/news/news-story/article/cost-of-docs-100-survey-trends-and-challenges-facing-documentarians-in-todays-market/?tx_ttnews%5BbackPid%5D=111&cHash=af111081414842c39781ec199c7e25f6.

Fagerholm, Matt. "Hot Docs 2017 Interview: Theo Anthony on 'Rat Film.'" RogerEbert.com (April 28, 2017). https://www.rogerebert.com/interviews/hot-docs-2017-interview-theo-anthony-on-rat-film.

FLM Magazine. "Errol Morris Interviews Errol Morris" (Winter 2004). Reprinted at http://www.errolmorris.com/content/eyecontact/interrotron.html.

Follows, Stephen. "The Seismic Shift in the World of Film Festivals." Stephen Follows: Film Data and Education (April 3, 2016). https://stephenfollows.com/the-revolution-in-film-festivals/.

———. "What Film Festival Directors Really Think." Stephen Follows: Film Data and Education (September 1, 2013). https://stephenfollows.com/what-film-festival-directors-really-think/.

Foundation Henri Cartier-Bresson. Biography page. http://www.henricartierbresson.org/en/hcb/.

Fox, Dan. *Pretentiousness: Why It Matters.* Minneapolis: Coffee House Press, 2016, 116.

Fraser, Nick. "The Act of Killing: Don't Give an Oscar to This Snuff Movie." *Guardian* (February 22, 2014). https://www.theguardian.com/commentisfree/2014/feb/23/act-of-killing-dont-give-oscar-snuff-movie-indonesia.

Hampe, Barry. *Making Documentary Films and Videos.* New York: Holt Paperbacks, 2007, 27, 50.

Hewitt, John and Vazquez, Gustavo. "Paying for It: Fundraising." In *Documentary Filmmaking: A Contemporary Field Guide*, 2nd ed. Oxford: Oxford University Press, 2014, 62, 68.

Impact Partners. About Us page. https://www.impactpartnersfilm.com/about-us.

Independent Feature Project. Website home page. http://www.ifp.org/.

International Documentary Association. The Documentary Core Application Project. International Documentary Association. https://www.documentary.org/funding/documentary-core-application-project.

Isler, Tom. "Making the Cut." *Documentary* magazine (February 28, 2008). https://www.documentary.org/feature/making-cut.

Jaglom, Henry. *The Movie Business Book*, 4th ed. Edited by Jason E. Squire. Milton Park: Taylor & Francis, 2016.

Kachka, Boris. "How Alex Gibney Is Reinventing Documentary Filmmaking." Vulture (June 29, 2016). http://www.vulture.com/2016/06/alex-gibney-is-reinventing-documentary-filmmaking.html.

Kahana, Jonathan, ed. *The Documentary Film Reader: History, Theory, Criticism.* Oxford: Oxford University Press, 2016.

Kaufman, Anthony. "Reality Checks: This Year's Sundance Showed How the Documentary Film World Is Changing." *IndieWire* (January 29, 2016). http://www.indiewire.com/2016/01/reality-checks-this-years-sundance-showed-how-the-documentary-film-world-is-changing-30443/.

————. "This Documentary Executive Produced by Brad Pitt Is Struggling at the Box Office. Here's Why." *IndieWire* (March 18, 2014). http://www.indiewire.com/2014/03/this-documentary-executive-produced-by-brad-pitt-is-struggling-at-the-box-office-heres-why-28902/.

————. "The Top 8 Pitches at the Hot Docs Forum: What Worked and What Didn't." *IndieWire* (May 1, 2015). http://www.indiewire.com/2015/05/the-top-8-pitches-at-the-hot-docs-forum-what-worked-and-what-didnt-62464/.

Kohn, Eric. "Sundance 2013: Robert Redford Says There Are Too Many Film Festivals." *Indiewire* (January 17, 2013). http://www.indiewire.com/2013/01/sundance-2013-robert-redford-says-there-are-too-many-film-festivals-241604/.

Kramer, Lance. "The Messy Truth Behind a Day Job as a Documentarian." *Documentary* magazine (April 26, 2017). https://www.documentary.org/feature/messy-truth-behind-day-job-documentarian.

Lang, Jamie. "My French Film Festival: Spotlighting Swiss Doc 'Before Summer Ends' and Director Maryam Goormaghtigh." *Variety* (January 18, 2018). http://variety.com/2018/film/festivals/spotlighting-swiss-doc-before-summer-ends-1202669281/.

Leary, Stanley. "If Your Pictures Aren't Good Enough, You're Not Close Enough." *Black Star Rising* (January 7, 2009). http://rising.blackstar.com/if-your-pictures-arent-good-enough-youre-not-close-enough.html.

Leipzig, Adam. "Park City Climate: Sundance Infographic 2017." *Cultural Weekly* (January 23, 2017). https://www.culturalweekly.com/sundance-infographic-2017/.

————. "Park City Climate: Sundance Infographic 2017." *Adam Leipzig* (blog) (January 19, 2017). https://www.adamleipzig.com/blog/park-city-climate-sundance-infographic-2017-million-piracy-losses-distribution-changes-and-slamdance-stats/.

————. "Sundance Infographic 2018: As Climate Changes, Indies Retrench." *Cultural Weekly* (January 17, 2018). https://www.culturalweekly.com/sundance-infographic-2018-climate-changes-indies-retrench/.

L'Heureux, Catie. "Mississippi's Last Abortion Clinic, Captured." The Cut. https://www.thecut.com/2016/06/jackson-documentary-last-abortion-clinic-mississippi.html.

MacDonald, Muriel. "Don't Drive Here." *The City Fix* (blog) (September 5, 2013), http://thecityfix.com/blog/dont-drive-heretelevision-takes-on-road-safety-peru-muriel-macdonald/.

MacDonald, Scott. *Avant-Doc: Intersections of Documentary and Avant-Garde Cinema.* Oxford: Oxford University Press, 2015, 147, 182, 183, 254, 259, 403.

MacDougall, David. "Beyond Observational Cinema." In *The Documentary Film Reader: History, Theory, Criticism,* edited by Jonathan Kahana. Oxford: Oxford University Press, 2016, 566.

Master Class. Werner Herzog Teaches Filmmaking, "Lesson 5: Financing First Films"; "Lesson 10: Camera Shooting Strategy." https://www.masterclass.com/classes/werner-herzog-teaches-filmmaking.

McLane, Betsy A. "Video Arrives." In *A New History of Documentary Film,* 2nd ed. London: Continuum, Page 273.

Minow, Nell. "Look & See: A Portrait of Wendell Berry." RogerEbert.com (June 30, 2017). https://www.rogerebert.com/reviews/look-and- see-a-portrait-of-wendell-berry-2017.

Moody, Luke. "The Silent Return of the Voice of God in Documentary." *11Polaroids: Journal of Film, Sound & Art* (n.d.). https://11polaroids.com/2016/07/21/silent-return-of-voice-of-god-in-documentary/.

Murch, Walter. *In the Blink of an Eye: A Perspective on Film Editing,* 2nd ed. Hollywood: Silman-James Press, 2001, 18.

Nichols, Bill. *Introduction to Documentary,* 2nd ed. Bloomington: Indiana University Press, 2010, Pages 30–33, 161–162.

PBS, *POV.* Filmmaker interview, Jesse Moss, "The Overnighters." http://www.pbs.org/pov/theovernighters/interview/.

Peter Hamilton Consultants. "Inside PBS's POV Strand." *Documentary Television.com* (May 5, 2013), https://www.documentarytelevision.com/commissioning-process/inside-pbss-flagship-pov-strand-12-how-many-projects-are-funded-what-do-they-pay-for-which-rights/.

Power, Samantha. "Ambassador Samantha Power's 2016 Class Day address." *Yale News* (May 22, 2016), https://news.yale.edu/2016/05/22/ambassador-samantha-powers-2016-class-day-address.

Pryluck, Calvin. "Ultimately We Are All Outsiders: The Ethics of Documentary Filming." In *New Challenges for Documentary*, edited by Alan Rosenthal and John Corner. Manchester: Manchester University Press, 2005, 197, 207.

Ravid, Orly. "About" page. The Film Collaborative. http://www.thefilmcollaborative.org/about/.

Ravindran, Manori. "The Risks and Rewards of International Pitch Forums." *Documentary* magazine (January 17, 2017) https://www.documentary.org/feature/risks-and-rewards-international-pitch-forums.

Rosenthal, Alan and John Corner, eds. *New Challenges for Documentary*, 2d ed. Manchester: Manchester University Press, 2005, 154, 286.

Rossi, Fernanda. "Doc Doctor's Story Strategies: Is Narration a Storytelling Red Flag?" *Independent* (November 23, 2009). http://independentmagazine.org/2009/11/narration/.

Sontag, Susan. "America, Seen Through Photographs Darkly." In *On Photography*. New York: Picador, Page 41.

"State of the Field: A Report from the Documentary Sustainability Summit." National Endowment for the Arts and International Documentary Association (August 2017). https://www.documentary.org/sites/default/files/images/articles/Stateofth eField_mediaartssummit2017.pdf.

Steyermark, Alex. "Here's How These Filmmakers Self-Distributed Their Documentary . . . And Actually Made Money." *IndieWire* (June 12, 2015). http://www.indiewire.com/2015/06/heres-how-these-filmmakers-self-distributed-their-documentary-and-actually-made-money-61050/.

Stubbs, Liz. *Documentary Filmmakers Speak*. New York: Allworth Press, 2002, 133, 182.

Suchorsky, Chris. "How to Make Sure Film Festivals Actually Watch Your Movie—And Hold Them Accountable." No Film School (May 9, 2017). https://nofilmschool.com/2017/05/film-festivals-submissions-actually-watch-your-movie.

Sundance Institute. Funding submission FAQ #29: What Percentage of Applications Are Actually Funded? http://applications4.sundance.org/res/p/faq/#29.

Svoboda, Martin. Interview with Kim Longinotto for the D-Word. The D-Word (March 20, 2018). https://www.d-word.com/topics/62-Documentary-Festivals?post=359149.

Tajima-Peña, Renee. "#DocsSoWhite: A Personal Reflection," *Documentary magazine* (August 30, 2016), https://www.documentary.org/ feature/ docssowhite-personal-reflection.

Taylor, Kate. "Why the Narrating Voice of God Has Disappeared at Hot Docs." *Globe and Mail* (April 24, 2015). https://www.theglobeandmail.com/arts/film/kate-taylor-why-the-narrating-voice-of-god-has-disappeared-at-hot-docs/article24106026/.

Thompson, Rustin. "Too Much? A Movie Gives Us an Inside View of Poverty." *Crosscut* (August 14, 2014). http://crosscut.com/2014/08/poverty-what-movie-can-tell-us-rich-hill/.

True/False Film Festival. Call for entries page (2018). https://truefalse.org/submit/features-and-shorts.

Walber, Daniel. "Notes from Art of the Real: What Critics Can Learn from Great Programming." Nonfics: Real Stories, Real Insight (April 22, 2017). https://nonfics.com/art-of-the-real-2017-d15cd00d2e37.

Walker, Dave. "The *Church on Dauphine Street* Celebrates the Spirit of Volunteers." *New Orleans Times-Picayune* (October 19, 2007).

Wenguang, Wu. "Individual Filmmaking." In *The Documentary Film Reader: History, Theory, Criticism*, edited by Jonathan Kahana. Oxford: Oxford University Press, 2016, 959.

Whicker's World Foundation. "Challenges for Freelance Documentary Filmmakers in Today's Market" (February 2016). https://whickersworldfoundation.com/2016/02/challenges-for-freelance-documentary-filmmakers-in-todays-market/.

Wissot, Lauren. "Shooting under Fire: Running and Gunning with the Renaud Brothers." *Filmmaker Magazine* (December 17, 2013), http://filmmakermagazine.com/82852-shooting-under-fire-running-and-gunning-with-the-renaud-brothers/#.WjU-gFQ-fx4.

INDEX